Political Bribery
in Japan

POLITICAL
BRIBERY
IN JAPAN

RICHARD H. MITCHELL

UNIVERSITY OF HAWAI'I PRESS, HONOLULU

96 97 98 99 00 01   5 4 3 2 1

Library of Congress Cataloging-in-Publication Data
Mitchell, Richard H.
Political bribery in Japan / Richard H. Mitchell.
p.   cm.
Includes bibliographical references and index.
ISBN 0–8248–1819–9 (pbk. : alk. paper)
1. Bribery—Japan—History.   2. Political Corruption—Japan—
History.   I. Title.
HV6321.J3M57   1996
364.1'323—dc20   96–25662
CIP

University of Hawai'i Press books are printed on acid-free
paper and meet the guidelines for permanence and
durability of the Council on Library Resources.

Book design by Kenneth Miyamoto

About the Author

RICHARD H. MITCHELL, who received his Ph.D. from
the University of Wisconsin-Madison in 1963, is professor of modern Japanese history at the University of Mis-
souri-St. Louis. He is author of *The Korean Minority in
Japan* (1967), *Thought Control in Prewar Japan* (1976),
Censorship in Imperial Japan (1983), and *Janus-Faced Justice: Political Criminals in Imperial Japan* (1992).

In memory of K. M.

Contents

A Note on the Transliteration
of Japanese Words

IN THE TRANSLITERATION of Japanese, Korean, and Chinese names, the standard form is used, with family name first. In notes taken from English language sources, however, I follow the order used in the source. The names of Japanese Americans are cited with personal names first. Macrons are used to mark long vowels except for common words found in collegiate dictionaries (e.g., Shinto, Taisho, Showa, Tokyo, Kyoto, and Osaka).

tion," but only postwar scandals are cited.[5] Therefore, badly needed
to properly understand the current political crisis is a historical view
of political bribery, which is one of the "traditional" practices under
attack by political reformers. Unfortunately, misinformation about
pre-1945 cases of political bribery abounds. Edwin O. Reischauer,
the distinguished diplomat and Harvard University professor, wrote,
"But the Japanese are very rigid about the sort of corruption alleged
in the Lockheed case. Corruption is often a political issue in Japan,
but that is because standards are so high. The last major scandal
involving bribery in high places was the Siemans affair of 1914. . . .
Where bribery is not part of the system, as in Japan, it is even greater
folly to tolerate shenanigans like those Lockheed engaged in."[6]
There were, of course, major political bribery cases after 1914, including the Teijin scandal (which caused the collapse of the Saitō
Makoto cabinet in July 1934) and the Showa Electric Company scandal (which destroyed the Ashida Hitoshi cabinet in October 1948).
Moreover, many scholars view bribery as "part of the system." Jerome
A. Cohen, former director of East Asian legal studies at Harvard
University, wrote about the Lockheed scandal, "At first, many jaded
observers of the Japanese scene expected a repetition of earlier
scenarios—including a famous Navy bribery scandal [Siemans affair
of 1914] involving British and German arms manufacturers just
before World War I—in which *those in power avoided serious exposure*
[italics added]."[7] In fact, this sensational navy bribery scandal did
cause those in power "serious exposure." First, it badly weakened the
cabinet of Admiral Yamamoto Gonnohyōe and contributed to its fall
in March 1914. Second, it left an indelible stain on the imperial navy.
Prime Minister Yamamoto and Navy Minister Saitō Makoto were
retired into the reserves; Vice Admiral Matsumoto Kazu, who was
rumored to be the next navy minister, was sentenced to three years
imprisonment; Rear Admiral Fujii Mitsugorō was sentenced to four
years; Captain Sawasaki Hirotake was given one year. Misinformation
about postwar political bribery also circulates. For example, in the
obituary of former prime minister Tanaka Kakuei, the *New York Times*
wrote, "He was Prime Minister for just two years, from 1972 to 1974,
when he was forced to resign because of allegations that he used his
office to enrich himself. Two years later he became the only politician to be charged with wrongdoing while in office."[8] More unexpected was this comment written in 1984 by two eminent political
scientists: "The Lockheed incident was the first occasion on which
any politician near the level of a former prime minister had been
indicted and prosecuted."[9] Former prime minister Ashida Hitoshi,
whose cabinet was destroyed by the Showa Electric Company scan-

dal, resigned from office on October 15, 1948, and was prosecuted on December 16 for accepting bribes and for tax evasion.

Authors who speculate on the amount of political bribery in Japan are not rare. In a book published in 1991 a journalist wrote, "Such scandals, of course, are a feature of any government in which politicians have favours to dispense. But if the measurements of corruptions are frequency of scandals, the prominence of those involved, and the amounts of money changing hands, it would seem that Japan's politics is the world's most corrupt."[10] Reischauer, writing three years earlier, said, "Political corruption is less widespread in Japan than in many other countries and is probably much less than in local government in the United States. . . . Major corruption cases like the two involving Tanaka [Kakuei] are rare. . . . Attacks on corruption and political misconduct have been a constant feature of postwar politics."[11] Gerald L. Curtis, writing in 1975 about postwar illegal financing of political activities, stated that Japan "traditionally has been relatively free of corruption."[12] John W. Dower, writing the same year, noted, "The Tokugawa bureaucracy was among the most corrupt and avaricious to be found anywhere."[13] Following the sage advice of John T. Noonan, Jr., in the monumental book *Bribes,* this author resists the almost irresistible temptation to quantify, leaving such speculation to journalists, tourists, and some scholars. As Noonan points out, quantification "has never been systematically attempted. There are no existing sets of figures by which one could conclude that the Roman Empire, for example, was more or less corrupt than the British Empire or the United States. In the absence of this kind of data it is wrong, I believe, to create an illusory certainty by using comparative terms."[14] Noonan notes the difficulties involved in compiling an index of corruption: many acts of bribery remain secret; accusations of bribery may be politically motivated; antibribery laws do not equal enforcement of the laws; and so on.[15]

A proper analysis of political bribery in Japan demands comparison with other national experiences. Such a comparison is difficult given different social and political atmospheres, but it must be done to clarify what is typical and what atypical in the Japanese experience. China, Korea, England, and the United States are selected for this cross-cultural perspective.

Political bribery is a slippery term, but "[t]he core of the concept of a bribe is an inducement improperly influencing the performance of a public function meant to be gratuitously exercised."[16] Bribery is viewed as a legal concept, with laws and regulations as interpreted by procurators and judges, determining what constitutes a criminal act. Thus, the numerous cases of political bribery analyzed are the products of the law enforcement standards of the time. For the most part, this book excludes local and prefectural bribery cases and concentrates instead on cases involving central government politicians and bureaucrats and the businessmen with whom they deal.

Not too many decades ago scholars writing on political bribery condemned ethical and political systems that permitted it to flourish. During the postwar era another approach was tried, one that broke away from the wholesale condemnation of political corruption. This "revisionist" school sought to discover the positive aspects of corruption in economic and political development.[17] It appears, however, that the pendulum is swinging back, as more economists and others view political corruption as a major impediment to development.[18] I have followed neither approach.

After briefly surveying political bribery in traditional Japan, I concluded that in the face of moral restraints, antibribery laws, and occasional harsh punishments, bribery seems to have been ubiquitous. Low salaries for officials and the long-standing custom of gift-giving contributed to this situation. The new Meiji state (1868–1912) outlawed political bribery, but the old pattern of corruption continued nevertheless. In 1890 Japan began an experiment with constitutional government; the first parliament met that year. Although many scholars support the view that compromise was the hallmark of the Meiji parliamentary system, as do I, it is clear that political bribery played an important role in the political process; bribery can be likened to grease that kept the gears of the political machinery turning smoothly. Rumors about businessmen making deals with politicians appeared in newspapers year after year, but the public got its first good look at a bribery transaction in 1907–1908, when Justice Ministry officials began an unprecedented investigation and trial of businessmen and politicians involved in the Greater Japan Sugar Refining Company scandal. A central figure in this investigation was Hiranuma Kiichirō, head of the Justice Ministry's Criminal Affairs Bureau. This case made Hiranuma and the procuratorial clique he led an important political force, whose strength increased over the following years.

This book also deals with election laws and vote buying, from the first election in July 1890 to the present. In the face of strict regulations, politicians and voters engaged in widespread bribery during the first election campaign. Over the following decades the pattern of politicians bestowing money and gifts upon voters became a regular feature of political life. As the suffrage was extended, and as elections became more expensive, a class of election brokers developed who sold blocks of votes to the highest bidder. A successful politician was forced to grease the local elite before each election and to dig deeply into the national pork barrel during his tenure in office. Hence, the so-called money politics, a topic frequently discussed among Japanese during recent years, was well entrenched by the early part of this century. Central government officials reacted to electoral corruption by enacting stricter voting laws and by purification programs aimed at weening voters away from illegal acts. Although government purification efforts did reduce discovered cases of bribery, the old-style politicians survived the various reforms, and electoral corruption remained a problem during the postwar era.

During 1914 and 1915, two serious political bribery cases filled newspaper pages. The first scandal involved high naval officers who were convicted of accepting bribes; the second focused on an important politician who handed out bribes to pass a government bill and who tried to rig an election. The corruption scandal involving naval officers contributed to the collapse of the Yamamoto Gonnohyōe cabinet; the second case resulted in a deal between the Hiranuma clique and the cabinet of Ōkuma Shigenobu, in which the offending home minister (Ōura Kanetake) was forced from not only his office but from political life. These important cases propelled the Justice Ministry, especially the Hiranuma clique, into a position of political influence.

As the nation's founding fathers aged and died, party leaders replaced them as prime ministers. This transition in leadership, however, did not mark a decrease in political bribery. In fact, during this period politicians engaged in an orgy of mutual vilification, with opposition politicians trying to discredit cabinet officers and their Diet supporters by charging them with political bribery. Among the numerous politicians and businessmen caught up in ugly corruption scandals was former justice minister and Seiyūkai politician Ogawa Heikichi. Ogawa's trial held public interest from November 1930 until the appeal to the Supreme Court; he was sentenced to prison in 1936, the first minister-level official to be imprisoned. The various corruption scandals of the party government era weakened the political grip of party government; those who, like Hiranuma Kiichirō, opposed party cabinets, were delighted at the spectacle of party self-destruction and were happy to add to party woes by charging politicians with ideological deviation (i.e., being soft on communism).

Scholars writing about Japan use the term "structural corruption," meaning that the structural nature of corruption is built into the political system to the point that to survive, politicians are forced to exchange favors with businessmen in return for funds to pay members of their faction and to use for elections. Furthermore, because structural corruption is so deeply embedded in the political system, reform programs are doomed to failure unless the entire system is destroyed. Some scholars contend that the "iron triangles" formed by politicians, bureaucrats, and businessmen, which resulted in the system of structural corruption, were forged in the postwar era; others see the origins during the Pacific War years. A careful look at the prewar period suggests otherwise. For example, the Teijin incident of the 1930s well illustrates the inside workings of the system of structural corruption. This neglected incident, which was the longest trial and the most sensational bribery case of the pre-1945 era, not only destroyed the Saitō Makoto cabinet but resulted in the trial of sixteen defendants: cabinet officers, Finance Ministry bureaucrats, and businessmen. Like the Siemens incident, this case left an indelible mark on the public mind. For instance, political critic Yayama Tarō, commenting on a political bribery case of the late 1980s, began the article with "The Lesson of the Teijin Affair."[19] There is another reason to look clearly at the Teijin incident. Itō Takashi, considered by many scholars to be the outstanding authority on this era, regards the Teijin incident as a very puzzling affair. As he puts it, "[T]he facts about it are not clear."[20] It is hoped that this book will help clarify this important trial.

Political bribery continued to flourish during the Allied Occupation. Among the corruption cases of this period the most important was the Showa Electric Company scandal, which caused the Ashida Hitoshi cabinet to fall. An examination of the trial of those indicted in this incident illustrates that procurators faced an uphill battle in gaining convictions. Not only did they have to prove that an official accepted money and was in a position to do the briber a favor, but they had to convince three judges that the official regarded the money as a bribe. Defendants, not eager to help the prosecution, usually claimed that the money was merely a loan, or a political contribution, or a gift.

Japan regained sovereignty in April 1952. The first of numerous corruption scandals caught public attention two years later. In the Shipbuilding scandal, thirty-four businessmen and politicians and seventeen bureaucrats in the Transport Ministry were prosecuted for bribery. Although exposure of this case was not the main reason for the fall of the fifth Yoshida Shigeru cabinet in December 1954, it was a contributing factor. The unification of conservative political forces in November 1955 marked the beginning of Liberal Democratic Party dominance that lasted nearly four decades. Throughout this era bribery scandals periodically shook the political world, but the public, which was satisfied with the nation's economic success, remained supportive of conservative political forces. Occasionally, a reform-minded politician would attempt to reform the political system, with little effect upon money-power politics. In recent years, however, the sensational Recruit scandal followed by the Tokyo Sagawa Express Company scandal converted more and more politicians to the idea of making real political reforms. Eventually, infighting among Liberal Democrats over proposed political reforms caused an ever widening split in the party, which in turn produced seven prime ministers in a period of seven years. The last of these cabinets was a coalition government led by Murayama Tomiichi, head of the Social Democratic Party.

During the last several years there has been much talk about political reform. For many people, political reform means stricter control of political funds and a change in the electoral districts system. These, however, are cosmetic changes: real reform demands a reorganization of political parties and new attitudes among citizens. For a reform that rejuvenates democratic politics, the iron triangles linking politicians, bureaucrats, and businessmen, formed to gain mutual benefits at the expense of taxpayers, must be broken.

Japanese for a "bribe" is *"wairo."* In the Penal Code (Article 197), "acceptance of a bribe" is *"wairo o shūju shi."* Scholars and others describing "acceptance of a bribe" often use *"shūwai,"* which has the same meaning. Thus, *"shūwaizai"* translates as "the crime of accepting a bribe." The Penal Code (Article 198) uses *"wairo o kyōyo shi"* to describe the action of a person who gives a bribe. People writing about this crime also use the term *"zōwai"* as synonymous with *"wairo o kyōyo shi."* Thus, *"zōwaizai"* translates as "the crime of giving a bribe." The section of the Penal Code that includes Articles 197 and 198 is entitled "Crimes of Official Corruption" (*"Tokushoku no tsumi"*). Besides meaning "corruption," *"tokushoku"* also carries the meanings of "bribery" and "graft." Interestingly, the character for *"toku,"* when used as the verb *"kega(su),"* means "to defile, pollute, or stain." The colloquial language has a number of terms for bribery—for example, *"sode no shita."* Since *"sode"* means "sleeve" or "sleeve pocket," a literal translation would be "under the sleeve" (i.e., concealed by the kimono sleeve). *"Hanagusuri"* means "bribe" or "hush money" (a literal translation is "nose medicine"). *"Nigiraseru"* means "to slip money into one's hand," "to grease one's palm," or "to bribe."

1. Legacies

DURING THE SEVENTH CENTURY the Yamato kingdom, which regarded itself as Japan's central government, tried to build a strong centralized state, using Chinese techniques for expanding political power. The Yamato political leadership was attracted to Chinese ideas and methods for state building because the Chinese system was based on a rational hierarchical authority, which the leadership wanted to use to end endemic strife among rival political forces. One of the strongest proponents of the Chinese-style state was Prince Shōtoku, who introduced a system of court ranks similar to those in Korean kingdoms (603) and who reopened diplomatic exchange with China (607–608). By creating a Chinese-style ranking system for officials based on merit, the central government aimed at strengthening its control.[1]

Prince Shōtoku is perhaps best remembered for the so-called Seventeen-Article Constitution (604). Although historians are at odds on its date and some feel that the prince had no hand in writing these articles, it is certain that the central government issued either these injunctions or similar rules to local officials. These seventeen injunctions, based on Chinese theories of state, created a new set of political ethics for the ruling class. Japan's ruler was equated with heaven, and officials were ordered to obey imperial decrees.[2] Article 5 of the injunctions illustrates that authorities at the capital were concerned about officials taking bribes. This article reads in part, "Abstain from gluttony and discard the desire for wealth; you must judge lawsuits impartially. . . . Nowadays (konogoro) it is common for authorities, who aim at making profit, to look at the size of a litigant's purse before making a decision."[3] The use of the term "nowadays" in this article is significant, because that word would be used for a current situation. Its use suggests serious complaints about officials from farmers.[4]

1

Orders to be honest and threats of punishment notwithstanding, provincial governors for the most part continued to accept perquisites, commissions, and bribes. Indeed, by the Heian era (794–1185) governors were notorious for squeezing wealth out of their domains.[5] Faced with disobedient local officials, the central government adopted various measures to reduce corruption and to increase tax revenues, but for the most part these measures were futile.[6] The government also attempted during the reign of Emperor Kanmu (781–806) to stop the purchase of court rank by officials. In this decree of 799, the word *"wairo"* (bribe) is first recorded.[7]

Hōjō Shigetoki, one of the leaders of the Kamakura regime (1185–1333), wrote on proper governing methods that "[a]varice is part of man's nature, but you must not give in to it. Regard the stirring of avarice as a messenger from the gaoler of hell. . . . For every scrap of profit gained through avarice you will lose a hundred or a thousand times as much in this life, and your next existence will be in hell."[8] In addition to this order to avoid bribery, judges by 1232 took an oath not to permit personal feelings or fear of powerful families to sway their rational decisions.[9] Judges during the first century of the Kamakura era appear to have followed the regime's antibribery ethic; "blantant miscarriages of justice in which wealth or influence overrode the clear weight of testimony seem decidedly rare. Naturally this does not mean that bribery or deliberate negligence were nonexistent; but cases in which these factors constituted real problems were probably minor ones."[10] It appears that the ruling elite complied with Shigetoki's strict rules until at least the two invasions by the Mongols (1274 and 1281), after which incompetence and bribery weakened judicial integrity.[11]

Ashikaga Takauji, who eliminated the Hōjō, created a new shogunal line in 1338. The tenth article of the Ashikaga code of conduct for officials sternly prohibited bribery: "Although this is not a new law, the Shogun must be especially strict in enforcing it. Even if the sum involved is only 100 *mon,* those guilty of bribery must be forever excluded from holding office. If a large sum is involved, they must be executed."[12] Traditionally, scholars have treated Ashikaga Takauji with contempt because he overthrew the reigning emperor and installed a puppet;[13] this treachery has colored most accounts of the Ashikaga shogunate. The *Chronicle of Ōnin* begins,

> In the first year of Ōnin, 1467, the country was greatly disturbed. . . . The fault lay with . . . the Shogun Yoshimasa [seventh Shogun] . . . [who] governed solely by the wishes of inexperienced wives and nuns. . . . Yet these women did not know the difference between right and wrong and were ignorant of public affairs and the

ways of government. Orders were given freely from the middle of drinking parties and lustful pleasure-seeking. Bribery was freely dispensed.[14]

Motoori Norinaga, a leading figure in the national revival movement, wrote in the late Tokugawa period (1603–1867), "By the end of the Ashikaga era, the empire was in an unprecedented condition, plunged, as it were, in perpetual darkness. Everything was in decline, and corruption reached its extreme."[15] Hiraizumi Kiyoshi, writing in 1979, agrees with Norinaga:"[T]o understand what a meaningless period the Ashikaga period was, we must make clear who the Ashikaga were and what their essence was"; it was an era "synonymous with personal gain and greed."[16] It should be noted, however, that the Ashikaga shogunate was never institutionally strong and that for only a few decades in the late fourteenth century and the early fifteenth did the Ashikaga come close to ruling the nation.

The Tokugawa shogunate, like earlier regimes, exhorted officials to obey regulations and to hold money in contempt. A basic code of regulations for the daimyo, the Buke shohatto, was issued in 1615. This code aimed primarily at stopping warfare between daimyo and preventing subversive activities against the Tokugawa. Over the following years, as the Tokugawa regime sought to expand moral authority and political control over several hundred daimyo, new articles were added to the Buke shohatto. Strangely, instructions to the various military houses did not mention bribery, but this oversight was corrected in March 1710 by Ienobu, the sixth shogun.[17]

The drafter of the revised Buke shohatto of 1710 was Arai Hakuseki, a Confucian scholar and personal adviser to the shogun who played an important role in politics between 1709 and 1716. Because Hakuseki's overriding aim was an increase in shogunal power, the expanded code aimed to impresss upon daimyo that their domains were part of a national polity headed by a monarch who held comprehensive authority over them.[18] Article 7 stated in part, "To offer bribes and seek to borrow the influence of those in powerful positions, to engage in private schemes and pursue personal connections is to open the road to corruption and obstruct the correct path. Such are the means by which government is destroyed. All should be strictly avoided."[19]

Hakuseki's concern with official corruption was probably prompted by the rapid growth of a money economy and a corresponding increase in consumption promoted by the expanding merchant class. The Confucian scholar Ogyū Sorai, who was frequently consulted by shogunal authorities on social policy, wrote in the early eighteenth century that the military class valued only money.[20] Motoori Norinaga, at the end of the same century, wrote, "[I]t has become the trend of the times that people in the world, no matter whether they are samurai, peasants, craftsmen, or merchants, neglect their own occupation and are interested merely in obtaining gold and silver easily and quickly."[21] One government response was the 1742 legal code called the Kujikata-Osadamegaki. Bribery was covered in Article 26: "Any one who, in connection with a lawsuit, a petition to the authorities, or a contract for the undertaking of some public work gives a bribe, or who as intermediary conveys a bribe, is to be sentenced to minor deportation."[22]

Although it is impossible to prove that the Tokugawa bureaucracy was more corrupt than that of earlier regimes, it appears that political bribery was widespread.[23] Arai Hakuseki explained how bribery was handled when the government was taking bids for work. Before submitting bids for the work, merchants gave magistrates money, calling it a "gift in anticipation." Merchants who got contracts then gave a "thank-offering." Even though Hakuseki was not a bureaucrat, in 1715 a middleman saying that he represented someone who wanted to be placed in charge of trade at Nagasaki came to his home. A large "gift in anticipation" was offered in gold, and a "thank-offering" was promised.[24] Hakuseki wrote, "Such proposals were made even to people like me. You can imagine what happened in the case of people who had great influence."[25]

The most celebrated example of warrior loyalty during the Tokugawa was set in motion by an inadequate bribe. The tale of the forty-seven masterless samurai began in 1701, when Daimyo Asano Naganori was ordered to act as one of two shogunal representatives to receive imperial court officials bearing New Year's greetings. It was the duty of Kira Yoshinaka, a direct retainer of the shogun and the chief of protocol, to instruct the two representatives on unfamiliar points of protocol. Both daimyo and their advisers well understood that Kira expected "gifts" in exchange for instruction. Indeed, from Kira's viewpoint such gifts were indispensible for maintaining his status.[26] One scholar notes that Kira used "every opportunity [for] . . . getting bribes from rich daimyo. This was an almost open secret, winked at rather leniently as a fault that a man in his circumstances was apt to commit." Therefore, "on the appointment of two daimyo unused to these ceremonies, he must surely have smiled to himself and counted on his ship coming in full laden."[27] One daimyo gave Kira costly gifts, but Asano presented only a box of dried fish. Why did Asano, who badly needed Kira's assistance, give such an inexpensive "gift"? One scholar writes that he did so because "he was a man naturally averse to bribery and now all the more so because he thought the occasion too solemn for such petty tricks." Moreover, Asano was not well served by his councillors, who "were men badly wanting in worldly wisdom."[28] Kira's anger over the small gift was a natural reaction. He refused to act as a guide through the ceremonial maze, and when Asano made errors, Kira taunted him. Finally, Asano lost his temper and cut Kira with a sword. This illegal act resulted in Asano's forced suicide and the confiscation of his property. Most Japanese pay little attention to the bribery part of this sad story, instead focusing on Asano's loyal retainers as they planned revenge against Kira. On January 31, 1703, forty-six of them (one dropped out) attacked Kira's home, killed him, and presented his head at Asano's grave. Despite popular acclaim, the warriors were ordered to commit suicide.[29]

Those who depict Tokugawa officialdom as utterly corrupt focus on Yanagisawa Yoshiyasu, a contemporary of Hakuseki's, and Tanuma Okitsugu, who was politically important a long generation later. Yanagisawa had a spectacular rise from a lowly page in attendance on Tokugawa Tsunayoshi, who became shogun in 1680, to high official status as the shogun's most trusted adviser. Near the end of his career Yanagisawa was granted the use of the original Tokugawa surname (Matsudaira) and given a large domain in an area held by the main line of the Tokugawa family.[30] Although Yanagisawa's name is synonymous with corruption, some historians express doubt about this traditional image.[31] Indeed, one revisionist sees Yanagisawa as "the first and most remarkable of a series of shogunal retainers who rose from obscurity to positions of power as shogunal favorites. His career established the pattern of an alliance between shogun and personal attendants against the entrenched interests of the shogunate bureaucracy and the high-ranking hereditary vassals."[32] Another scholar agrees, writing that the great daimyo were angry at Yanagisawa and his followers because the newcomers had pushed them out of influential government positions.[33] Nevertheless, even before Yanagisawa's death in 1714, popular gossip painted the picture of a corrupt and evil man who encouraged the shogun's baser instincts and who was eager to prostitute his wife so that his own son might become Tsunayoshi's heir. Contemporary government officials knew that much of this gossip was pure fiction, but after Yanagisawa's death the gossip gradually turned into "fact."[34]

Tanuma Okitsugu was the dominant political figure in the shogunate from the mid-1760s until 1786. Like Yanagisawa, Tanuma acquired the confidence of the shogun and used it to rise from the low status of a page to the high status of senior councillor. Conrad Totman views Tanuma as "the most powerful non-shogunal leader in

the history of the Tokugawa regime."[35] Tanuma has been portrayed
as the outstanding example of corruption in an age of extravagance
and venality, a person who rose to power by ingratiating himself with
high officials and ladies of the shogun's court. Supposedly, he based
each decision on the size of the bribe.[36] He also supposedly said,
"Gold and silver are more estimable than life, and those who wish to
serve me by presenting gifts of money are, of course, the most loyal.
One can judge the warmth of another's intentions by the amount of
gold he gives. . . . I attend the Shogun in his castle daily and have no
rest from my arduous tasks. But when I return to my house and find
presents from various people heaped up in the corridor, then all my
pains are forgotten and I feel at ease."[37]

A different view of Tanuma is that of a skilled politician who used
gifts given by those seeking preferment to build a powerful vertical
political clique. Indeed, the government was packed with officials
who owed Tanuma favors. Tanuma's real "sin," as perceived by his
contemporaries, was not taking bribes, but rising from modest
origins; this in itself was a mark of "corruption." Moreover, many of
Tanuma's financial and other policies were not in conformity with
classic ideals. As in the case of Yanagisawa, powerful lords displaced
by Tanuma attacked his morals.[38] Tanuma's biographer writes, "Certainly Tanuma cannot be blamed for all the innumerable ills which
beset the country during his years of power. . . . On the contrary,
Tanuma brought to the shogunate certain qualities which were most
rare for the rest of the Tokugawa period. The liberal atmosphere
which he fostered, the spirit of enterprise and inquiry which he
inspired, were valuable gifts for an age too much under the shadow
of the past."[39] Another historian agrees and sees Tanuma as a man
ahead of his times who sought to promote industry and trade and to
tax the profits in order to recover the shogunate's control over the
national economy.[40]

After the death of Shogun Ieharu in 1786, Tanuma was crushed by
a reform group led by Matsudaira Sadanobu. Tanuma's domain was
drastically reduced in size, and he was placed under house arrest.
After his death his heir was assigned a small northern domain. Moreover, Tanuma's policies were overturned and his political supporters
purged. In December 1787, Tsuchiyama Sōjūrō, a former section
head in the Finance Department, received the first death sentence,
for involvement in a rice scandal and for falsifying census records.
Other death penalties were handed down in the following months.[41]
Simultaneously, the reform clique issued a flood of regulations in
which bribery, lewd literature, prostitution, elaborate hair styles, and
expensive clothing were condemned.[42] However, Matsudaira's aus-

tere economic retrenchment program, which was designed to cut consumption and lower inflation, met with public opposition. Gambling simply went underground, and street prostitution continued, because government enforcement agents were easily bribed.[43] Indeed, by the late eighteenth century, corruption among enforcement agents was widespread. Police constables depended upon *meakashi* (private individuals who aided in the prevention of crime and apprehension of criminals). An official report prepared late in the Tokugawa period noted that only the leaders of groups of *meakashi* received a salary; underlings got money from houses of prostitution, from streetwalkers, from businesses, and from gambling houses. Bribes were also squeezed from suspected criminal offenders and their families.[44] By 1793 unpopular sumptuary regulations coupled with Matsudaira's stern treatment of the imperial court forced his resignation.[45] Although Matsudaira is famous as an incorruptable model ruler, one biography mentions that "he had received a high promotion beyond what he could normally expect because of a generous 'gift' to the Shogun's favorite."[46] Perhaps he did not consider this a bribe, because the constant giving of gifts of a prescribed nature was well formalized by late Tokugawa times.

Although the shogunate did not tax the daimyo directly, various contributions to reinforce the elaborate status system were regularly required.[47] As a senior councillor, for example, "Tanuma was under orders to be the recipient of periodic gifts from the daimyo."[48] Tanuma, as the shogun's gatekeeper, was beseiged by petitioners. Therefore, Tanuma's control over the channels of preferment automatically brought to him many expensive gifts. Tanuma, however, went one step further and "actually cultivated this source of income."[49] Despite government orders to curb the abuse of gift giving, some of the Tokugawa leadership thought that gift giving by daimyo should be encouraged in order to absorb their surplus wealth. In March 1787 most daimyo were sent an official notice complaining that official gifts meant for people close to the shogun were inferior in quality and not in the proper quantity. In some cases the required gifts were not given. Daimyo were told to correct this situation.[50]

Tanuma, like his predecessor Yanagisawa Yoshiyasu, rose from humble origins to a powerful position beside a shogun. Both men were hated and feared by the old guard with a long hereditary status in the hierarchy. Although the old guard used charges of individual corruption as an excuse to attack Tanuma and Yanagisawa, in fact the "immorality" that most bothered them was the transgression against the status system.[51]

From these examples we can see that antibribery laws were established from early times and that moral rules for integrity were also put into place. Officials were threatened by Buddhist hellfire and lectured on proper government by Confucianists. Besides Hōjō Shigetoki's warning about perdition for officials swayed by avarice (written between 1256 and 1261), judges who swore in 1232 to follow regulations and to give just decisions did so on pain of "punishment and retribution by each of the following divinities: Brahma, Indra, the Protector Gods of the four Directions, the greater and lesser gods of the more than sixty provinces of Japan, and in particular the Manifest Bodhisattvas of Itō and Hakone, the Great Deity of Mishima, the Great Bodhisattva Hachiman, the diety Tenjin dwelling in the Temman Shrine, and the kin of these deities."[52] Tokugawa Confucian scholars saw the government and laws as a reinforcement of codes of moral conduct and regarded bribery as an immoral act. Arai Hakuseki's attack on the general state of official corruption and in particular on the personal corruption of financial expert Ogiwara Shigehide, whom he forced out of office, are examples.[53]

To what extent were antibribery regulations enforced? Evidence for earlier periods is thin, but there are examples of harsh punishments during the Tokugawa. In 1642 a group of Edo merchants who conspired with high shogunate officials to raise rice prices were exiled, and their children were executed.[54] During the late eighteenth century two Tokugawa treasury officials in Osaka were exiled for taking bribes from merchants.[55] A few years later Matsudaira Sadanobu not only executed Tsuchiyama Sōjūrō, a former section head in the Finance Department, but also punished numerous underlings with sentences ranging from fines to death.[56]

Despite antibribery laws, moral restraints, and harsh punishments, however, bribery appears to have been ubiquitous. Two details in particular contributed to this situation: low salaries for officials and the long-standing custom of giving gifts. Within a century of its founding the Tokugawa regime was in serious financial straits, with the result that some groups within the upper class became impoverished. John Hall illustrates how this financial problem affected the lower-ranking bannermen from whom the shogunate's local representatives were chosen. "Their personal salaries were small and the funds allotted them for official expenses were insignificant. Yet each one administered a domain of some 100,000 koku." Because their duties kept them in Edo, "the actual supervision of the peasants [was left] to subordinates. . . . As the number of intermediary officials increased and as the Deputies lost touch with the localities under their jurisdiction, opportunities for corruption . . . naturally multiplied."[57] This problem of poorly paid officials who found illegal means to supplement their salaries was not new. An imperial edict of 775 noted that "the functionaries at the capital are poorly paid and cannot escape the hardships of cold and hunger, [whereas] provincial governors make great profits. In consequence all officials openly covet posts in the provinces."[58]

By Tokugawa times gift giving was a long-established custom; the hairline between bribery and etiquette was difficult to ascertain. Shortly after Tanuma Okitsugu's fall, Kanazawa Tokō wrote that "each official sought by the use of gifts and favors to improve his private interest. The dominant ambition of most officials was to rise to a position where they in turn could become the recipients of such gifts. . . . [T]hose who refrained from bribe-giving were treated with scorn."[59] Under such conditions it is possible that many officials were not even conscious of the corrupt nature of their "gifts."

In traditional Japan bribery was considered a wrongful act for two reasons: the state had declared it illegal and Confucianists had stigmatized it as immoral. Nevertherless, bribery flourished and had become a way of life by the Tokugawa era. Were officials unable to understand the state's laws, or immune to moral censure, or unusually corrupt? Probably, some officials were simply dishonest, refusing to follow legal and ethical standards. Many officials, however, appear to have reconciled their illegal actions by regarding bribes as part of their normal salary or as "gifts." Hence, the widespread custom of gift giving masked the illegal and immoral nature of bribery. In a classic study of bribery in the West, the author notes that a bribe is kept secret because lies and deceit are involved. A "gift" may be disclosed, but a bribe must remain concealed.[60] This comment aptly applies to Tokugawa Japan: bribes, if they were categorized as "gifts," could be displayed in public.

2. The New State

THE MEIJI STATE, which replaced the Tokugawa shogunate in 1868, admonished officials to strive for national glory; like earlier regimes, however, the new government prescribed punishment for those whose devotion to duty permitted the taking of bribes. Nevertheless, in spite of official exhortations and new antibribery laws, the old pattern of corruption continued.

The Shinritsu Kōryō (Essence of the New Code) of 1871, which was in force until 1882, stipulated punishments for officials who accepted bribes, persons who offered them, and persons who promised them. Depending upon the amount of the bribe and the person involved, punishment ranged from beating to strangulation. Confession prior to discovery would earn a reduction in punishment.[1]

On January 1, 1882, the Keihō (Penal Code) was implemented as the first Western-style law. Articles 284 through 288, in the section "Crimes of Official Corruption," outlined punishments for officials who took bribes. Penalties ranged from one month to two years' imprisonment.[2]

A new civil service system was introduced in 1885. Emperor Meiji decreed on December 23 that disciplinary rules would be strictly enforced. Three days later Prime Minister Itō Hirobumi announced that incorruptibility of officials was of vital concern to the government. "Regulations Concerning the Personal Conduct of Officials" were issued on July 30, 1887. In Article 1, officials were ordered to obey all ordinances and laws.[3] According to Article 8, "officials may not receive, in connection with their official functions any present whatever from others, be it as an acknowledgment of service rendered, as a fee, or in any other name or under whatever pretext."[4] Officials also were prohibited from taking free passes from transportation companies and from accepting free meals. Violators of these regulations were subject to disciplinary actions: removal from office, reduction in salary, or reprimand.[5]

Reflecting on the Tokugawa administrative system in the 1870s, Nishi Amane, a scholar and government official, wrote that the new government must be on guard against graft and strive for clean government.[6] Tsuda Mamichi, who published the first Japanese book on Western law and who played an important role in the development of legal thought, urged in an article on government (August 1874) that the Meiji leaders give proper authority to the new Audit Bureau within the Finance Ministry. He emphasized that the Tokugawa had made a mistake by not giving audit officials enough investigatory powers to expose corruption.[7] He wrote, "There is nothing finer than thus to clarify to all the people of our empire the fact that, while the imperial court, of course, is upright and enlightened, there is elsewhere no leakage of even the smallest sums into private pockets, as the officials are also all honorable and forthright."[8] Meiji statesmen, at least in public pronouncements, were in agreement with Nishi and Tsuda: government officials had not only a legal but also a moral obligation to discard self-interest and to work for the benefit of the nation.[9] The statesman Yamagata Aritomo, writing a generation later than Nishi and Tsuda, warned that progress could be achieved only if political leaders were superior "men who would not be corrupted by thoughts of personal gain or fame . . . [and] who would not falter in their public devotion."[10]

Despite antibribery laws and exhortations to refrain from corrupt acts, some in the political oligarchy viewed administrative positions as platforms from which to harvest the rich spoils of office. This attitude was mainly due to the Tokugawa legacy of ignoring antibribery regulations coupled with the arrogance of a victorious elite.

The new state's relationship with business leaders, the so-called political merchants, in which the initiative usually came from the government, resulted in "special privileges for special services."[11] Although such deals ordinarily did not stem from government corruption, once a special arrangement was made, corruption usually crept into the relationship. One scholar of the rise of political merchants notes that although close ties to the government were financially rewarding, "[s]uch firms were required to pay kickbacks in return for the special privileges received."[12]

Among the political merchants the oldest and most famous was the House of Mitsui, which arose in the late seventeenth century. During the early Meiji era, the Mitsui Bank acted as a depository for public revenues, using this interest-free money to expand the firm. Political leaders who provided this official patronage expected bank loans in return. Many of these "loans" eventually were written off as "gifts." The Mitsubishi Company was another political merchant.[13] The special relationship began after the government chose Iwasaki Yatarō's shipping company to transport an expeditionary force to Taiwan in 1874. Key government leaders were so impressed with Iwasaki's execution of the commission that they gave him the ships used in the expedition, paid him an annual subsidy, and loaned him other ships.[14] Over the following years, Iwasaki's Mitsubishi Company resorted to bribery to maintain its near monopoly of coastal shipping: money went to supporters in prefectural assemblies and to important newspapers. Although not documented, some of the "gifts" must have gone to Ōkuma Shigenobu, head of the Finance Ministry, who for years acted as Iwasaki's protector.[15] By the mid-1880s it was reported that Mitsubishi had a special fund of 400,000 yen to bribe government officials. That bribes were still being given to influence government decisions two decades later is illustrated in the minutes of a company (by this time the company was called Nippon Yūsen Kabushiki Kaisha) meeting in which it was agreed to bribe key members of a political party.[16]

Before the establishment of the national Diet the government was dominated by the *hanbatsu,* a clique of former samurai from western Japan. With the election of three hundred members to the House of Representatives in July 1890, however, the old political balance was changed. Rules for the first national election campaign were set out in the Election Law of February 11, 1889. Bribery as a criminal offense was listed in Article 91: "Any person who has either obtained a vote for himself, or has enabled another person to obtain the same, or has prevented an elector from voting for another person, by either directly or indirectly giving or promising to give the elector money, goods, notes, or public or private employment, shall be dealt with according to the provisions of Art. 234 of the Criminal [i.e., Penal] Code. Any person, who has voted or who has refrained from voting in consideration of such a gift or promise shall be dealt with in a like manner."[17] Violators of Article 91 faced from two months to two years in prison and a fine of three to thirty yen.[18] On May 29, 1890, the government promulgated the Supplementary Penal Regulations for the House of Representatives Election Law. These regulations widened the definition of bribery to cover the serving of drink or food to electors near the polling stations and similar acts.[19]

Prison terms and fines notwithstanding, bribery was widespread. Journalists and others agreed that it had "reached new heights of refinement, as candidates vied with one another to give away just enough—but not more than was necessary—to secure the votes of their fellow men of influence. Songs and limericks caricatured the high costs of electoral politics."[20] R. H. P. Mason, in a study on this first national election, concludes that bribery, although widespread, should be divided into two classes: small bribes indiscriminately distributed and big ones aimed at a selected few. Small bribes consisted of small amounts of money, handkerchiefs, packets of sugar, hand-towels, dried fish, boxes of cake, and the like.[21] Mason thinks that these items

> were generally regarded by the candidates and voters alike as something in the nature of a discreetly timed present designed to ingratiate the candidate with the electorate, and not as a calculated and binding attempt to suborn it. The giving of little presents has long been an established convention in business and social relationships in Japan, and although based on an ethic of strict reciprocity, has also developed into a means of advertisement that does not entail any particular obligation for those receiving them.[22]

Bigger bribes, between three and ten yen, were serious efforts on the part of candidates to buy particular votes. Although some Diet seats were won by copious bribes, Mason thinks that overall the composition of the lower house was not decided primarily by bribery.[23]

That party politicians were not alone in the frenzy of bribery on the eve of the first national election is illustrated in the late 1889 letter, requesting secret funds, from Nakai Hiroshi to Agriculture and Commerce Minister Inoue Kaoru, who was a long-time member of the postrestoration elite. Nakai said,

> [T]he time for next spring's elections is approaching, political parties will have to plan to exert all their efforts including paying sums of money, large and small, to attract businessmen . . . and to expand their party strength. Happily in Kyoto and its hinterland . . . [various business associations] have not yet affiliated with any political parties. Naturally, however, if we neglect them the situation for us may become quite irretrievable. Hitherto we have had enough money. *Even a small amount of gifts can make a certain difference to the direction in which a given party member goes, and we are putting some effort into this.* . . . For the future we deeply desire to work out a plan whereby distinguished people should be sent to the Diet. Without a certain amount of money this is impossible, but if evidence of this is revealed it may on the contrary create a hostile reaction, in which case the scheme would lose its effectiveness. Therefore our present duty is to keep the details strictly secret.[24]

The first national election ushered in Japan's experiment with constitutional government. Newly elected members of the House of Representatives, in which opposition politicians outnumbered government supporters 171 to 129, were united on the issues of the need for cabinet responsibility to the Diet and of the need to reduce the land tax. The government, which was dominated by *han* cliques *(hanbatsu)* determined to move ahead with an ambitious program of industrial development and military expansion, was soon locked in confrontation with the "popular parties" *(mintō).* Lower house members quickly used the new unrestricted right to disagree publicly with the government and attacked the inviting target of the cabinet's budget. As a result the early Diet sessions became one extended criticism of cabinet policy; the result was an era of bitterness and hostility. As time passed, however, popular parties moved toward the government position to the point of passing an increase in the land tax and supporting an increase in the size of the military. Moreover, as the popular parties gained strength they formed a cabinet led by Ōkuma Shigenobu with Itagaki Taisuke as home minister (June 30–November 8, 1898).[25]

George Akita, writing in 1962, took to task the traditional view of the development of parliamentary government. In part, this view was that after the first election "the oligarchs, made even more powerful by the Constitution, adroitly manipulated the existing institutions such as the Emperor and the Privy Council, and exploited the inherent weaknesses of the parties—factionalism and lack of principles. This forced the parties to compromise on their primary goal of party cabinets and to accept instead a taste of public power dispensed in a niggardly manner by the oligarchs." The traditional view concludes that the results "of these factors were the effective frustration of democratic government and the party movement in Japan prior to the end of the Pacific War."[26] In fact, states Akita, from the beginning the oligarchs accepted the idea of power sharing that is central to parliamentary government, even though it meant the introduction of what they regarded as selfish and irresponsible elements into the state administration. The compromise on the conflict over the budget that emerged in the first session of the Diet illustrated that the oligarchs were not fully in control of the parliamentary experiment. This early compromise set the pattern for the following Diet sessions. Akita sees this outcome as a result of factionalism within both the oligarchical camp and the ranks of the politicians.[27]

Others support this view that compromise was the hallmark of the Meiji parliamentary system. R. H. P. Mason notes that "a sizeable and notable group among the Liberals were anxious from the outset to reach an agreement with the government on the matter of the budget; and consequently the question of whether any more of their number had to be bribed as a last resort to secure passage is of little more than secondary importance. The fundamental process was government by compromise, and not government by corruption."[28] J. A. A. Stockwin, commenting on the decade of the 1890s, writes, "It is also the story of politics of compromise, pragmatism and fine calculation, in which political actors confronted by superior force rarely maintain rigid positions for ideological reasons, but rather trim their sails to the wind of reality, preferring even limited access to political power over principled confrontation." As for the *hanbatsu*, Stockwin notes that they "learned how to use the weaknesses of the parties—and particularly their pragmatism (or, if one prefers, venality)—in order ultimately to spike their guns."[29]

It is clear that the main theme in the history of political parties is not corruption, but as the following pages make clear, bribery did play an important role in the political process. It greased the gears of the political machinery.

The stormy First Diet session opened on November 29, 1890. Prime Minister Yamagata Aritomo, who faced an antagonistic lower house, viewed political parties with distaste and suspicion. Yamagata's call for unity in support of the government's legislative program was met by hostility and an attack upon the proposed budget. Yamagata used a variety of tactics to split the opposition, including bribery. One source states that "Yamagata seems to have agreed reluctantly to the buying of Diet votes by his lieutenants, but the bad aftertaste of such dealings only confirmed his detestation of party politics."[30] Another scholar notes that there is "little doubt that the ministry employed open bribery. Hayashida [Kametarō] writes that twenty-eight Tosa faction men switched sides temporarily *after* a visit to the finance minister's official residence."[31] About this bribery incident, Akita writes, "It is an almost universally accepted belief that the Tosa faction was bribed to support the government. However, Oka [Yoshitake] categorically states that: 'To this date, no historical material has been discovered to substantiate this rumor.' "[32] As a footnote, however, Akita adds, "There seems to be one piece of indirect evidence that bribery may have been used sometime during the first session. In a letter to Itō, dated December 12, probably in 1891, Mutsu [Munemitsu] speaks of 'the customary method of corruption' with which the government hopes to inveigle the Diet members, and Mutsu expressed fears that this method would prove effective 'in this session.' "[33] Unfortunately, Akita, in an eagerness to downplay the role of bribery and to emphasize the spirit of compromise in the political process, ignores the view of Hayashida Kametarō. Political bribery, by its very nature, is kept secret, so the lack of paper documentation is not surprising. In Hayashida, however, we have an "eyewitness" to this event. Hayashida, a graduate of Tokyo Imperial University, worked as a bureaucrat attached to the Privy Council and later was employed by the Legislative Bureau. In 1890 he was appointed the first secretary of the lower house.[34] Given Hayashida's position and Mutsu's comment, it appears likely that the pattern of bribery discernible in later sessions of the Diet had its beginning in this first session.

The Yamagata cabinet, after much political maneuvering, managed to pass a reduced budget; the next cabinet, of Matsukata Masayoshi (May 6, 1891–July 30, 1892), was determined to break the power of the popular parties. At the recommendation of Yamagata, Matsukata picked Shinagawa Yajirō, one of the elder statesman's political disciples, for home minister. Another follower of Yamagata, Shirane Sen'ichi, was chosen for vice-minister. The business of the Second Diet soon was halted by a debate over the government's issuance of an emergency imperial ordinance to suppress publication; this acrimonious dispute spilled over into discussions about the budget bill. With his budget rejected, Matsukata ordered the Diet dissolved. Encouraged by Matsukata, Home Minister Shinagawa ruthlessly interfered in the election planned for February 15, 1892, by arresting candidates, having gangs of toughs molest voters, burning antigovernment politicians' property, and giving bribes. Prefectural governors and police chiefs were secretly ordered to disrupt campaigns of anticabinet politicians and to aid government supporters. These tactics resulted in the most brutal election in Japanese history: twenty-five were killed and more than three hundred wounded. In spite of this, most of the previous representatives were reelected, and the government faced an angry lower house in the next Diet term. Indeed, even members of the House of Peers were outraged, and in May a majority of members urged the cabinet to punish those who were behind the election disturbances. Eventually, after getting a reduced budget passed and after the forced resignation of Shinagawa in March 1892, Matsukata dissolved the cabinet in August.[35]

By the time of the Yamagata second cabinet (November 8, 1898– October 19, 1900), the giving and receiving of "gifts" and bribes was a standard feature of political life. Yamagata's second tour as prime minister, however, was a period of unprecedented corruption and bribery among politicians: a fixed sum of money was guaranteed for each vote supporting a government bill. The going rate for one tax bill, for example, was five hundred to fifteen hundred yen per vote.[36]

Despite a strong distaste for politicians, Yamagata made a secret deal with Hoshi Tōru, who was a leading figure in the Kenseitō. Working through Hoshi, Yamagata passed out funds to lower house members for their votes on a tax bill. Army Minister Katsura Tarō was the conduit for bribes to upper house members. To obtain the large amounts of money required for vote buying, Yamagata turned to businessmen and the Imperial Household Ministry. According to the diary of Hara Kei, Yamagata got the money used to buy up Kenseitō politicians from the emperor's privy purse (Yamagata received the huge sum of 980,000 yen). At least 80,000 yen went to Hoshi. That Yamagata spread around such large sums to buy votes shocked even Hara, who was known as a very practical politician who did not disapprove of bribery to gain a political objective. Hara also noted that although Yamagata acted as a pure man, he must have pocketed a good portion of the money. Until his death in 1922, Yamagata strove to keep the money pipeline open by having his followers appointed head of the Imperial Household Ministry.[37] Three months before the Yamagata cabinet resigned, Ōkuma Shigenobu, in an interview with a reporter from a Kobe newspaper (printed on July 18, 1900), stated that "there is scarcely any one form of political corruption known in the whole history of parliamentary institutions in the west that has not shown its head here. I do not mean to say that all, or even a majority, of our legislators and electors are corrupt, but the minority prone to being corrupted is large enough to make things look very ugly and very disquieting."[38] Ōkuma's were not the only negative remarks about political corruption to appear in print. First in January 1899 and then in April 1900, the social critic Toyabe Shuntei attacked both politicians and Yamagata, saying that the latter got his way via two methods: bribery and rewards. Toyabe pointed out that the Diet had become almost like a stock market where shares were traded. Thus, Yamagata's vote buying was exposed publicly. How the general public felt is difficult to discover. Among the political elite, however, Yamagata's source of funds and use of the money became common knowledge, and although there was some muttering, few people were willing to call this sort of thing corruption; no one spoke up and called it a criminal act. Hara Kei, speaking to his diary, wrote that from this time onward most people holding public positions were openly taking bribes. Usually, they escaped punishment.[39]

By the late 1890s, Itō Hirobumi decided that the Diet could be controlled properly if he formed a political party. Thus, with Kenseitō support Itō formed the Rikken Seiyūkai in September 1900. These party politicians, eager to grasp political power, were the same men whom Yamagata had paid off with bribes and official positions.[40] Why had so many of the anti-*hanbatsu* group joined one of the foremost leaders of that group? "Partly because it had become apparent to the party leaders, from bitter experience, that under the Japanese Constitution, the only access to administrative authority was to come under the auspices of the elder statesmen whose keys opened the doors to political power."[41]

Hayashida, who was the first secretary for the House of Representatives and who became the chief secretary in 1897, was appointed a secretary for the Seiyūkai. The other secretary for the party was Samejima Takenosuke, who became chief cabinet secretary in Itō's cabinet formed the following month. Hayashida wrote, "It is necessary to have the strength of gold in order to produce party members. . . . During that time that was the common practice. Itō, however, did not like doing this sort of thing, but he realized that it was necessary to first have money, and second have money, and third have money in order to fight the war."[42] Besides tapping secret service funds, Itō also sought money from the Imperial Household Ministry. The most important source of money for the establishment of the party, however, was the Mitsui businessman Magoshi Kyōhei, who gave three hundred thousand yen, with the promise of more if needed.[43] Itō's decision to combine with party politicians marked a watershed in the development of political parties. Over the following years a growing number of civil bureaucrats entered the ranks of political parties. George Akita writes, "Despite the fact that he did not understand and could not cope with party politics, he *early* and *realistically* made the decision to combine with the parties and thus helped to shape the nature and style of Japanese politics that has continued to this day—the combination of bureaucrats and politicians."[44]

Itō formed his last cabinet on October 19, 1900. Almost immediately the new cabinet, a mixture of party politicians and bureaucrats friendly to Itō, was opposed by supporters of Yamagata in the House of Peers. When the Peers blocked a bill to increase taxation, however, Itō pressured them with an order from the emperor, and the bill passed. This attempt to block Itō's tax bill was not the only tactic used by the Peers to discredit the new party and to bring down Itō's government. On December 17, just before the Diet session opened, a majority of the Peers demanded the removal of Communications Minister Hoshi Tōru, a leading figure in the new party politician–bureaucrat combination. Hoshi, they charged, should be dismissed and prosecuted for corrupt actions as a member of the Tokyo city government.[45] In the main this attack on Hoshi was a roundabout method of hitting Itō; it is doubtful that many members of the upper house were deeply concerned about Hoshi's political deals with Tokyo city politicians. The Peers' method of attacking the Itō cabinet, in which the real political issues were hidden behind charges of corruption, became in the following years an all too common method of dealing with political foes.

The peers, however, were right on target when they charged Hoshi with corruption. Indeed, Hoshi was the personification of a corrupt politician. Hoshi was a leading figure in the Jiyūtō (Liberal Party) who was elected to the House of Representatives in 1892 and became speaker. During the Fifth Diet, which opened in November 1893 (Itō Hirobumi was prime minister), Hoshi was impeached for accepting gifts and money. The no-confidence vote was undoubtedly politically motivated, because of Hoshi's political deal with Itō, but nonetheless, the common perception was that Hoshi was guilty of corrupt practices. Several years later, when it was reported that Hoshi said that Diet members should take all offered bribes, most knowledgeable people must have accepted the statement as accurate.

Hoshi, of course, needed an enormous amount of money to build and maintain a political army in the lower house. Political payoffs worked well, and by 1900 his faction in the Kenseitō (formerly the Liberal Party) was dominant. The search for funds pushed Hoshi into closer ties with businessmen, and he encouraged followers to seek campaign funds and living expenses from businessmen. Indeed, Hoshi joined the Tokyo Municipal Assembly because most important businessmen were associated with the many companies seeking franchises from that body.[46]

On October 15, 1900, the *Tokyo Yokohama Mainichi Newspaper* published an article about a 3,000-yen bribe given to Tokyo city officials by a company manufacturing lead pipes. The three officials named were known as Hoshi's followers. Behind this newspaper attack was the politician-journalist Shimada Saburō, who was outspoken in condemning political bribery. Shimada, who held a lower house seat from the first election, practiced what he preached: he refused gifts from anyone except relatives and never accepted personal requests in connection with his political role. Shimada, who was president of the newspaper and a long-time foe of Hoshi, stepped up the newspaper attacks, identifying Hoshi as the chief of the robbers plundering the nation and urging justice authorities to indict him. In the midst of these attacks, Hoshi became communications minister in the fourth Itō cabinet. On December 19, Justice Minister Kaneko Kentarō announced at a general meeting of the Seiyūkai that Hoshi would not be indicted. Nevertheless, Hoshi resigned from the cabi-

net two days later.[47] On June 21, 1901, Hoshi was stabbed to death by
Iba Shōtarō, who justified the murder by stating that Hoshi, while
president of the Tokyo Municipal Assembly, had accepted bribes,
bringing disgrace to the nation. Iba was from a well-known wealthy
house that taught martial arts; he had been manager of the Nihon
Chochiku Bank and principal of the Tokyo Agricultural School.[48]
Although it is impossible to prove that Shimada's vitriolic newspaper
attacks stimulated Iba's murder of Hoshi, "public opinion" held Shimada responsible.[49]

Despite Itō Hirobumi's skillful maneuver to pass the tax bill,
external opposition to the cabinet mounted as fights over government spending on public works divided cabinet members. Itō
resigned after only seven months in office. As things turned out, this
was the last cabinet headed by a senior member of the old *hanbatsu.*
The next cabinet was led by General Katsura Tarō, a handpicked
protégé of Yamagata's.[50]

The new prime minister, whose first cabinet ran from June 2,
1901, to January 7, 1906, had considerable political experience as
minister of war in previous cabinets. Although Katsura enjoyed
domestic political success and foreign policy triumph, his first term
in office was marred by a sensational, widespread bribery case. The
Textbook scandal caught public attention on December 17, 1902, as
police exposed bribery cases involving textbook publishers and prefectural textbook examination committees. By March 1903 many
prefectural education officials, from most prefectures, had been
arrested. After investigations by procurators, 152 suspects went before preliminary trial judges. Of the 152 suspects, 28 were released;
the balance were tried at the Tokyo District Court. By the end of the
appeals process, 69 officials had been found guilty of accepting
bribes. Among the suspects in this case were the governors of Chiba,
Tochigi, Gunma, Miyagi, Niigata, and Shimane; former governors of
Miyazaki and Shimane were also arrested. Most of these big fish,
however, eluded the legal net, which probably surprised few among
the newspaper-reading public. The investigation of Governor Abe
Hiroshi (Chiba) is a typical example. Abe told investigators that the
large sum of money he received from the president of a textbook
publishing firm was merely a loan, which he planned to repay. Justice Minister Kiyoura Keigo, who was closely identified with Yamagata Aritomo, ordered Abe released from detention: the chief procurator in this case resigned in protest. Abe survived this scandal,
becoming mayor of Tokyo.[51]

This case not only exposed the fact that bribery had gone on for
many years but also stopped most opposition to the Education Minis-

try's drive to control totally the selection of elementary school textbooks. Up to this point the ministry offered "guidance" in the selection of textbooks, but with this case the ministry, on April 13, 1903, took full control of the process.[52]

A few years earlier bribery had appeared in the civil service examinations as well, especially in the bar examinations. To prevent fraud the government established detailed guidelines for examinations and tried to keep questions secret. Although this approach appeared to work for the civil service examinations, leaks of questions continued in the bar examinations. It took a major scandal in October 1892 to change the complacent attitude about this problem among the government and press. Because this scandal implicated a Justice Ministry clerk, occurred in Tokyo, and involved many candidates, it became a major news story. The clerk and seven candidates were prosecuted for accepting bribes and for giving them, but the Tokyo District Court ruled that no law had been broken. The clerk was punished, however, by dismissal from office for leaking official secrets. Newspapers, by now hungry to pursue a good story, charged that officials had for years ignored similar cases because they had occurred outside Tokyo.[53] Press charges were probably true; the Justice Ministry at this time was in a chaotic condition, and "many officials were notoriously irresponsible, some spending much of their time at the geisha houses of Yoshiwara, while others rarely appeared at the ministry for work before noon."[54]

As noted above, businessmen were involved heavily in the spreading pool of corruption. They did not have to look far to find willing takers of the bribes offered in exchange for government contracts and other favors. The Mitsui Company, for example, had close contacts with highly placed government leaders, including Inoue Kaoru, Yamagata Aritomo, and Gotō Shōjirō. Money lent by Mitsui to key government leaders was written off as "gifts." Mitsubishi favored Ōkuma Shigenobu and Ōkubo Toshimichi.[55] Indeed, as Robert Scalapino points out, although the corruption scandals involving politicians make it appear that they were more corrupt than Meiji Restoration leaders and their protégés, the "oligarchic leaders obtained personal funds from the capitalist class; whether it was by outright monetary bribery, shares in the company, or loans written off, they received sizable benefits."[56] Walter McLaren, writing at the end of the Meiji period, notes that the oligarchs "were originally in almost every case either poor samurai or the sons of men of very modest fortune, and have been all their lives in the service of the State, drawing small salaries. Their present immense properties are not the result of savings wisely invested but of peculations and bribes."[57]

Ōkuma Shigenobu, for example, who lived richly and ostentatiously, felt that people whom he had encouraged to achieve success should show their appreciation in the form of gifts. These gifts included land in Tokyo, a coastal villa, and a villa in the mountains. Among the political merchants, Ōkuma's closest tie was with Iwasaki of the Mitsubishi Company.[58] Yamagata Aritomo, who needed large sums of money for a network of followers in the bureaucracy and for manipulating politicians, drew upon Mitsui and the privy purse. Even though Yamagata supposedly used much of the money collected for politics, he somehow acquired great wealth. Although details about most of the money that flowed Yamagata's way remain secret, his many residences were an indication of great wealth. Chinzansō in Tokyo (18,000 *tsubo*) was famous for its garden. This stately home was built after the Satsuma Rebellion (1877). A home in Ōiso in Kanagawa Prefecture (5,000 *tsubo*) was constructed while Yamagata served as home minister during the 1880s. Another home was maintained in Koishikawa (Tokyo). This one, too, had a famous garden. In 1891, Yamagata purchased a residence in Kyoto and then built a new home near Nanzenji. The later home as well was famous for its garden. Another home (10,000 *tsubo*) with a famous garden was maintained in Odawara, Kanagawa Prefecture. Finally, there was Shinchinzansō (700 *tsubo*) in Tokyo. Next door was the home (2,000 *tsubo*) used by his mistress.[59] Inoue Kaoru, who began his rise to wealth and power in the Finance Ministry, became a confidant and adviser of the Mitsui family. Indeed, so deeply was Inoue involved with Mitsui's financial deals, one scholar applies the label "commander for Mitsui."[60] Itō Miyoji, who claimed that his fortune came from savings and wise investments, did not mention that he had acquired the *Tokyo Nichinichi Newspaper* at no cost from Itō Hirobumi and that he used the newspaper to blackmail businessmen, politicians, and others. A bribe to Itō Miyoji would silence the newspaper.[61] Unlike many of the political oligarchs, Itō Hirobumi had a reputation for financial honesty and was not plagued with unsavory rumors of bribery. Nevertheless, as a political leader he needed large sums of money, and it appears that these needs were met by gifts from the imperial family and other benefactors.[62]

Although rumors about bribery employed by businessmen appeared in newspapers year after year, their deals with politicians were usually hidden. Occasionally, however, the curtain was pulled aside, giving the public a detailed look at a bribery transaction. This is what happened in the Greater Japan Sugar Refining Company (Dai Nihon Seitō Kabushikigaisha or Nittō) scandal of 1907–1908.

This affair began because the company was not doing well and because lower house members were easy to bribe. This situation was not unusual: oil companies and railway companies were also trying to buy the votes of legislators in an effort to influence government policies. What was unusual about the sugar company's efforts was that company officials and lower house members were prosecuted, in the first large-scale prosecution of Diet members for bribery. An important result of this case was an expansion of the power of justice officials.[63]

In December 1906, company officials lobbied for the extension of a law that reduced the import tax on sugar, which was due to expire on March 31. The company, which wanted the temporary law extended until July 1911, rallied enough support to get a bill introduced in December 1906; Finance Minister Sakatani Yoshio supported the bill. Taiwan sugar companies, however, viewed the bill as a threat and got some Seiyūkai politicians to oppose it. To save the bill Nittō executives decided to bribe Diet members. Two executives, Isomura Otosuke and Akiyama Kazuhiro, approached lower house members; company president Sakanioi Takiaki handled members of the upper house. More than 120,000 yen went to lower house members (Seiyūkai ca. 53,000; Kenseihontō ca. 25,000; Daidō Kurabu ca. 35,000; others ca. 10,000). The bill passed the lower house on February 21, 1907, and the upper house on March 19.[64]

Unfortunately for the company, this successful effort did not stop the company's financial decline, so executives began to consider selling it, with the aim of persuading the government to become the buyer. After an unsuccessful effort to gain support among bureaucrats in the Finance Ministry and the Agricultural and Commerce Ministry, Nittō executives began to work on politicians, hoping that they would push the bureaucrats into buying the company. This activity began in December 1907, with special effort directed at Seiyūkai members Matsuura Gohei and Sawada Mamoru (Isomura gave them 30,000 yen). By the end of the month, seven other Seiyūkai members had part of this money. Besides this money up front, the Seiyūkai was promised 300,000 yen if the bill for the purchase of the company passed; another 300,000 yen was promised to political groups in the House of Peers. The smaller Daidō Kurabu was not neglected: Yokota Torahiko got 20,000 yen plus a promise of 100,000 yen. As part of this effort, the company hired Shibusawa Eiichi, a famous businessman, as a consultant and asked Finance Minister Sakatani to pick a worthy bureaucrat to join the company (company president Sakanioi was originally a bureaucrat in the Agricultural and Commerce Ministry). Despite this strong pressure, however, the cabinet of Saionji Kinmochi (January 7, 1906–July 14, 1908) refused to permit the purchase.[65]

Rumors of collusion between company officials and politicians prompted an investigation and prosecution by Justice Ministry officials. A central figure in these unprecedented investigations and trials was Hiranuma Kiichirō, head of the Criminal Affairs Bureau. Before this time Tokyo procurators had been handicapped by poor police cooperation and a lack of funds to carry out an independent investigation. Hiranuma solved a big part of this problem by obtaining a 70,000-yen fund for procuratorial investigation. With this money, procurators carried out a detailed investigation of the sugar company offices and the homes of suspects. The public and politicians alike were amazed at this unprecedented investigation. During the investigation, the Katsura cabinet (second, July 14, 1908–August 30, 1911) appeared content to watch procurators indict Seiyūkai politicians, but as the scandal reached people near the cabinet the prime minister threatened to stop the case.[66]

According to Hiranuma Kiichirō, the power of the Justice Ministry at that time was not strong enough to ignore an order from a prime minister to stop an investigation. Ordered by Katsura to do something about the investigation before it caused the cabinet a problem, Procurator General Matsumuro Itaru returned to the ministry and said it would be best to halt the investigation. The chief procurator for the case, Kobayashi Yoshirō, threatened to resign. At that point, Hiranuma decided to visit the prime minister. Their meeting resulted in a compromise: Katsura would not interfere in the case and Hiranuma agreed not to enlarge its scope. Kobayashi, too, agreed to these terms.[67]

Suspects in this case were tried in two groups: the company officials who gave bribes and the politicians who accepted them. Eight company executives were scheduled for trial until Sakanioi shot himself. On December 6, 1909, the remaining seven were found guilty. Isomura was sentenced to four years in prison, Akiyama to three and a half; five others received lesser prison terms but got stays of execution. Isomura and Akiyama appealed their sentences, which were reduced to three years. The Supreme Court rejected a final appeal on March 29, 1912. As for the politicians, twenty-two were tried; sixteen of them received some sort of punishment. Seven of the sixteen were sentenced to three years in prison, but they got stays of execution. Those who actually were imprisoned got between four and ten months. Matsuura Gohei, for example, was sentenced to ten months and fined 20,150 yen; Sawada Mamoru got eight months and was fined 3,000 yen.[68]

Reflecting on this case many years later, Hiranuma said, "From this time onward, the public began to fear justice authorities. . . . For the Justice Ministry, the Nittō incident was a watershed that marked a new period. Up to that time the office of the procurator was not influential in the [political] world."[69] Ohara Naoshi, who was a procurator at the Tokyo District Court, supports this viewpoint. In a postwar interview he noted that before the Nittō incident neither the police nor the public paid much attention to the Tokyo procurators and that before this case it was nearly impossible to arrest lower house members for corruption. This all changed, however, because of the actions of three men: Hiranuma, Matsumuro, and Kobayashi. The key to the successful prosecution of this case, he felt, was the fund of seventy thousand yen Hiranuma obtained. Like Hiranuma, Ohara viewed this case as a watershed in the development of the powers of Justice Ministry procurators.[70]

One close student of the rise of the Hiranuma clique within the Justice Ministry notes that the prosecution and conviction of politicians in the Nittō case

> made Hiranuma an important actor on the political stage. . . . We note, however, that Hiranuma did not launch a zealous moral crusade to eradicate moral corruption from government totally, but that he compromised with Katsura. . . . The agreement with Katsura assured the procuracy faction of a certain sphere of political influence and set a precendent for future political bargaining. Hiranuma . . . was always fully cognizant of any potential for political gain in procuratorial investigations. . . . [Hiranuma was able to rationalize these] tactical concessions for power by invoking the formula of "power perfects virture."[71]

Because Hiranuma exerted a strong influence upon the justice field and the world of politics over a very long period, a look at his motives is in order. The principles upon which he based his politics were derived mainly from his early training in samurai values and Confucianism. This traditional ethical system, he believed, remained valid even for a rapidly industrializing society. Hiranuma also believed, however, that Confucian values had to operate within a modern legal structure. It appears that Hiranuma regarded himself as a reformer dedicated to the promotion of traditional morality from the time he entered the Justice Ministry in 1888. Faced with a ministry crippled by official lassitude and factionalism, Hiranuma was happy to support Vice-Minister Yokota Kunitomi, who began an inhouse reform in 1898. Hiranuma became Yokota's key supporter in this difficult task. After Yokota became procurator general, Hiranuma was made his chief aide. Although some people may have regarded Hiranuma's professed Confucian ethics as anachronistic, a number of young justice officials did not, and he soon had a loyal

following. From the beginning of his career, Hiranuma resented the
hanbatsu, and later he added big business and political parties to the
list. Throughout his public career Hiranuma's zeal to raise the prestige of the emperor and the national polity *(kokutai)* matched that of
Yamagata Aritomo.[72]

Reflecting on the sensational Nittō case, Walter McLaren writes,

> The venality of the members of the Lower House, when contrasted
> with the peculations of the official class, appears extremely sordid.
> The bribes are smaller, and the transactions almost invariably take
> place in disreputable resorts in an atmospher of vulgar dissipation.
> . . . But it is impossible to blame the party politicians more severely
> than the Cabinet officers. All alike have their price. . . . There are
> and were some notable exceptions, but these merely serve to em-
> phasize the almost universal corruptibility of the Cabinet and the
> Diet.[73]

A new Penal Code was implemented in October 1908. Chapter 24
covered "Crimes of Official Corruption"; Articles 197 and 198 there-
in dealt with bribes. Any public official who demanded, or agreed to,
or received a bribe could be punished with up to three years in
prison. If after accepting a bribe an official either failed to perform a
required act or committed an improper act, the punishment could
be up to ten years in prison. Bribe money would be confiscated (Article 197). During the following years, Supreme Court decisions in
connection with bribery cases involving government officials were
listed after this article. These decisions made clear that taking a
bribe was risky. For example, a legislator who took a bribe and then
did not attend a meeting at which he was scheduled to vote could be
prosecuted for failing to perform a required act. Article 198 applied
to those who gave or promised to give bribes to public officials. The
penalty was prison for up to three years or a fine of up to three hundred yen. Several Supreme Court cases were appended to this article
as well. For example, a bribe offered indirectly to an official via his
wife was considered a violation.[74]

We have seen that money and gifts in exchange for votes played
an important role in the first national election of July 1890. Over the
following years the use of bribery to influence voters became a regular feature of political life. Another normal feature of national elections, as the size of the electorate expanded, was a sharp rise in the
money needed to win a campaign. Candidates were forced to
depend more upon local bosses who collected votes, and, starting
about 1908, the pressing need for money pushed candidates into the
arms of the business community.[75]

Voter qualifications for the 1890 election included payment of direct national taxes of at least fifteen yen, which produced an electorate of about 450,000 out of a population of about 40,000,000. The tax qualification was lowered to ten yen in 1900; by 1908 the number of voters was about 1,600,000. In the early elections, the size of each constituency was small, ranging from hundreds of voters to several thousand. Thus it was possible for each candidate to meet voters person-to-person at election time. The great jump in the size of the electorate in the early twentieth century, however, broke this pattern of personal interaction and fostered the growth of a class of election brokers who sold blocks of votes to the highest bidder. These changes not only pushed up the cost of elections but also destabilized *jiban* (electoral bases) maintained by politicians.[76] Diet candidates responded to changing times by trying to create "iron *jiban*"—solid support among powerful headmen, mayors, landlords, and other respected local figures. A successful politician greased the *jiban* machinery before each election and dug deeply into the national pork barrel during his tenure in the lower house. Obviously, a successful politican required a constant flow of money into one hand so he could pass out funds with the other. The inflation of election costs also promoted the rise in party ranks of politicians who knew how to obtain and dispense large sums of money. The number of reported cases of bribery—1,338 in 1908; 3,329 in 1912; 7,278 in 1915—reflects the greater emphasis on vote buying.[77] A confidential Justice Ministry report notes that in the 1915 election, respected local figures who organized large-scale vote buying each received between ten thousand and fifteen thousand yen from candidates.[78] It appears that a good portion of this money found its way "into the hands of voters who, by and large, were indifferent as to the outcome of the election."[79]

Hara Kei is the premier example of a politician who understood the new money politics. Hara joined Itō Hirobumi's new Rikken Seiyūkai in 1900 as a member of the board of directors and secretary-general. Fortune smiled on Hara, as he rose rapidly in the political world: communications minister (1900), home minister (1906, 1911, 1913–1914), and head of the Seiyūkai (1914).[80] Hara's success depended upon skillful political maneuvering, especially upon the operation of a complex system of patronage. As a patron Hara granted political offices to those who showed promise; to build a solid voter base he pushed pork-barrel legislation for selected local areas. Crucial to the Seiyūkai's power base was the continued flow of funds from Hara to all parts of the patronage network.[81] "Hara dispensed money with grace. He would patiently listen to the petitioners' reasons for their need of funds so that they 'would not lose face.' "[82] Hara, the ultimate political realist, understood that men were best moved by money, official posts, and various favors. It appears that the large sums of money that flowed through Hara did not stick to his fingers. One source notes that he was personally frugal, and another notes that the money raised was given to others.[83]

During the late Meiji and the early Taisho (1912–1926) era, rumors of corruption among high bureaucrats and party politicians were common newspaper fare, but proof of illegal actions seldom became public. In 1914 and 1915, however, facts about two serious bribery scandals filled newspaper pages and rocked the political world. The first sensational scandal focused on high naval officers who were convicted of taking bribes; the second, the so-called Ōura incident, involved a home minister who handed out bribes and who tried to rig an election, plus many politicians who both gave and took bribes. Hiranuma, who was by now procurator general, was quick to use these incidents to expand the powers of the procuracy.

The first scandal hit the cabinet of Admiral Yamamoto Gonnohyōe (prime minister from February 1913 to April 1914) on January 23, 1914. Morning editions of Tokyo newspapers quoted a Reuters dispatch of January 21 from London about the Berlin trial and conviction of a German who had worked for the Siemens, Schuckert, and Company office in Tokyo; he received two years' imprisonment for stealing Siemens documents, which he used to blackmail company officials. According to Reuters, the trial revealed that Siemens was bribing Japanese navy officers to obtain naval contracts. The trial also implicated the British firm of Vickers and Company in a kickback arrangement with naval officers. Foes of the Seiyūkai-dominated Yamamoto cabinet seized this hot issue as a weapon with which to attack the government. The timing of the Reuters dispatch was most unfortunate for the cabinet, which was urging the Diet to approve a budget with a large sum earmarked for naval expansion.[84]

Navy prosecutors began an investigation soon after the scandal surfaced. Vice Admiral Matsumoto Kazu was accused of taking a bribe of 400,000 yen from Vickers and Company in connection with the building of the battleship *Kongō*. The money was distributed by Mitsui Bussan (Mitsui's trading company), which acted as a go-between. Both Vickers and Siemens had contracts to help construct the *Kongō*. Rear Admiral Fujii Mitsugorō and former captain Sawasaki Hirotake were also charged with taking bribes. As this pool of corruption expanded, newspapers carried cartoons satirizing greedly naval officers who demanded a "commision" on ships under construction. Moreover, rumors circulated that Navy Minister Saitō

Makoto and Prime Minister Yamamoto had either taken money or at least had known about the bribes. On March 30, Vice Admiral Matsumoto, who was rumored to be the next navy minister, was arrested. Matsumoto confided to a fellow officer that the money was not taken for personal gain but to help the navy when he became minister. Also, he said that he got only a third of the money from Vickers: Mitsui kept the rest. The court-martial on May 29 sentenced the admiral to three years in prison and to a fine of 409,800 yen. Sawasaki received a one-year sentence and a fine of 11,500 yen. Rear Admiral Fujii, who was charged with bribery in not only the *Kongō* construction case but in connection with the battleship *Hiei* as well, was sentenced on September 3 to four years and six months in prison and fined 368,000 yen. Procurator General Hiranuma, who closely followed the naval trial as his procurators were investigating civilians involved in this scandal, knew that the naval court-martial did not reach high enough, because Navy Minister Saitō had received 100,000 yen from Matsumoto. He said nothing, however, about this. Hiranuma also knew that the rumors of Prime Minister Yamamoto's involvement were not true. Although Admiral Saitō escaped the wrathful navy procurators, he was punished by being forced from the active list into the reserves.[85]

Civilians in this scandal were investigated by procurators from the Tokyo District Court, with Ohara Naoshi in charge. Although justice officials moved with extreme care, Hiranuma nevertheless was worried that the navy might close ranks and attack the Justice Ministry. He visited Prime Minister Yamamoto and Navy Minister Saitō to guarantee their cooperation and conferred with navy procurator Uchida Shigenari, who pledged full cooperation. With this backing, Hiranuma and Ohara went to the Kure Naval Station to search for evidence linking civilians to the navy case. This search of a military installation by civilians was unprecedented. Procurators also searched the homes of Mitsui employees and seized an account book that had been altered after the scandal began. Faced with this concrete evidence, Mitsui personnel confessed. A director of Mitsui, Yamamoto Jōtarō, however, complained about the attitude of the procurator's office. Inasmuch as Mitsui's only aim was to make money, Yamamoto saw nothing wrong with taking a "commission."[86] On July 18, 1914, five Mitsui employees were sentenced to prison terms ranging from two years to three months; two were put on probation. The five cases moved to the appeals court and on April 30, 1915, one sentence was reversed, one defendant paid a forty-yen fine, and three were put on probation. These were very light sentences. Director Yamamoto, however, was removed abruptly from his position by Mitsui.[87] Yoshida

Shūkichi, who acted as Siemens' clerk for transactions with the navy, was also prosecuted, but his case did not go to trial: someone strangled him on March 17, 1914, at the detention house.[88] During their investigation of civilians, procurators heard rumors of bribery by former vice admiral Yamanouchi Masuji, who had become a top official of the Muroran Steel Company after retirement, so they interrogated him. Afterwards the former admiral tried to kill himself. Because Ohara regarded him as a living corpse, there was no prosecution.[89] Hiranuma Kiichirō, in his memoirs, noted that as a result of this incident Mitsui began a new bookkeeping policy to better cover up the movement of illegal funds.[90] One scholar, discussing the political activities of Mitsui in the 1930s, notes that political work was carried out by the so-called research department. The "research" was in fact political maneuvering with civilian and military bureaucrats and politicians. "The finances of the research department were handled on a cash basis for which no records were kept."[91] Obviously, Mitsui never forgot Hiranuma's seizure of its account book.

It is difficult to ascertain what the general public thought about the naval bribery scandal, but protests by politically engaged citizens furnish a partial answer. On February 5, 1914, opposition political parties held a rally condemning the cabinet; fifteen thousand people attended. On February 10 about fifty thousand people filled Hibiya Park and marched on the Diet building, where they clashed with four thousand police. Demonstrators also surrounded two buildings belonging to progovernment newspapers.[92] Police reported the following impromptu speeches by demonstrators: An angry tradesman said, "Prime Minister Yamamoto took a commission. The *Maiyū* [a newspaper] supports the government, so it takes a commission, too. I'm a former soldier, and we should all rise in anger now for the sake of the nation. The police are running dogs of the bureaucrats."[93] A tailor yelled, "Overthrow the Yamamoto cabinet! Yamamoto . . . is a great thief who gained millions in riches through his 'commission.' Overthrow Yamamoto! We must sever Gonnohyōe's head from his body."[94] One newspaperman-historian, commenting on this scandal, wrote that although the public expected commercial morality to be low, the navy was highly regarded, so its venality came as a great shock.[95] Home Minister Hara Kei responded to public criticism of the cabinet by banning critical newspaper articles and calling out troops to control the crowds demanding Yamamoto's resignation.[96]

Tetsuo Najita points out that although the bribery scandal badly damaged the Yamamoto cabinet, the real cause of its collapse was much more complicated than the exposure of corrupt admirals. The Seiyūkai blocked a no-confidence vote in the lower house on February 10, but the Yamagata Aritomo clique in the upper house, which wanted to destroy the hated Yamamoto cabinet and its Seiyūkai supporters, vetoed the government's budget bill. The cabinet resigned on March 23, 1914.[97]

The Ōkuma Shigenobu cabinet (April 1914–October 1916) was established on the ruins of Admiral Yamamoto's government. Yamagata Aritomo and other elder statesmen chose Ōkuma because he was not from the former Satsuma fief, was opposed to the dominant Seiyūkai, had popular support, was amenable to Yamagata's general program, and supported Japanese interests in China.[98] Although Ōkuma was a long-time foe of cabinets dominated by statesmen from the former fiefs of Satsuma and Chōshū, he also hated the Seiyūkai and was willing to become Yamagata's vehicle to crush the despised party.[99] Ōkuma, who was famous for denouncing corruption within political parties, was hailed by the public as the champion of honest representative government.[100]

At the Thirty-fifth Diet (from December 1914), the cabinet presented a budget that included the addition of two army divisions and expansion of the navy. Inasmuch as the Seiyūkai had a majority in the House of Representatives, the government tried to split the opposition. Agriculture and Commerce Minister Ōura Kanetake, a leading figure in the Yamagata clique and a powerful political force in his own right, worked through Hayashida Kametarō, chief secretary of the lower house, to bribe members. Hayashida passed on forty thousand yen from Ōura to Shirakawa Tomoichi and Masuda Jōzō, who in turn handed out money to seven others. Besides that money, Ōura directly gave ten thousand yen to Itakura Chū. Using this money, plus more from Shirakawa and Masuda, Itakura bribed six colleagues. Despite this vote-buying effort the lower house would not approve two new army divisions; the Diet was dissolved, opening the way for a general election.[101]

After taking office, Ōkuma informed prefectural governors that it was a basic cabinet policy to prevent election campaign vote buying and other abuses. On the eve of the March 25, 1915, national election, Ōkuma called for a fair election. New Home Minister Ōura also denounced political corruption and vote buying. Nevertheless, the government manipulated the election in many illegal ways, marking it as the second most corrupt in the nation's history.[102] Ōura, who was put in charge of overseeing the election by being made home minister two months before the polling, used his police power fully: in some places police visited door-to-door to pressure voters. The going rate for a vote was between three and five yen.[103] Money was spread lavishly by the government and its allies. The funds were said to come from big-business interests and the Imperial Household Ministry. One estimate is that during the two days before the election about 1,600,000 yen was handed out in bribes.[104] Justice Minister Ozaki Yukio, however, ordered chief procurators to uphold the honor of the justice system by strictly punishing vote buyers. As a result, 10,012 people were arrested for bribery. Some of these suspects were released without being prosecuted.[105] Even though the cabinet won a great election victory, Ōura's excessive zeal provided the angry Seiyūkai with a political issue. Representative Murano Tsuneemon charged the home minister with bribery and other Election Law violations: the Seiyūkai passed a vote of no confidence. Procurators at the Tokyo District Court began investigating Ōura on May 25. When the bribery scandal became public, two cabinet members urged Ōura to resign to avoid arrest. The home minister replied that he had acted to support the cabinet's legislation and not for personal profit. Moreover, he noted, giving bribes had never been considered illegal.[106]

Procurators arrested lower house members Shirakawa and Itakura for election fraud in late June. In July, more representatives were under arrest. Eventually, Hayashida, Shirakawa, Itakura, and sixteen others (all but one were lower house members) went on trial at the Takamatsu District Court. All were judged guilty and sentenced on June 5, 1916. Hayashida, who resigned from the Diet, was fined 150 yen. Itakura got six months in prison and Shirakawa four months. Others received terms of two to three months. Eleven of them, however, were granted three-year suspended sentences. All were ordered to hand over bribe money to authorities.[107]

Justice Minister Ozaki, increasingly concerned about the spreading bribery scandal, called in Procurator General Hiranuma and justice Vice-Minister Suzuki Kisaburō to discuss the involvement of Home Minister Ōura. Ozaki noted that during the Meiji era, government officials often were involved in the crime of bribery and in violations of the Election Law but that none of these officials was prosecuted and that not even administrative punishment was applied. Nevertheless, Ozaki felt that something must be done in this case, so he asked Hiranuma and Suzuki to suggest a solution. Suzuki, who was on friendly terms with Ōkuma, dined with the prime minister and reported on the situation. Ōkuma expressed surprise.[108] The Hiranuma-Suzuki solution to the Ōura problem was a suspension of indictment *(kiso yūyo)* together with a complete withdrawal from public life. Ozaki presented this suggestion to cabinet members, who were not only surprised but angry: this kind of solution had never entered their thoughts. Indeed, it is doubtful that any of them thought that Ōura's actions had been anything but normal political business procedure. Certainly, Ōura believed his actions justified by political circumstances. The cabinet threatened to resign rather than accept the Hiranuma-Suzuki solution, but when Ozaki argued that this would be a mistake, they accepted the proposed solution. Ōura resigned from the cabinet (July 28, 1915), resigned from the House of Peers, and withdrew from all political activity. He turned over the headship of the family to his son and settled down in Kamakura.[109]

After excitement from this affair had abated Suzuki talked to the press: "I believe that the nation's ministers should never be made into prisoners in bonds. Not only is it a national disgrace in the eyes of foreign nations, but looked at from the viewpoint of national morality it is bound to have a bad influence on the people. Furthermore, Ōura has left public office, resigned his title, and withdrawn from the political field. Thus, he is expressing penitence. It is safe to assume that he has received social sanction."[110] The newspaper-reading public, however, which by this time was long familiar with politicians' and bureaucrats' corruption, viewed the Justice Ministry solution as too lenient and demanded the resignation of the entire cabinet.[111]

Ōkuma's cabinet and its supporters won an overwhelming election victory in March 1915 with a gain of sixty-two lower house seats. In July the prime minister offered to resign, but Yamagata and others urged him to stay in power. Finally, after seeing the military expansion program through the Diet, he resigned on October 8, 1916.[112]

About this sensational bribery scandal, Ōkuma's biographer writes, "It is not easy to argue that Ōkuma should be absolved of moral responsibility for Ōura's actions in the Diet. Ōkuma recognized his own laxity when he acknowledged his failure as 'imperfect supervision.' He submitted a token cabinet resignation, which was not accepted. . . . Some journalists were disillusioned that Ōkuma . . . who had held that elections were sacred and the basis of parliamentary government, had overlooked such malfeasance in his own cabinet."[113] Another scholar notes that to win the election "Ōkuma closed his eyes to bribery and chicanery."[114] Given that the prime minister approved the move of Ōura to the Home Ministry to supervise the election and that Ōura had a long career as a police administrator, Ōkuma must have suspected that there would be interference in the election. He probably expected, however, that such interference would be done in a "normal" manner and not on the massive scale employed by Ōura. It appears that the Seiyūkai looked at the abnornal interference in a similar manner; it did not anticipate that the home minister would alter the rules of the game and move "beyond the bounds of propriety in Japanese politics."[115] As for Ōura's preelection bribing of Seiyūkai politicians, one scholar notes that it was standard procedure for cabinets that did not have a lower house majority to give bribe money to the chief secretary of the lower house, who would dole it out to house members. There was no feeling among those passing out the money that a crime was being committed.[116] Certainly Ōura did not see bribing Seiyūkai members to split the opposition and to get defense bills smoothly passed as a crime.[117] Yamagata Aritomo's viewpoint surfaced in a conversation with Education Minister Ichiki Kitokurō: "It is not in the least bit wrong, because he did it for the sake of the nation."[118] Talking with Hara Kei, Yamagata justified Ōura's buying politicians' votes by pointing out that he and Itō Hirobumi did the same thing.[119]

Murano Tsuneemon, who charged Ōura with bribery on the Diet floor and who sent a document to the Tokyo procurators charging Ōura with election violations and bribery, explained his actions to journalists (carried in the June 5 issue of the *Chūō Newspaper*). These things were done, he stated, to preserve the concept of clean elections and to protect the reputation of justice. Ōura's bribery (both taking and receiving bribes) was especially disgusting because his police arrested several thousand people for very minor violations of the election regulations. Worse than that, Murano noted, some were even imprisoned. Murano, who claimed to harbor no personal animosity toward Ōura, pointed out that he had resigned from the board of the Seiyūkai before taking legal action. Furthermore, he had the lawyers Imamura Rikisaburō and Shiotani Kotarō, who had no ties to political parties, act as representatives in preparing the legal document submitted to procurators.[120]

Some of Justice Minister Ozaki's views on the Ōura incident are in an autobiography. When he first heard about the bribery investigation, he was shocked, even though as an old hand in the political world he was well aware that bureaucrats from a *hanbatsu* background believed that violating laws in pursuit of political objectives was acceptable. Ōura's actions, however, were serious breaches of the law and therefore required punishment. At least one friend pointed out to Ozaki that vote buying by cabinet members was an old custom. Torn by a desire to help a colleague and yet certain that some punishment was required, Ozaki discussed the problem with Hiranuma. Ozaki claims that it was from this meeting that the decision came not to arrest Ōura if he retired from politics.[121]

Reflecting on this case, Hiranuma noted that in the Ōkuma cabi-

net were a number of people under the influence of Yamagata Aritomo. Once this affair became public and a charge of bribery was
made against Ōura it was impossible to ignore it, and as the investigation progressed more evidence against Ōura was discovered.
Ōura's attempts to intimidate Hiranuma during the investigation
stiffened the procurator general's resolve to remove him from politics. No doubt Ōura's wheeling and dealing over the years had irri-
tated Hiranuma. He recalled, for example, that when Ōura was head
of the Metropolitan Police Board he freely used police power against
politicians and other political foes; material seized by policemen was
used as blackmail if a situation called for that sort of measure. In
summary, Hiranuma saw a man with bad political morals *(seiji dōtoku)*
who should be retired from office.[122]

The views of Hitotsumatsu Sadayoshi are preserved in a postwar
interview. Hitotsumatsu, who was a procurator at the Osaka District
Court, discovered evidence linking Ōura to bribed politicians in
Takamatsu, where he was sent to investigate election violations.
Returning to Osaka, he told Chief Procurator Kobayashi Yoshirō that
Ōura must be prosecuted. In Tokyo Kobayashi discussed the case
with Hiranuma Kiichirō and Justice Minister Ozaki, who agreed to
prosecute. However, Prime Minister Ōkuma argued that such prosecution would cause the cabinet to collapse. Back in Osaka the chief
procurator explained the situation to Hitotsumatsu, who suggested
that he might start the prosecution and then resign. The following
day Hitotsumatsu announced that he would drop the prosecution
on two conditions: Ōura would leave politics and return his titles to
the government, and the procurators who were to handle the bribery
trial of politicians at the Takamatsu District Court would be permitted to include a statement in the summation that Ōura was guilty of
the crime of bribery. Authorities in Tokyo agreed with this plan.[123]

The view of Izawa Takio, who at the time of the Ōura incident was
head of the Metropolitan Police Board, appeared in a postwar biography. Ōura was pushed into bribing politicians by Yamagata, who
was eager to get the bill to expand the army through the Diet. In
doing this, Izawa pointed out, Ōura was following a well-worn path:
bribing Diet members was a normal procedure. As the case grew
more serious, Izawa talked with Justice Minister Ozaki, asking if
there was not some way the problem could be solved. He also
pointed out that bribery was common, illustrating this point by noting that Hara Kei (by this time head of the Seiyūkai) had given a
bribe to someone in Gifu Prefecture (Izawa's men found a letter
proving this when they seized documents in a home during an investigation having nothing to do with Hara). This sort of thing, Izawa

noted, was trifling. Ozaki replied that a crime had to be punished and that the procurators were against suppressing the affair. Izawa suggested that a transfer of procurators might solve that problem. Izawa also talked with Ōkuma, suggesting that Ozaki be pressured to resign and that Vice-Minister of Justice Suzuki Kisaburō be moved to another position. Finally, Izawa noted that Ōura came out of this incident feeling that he had done nothing wrong.[124]

Hayashida Kametarō, a secretary and later chief secretary in the lower house from 1890, was one of those tried and convicted at the Takamatsu District Court. In his 1927 *History of Japanese Political Parties* he said that the Seiyūkai ran a skillful propaganda campaign against Ōura and the cabinet. The newspapers in turn featured the scandal, making small items into big ones. Consequently, the public came to see this as a very serious incident.[125]

One of the most interesting developments in this scandal was the bargain struck between justice officials and the cabinet: Ōura would not be prosecuted and instead would retire. Scholars discussing this agreement have usually seen it as coming from Hiranuma and Suzuki; some even credit Ozaki.[126] In fact, it appears that this novel solution was the result of Procurator Hitotsumatsu Sadayoshi's overnight reflection about how to handle this case. Another misconception grew out of this case: many people regarded Hiranuma and Suzuki as having ties with the Seiyūkai.[127] Of course, people had been whispering this sort of thing since the end of the Siemens incident in 1914, when Hiranuma tried to protect the Satsuma-Seiyūkai coalition in the Yamamoto cabinet.[128] In fact, the Hiranuma-Suzuki clique should be regarded as a nonaligned political force, willing to make deals to gain more political power. Finally, Ōura's removal from politics was less complete than planned. True, he never held public office again and after retirement to Kamakura he abdicated the headship of his family in favor of his son.[129] Nevertheless, he remained a player in the game of politics. For example, as the power brokers debated the matter of a new prime minister in 1918, Ōura's valued opinion was sought. According to Matsumoto Gōkichi, who on a number of occasions served as messenger for elder statesmen and other power brokers, on September 8 he asked Yamagata Aritomo if Hara Kei would be acceptable. On September 11, Matsumoto visited Hara and told him about the conversation with Yamagata. Then Matsumoto saw Ōura, who supported the idea of a Hara cabinet. When the next meeting with Yamagata occurred on September 17, Matsumoto explained Ōura's feelings about the appointment. Ōura's views, according to Matsumoto, deeply influenced Yamagata's decision to nominate Hara for the prime ministership.[130]

The outcome of the 1914 and 1915 bribery scandals was unprecedented: the Yamamoto cabinet collapsed, Prime Minister Yamamoto and Navy Minister Saitō were retired into the reserves, Yamamoto of Mitsui lost his directorship, admirals were convicted, Home Minister Ōura was forced out of politics, and Ōkuma's image was tarnished. Furthermore, these cases strikingly illustrated the disregard of laws by government bureaucrats, military men, politicians, and businessmen: it was a sorry example for those who thought Japan a nation ruled by law. The important people caught up in these scandals seemed puzzled about being charged with crimes, believing as they did that the money was for a high purpose. Admiral Matsumoto excused his greed and law breaking by saying that he did it for the navy; Ōura's excuse was the need to push the national defense legislation through the lower house; even the Mitsui man Yamamoto—who frankly said he did it for money—added that the money was for the company. Punishments for the Diet members and the Mitsui employees were very light, but the admirals were treated harshly (the maximum sentence under Article 197 of the Penal Code was three years). Ōura's punishment was either soft or harsh, depending upon one's perspective.

That careers, though damaged, survived these scandals is illustrated in several cases. Admiral Yamamoto formed a new cabinet in 1923, and Saitō Makoto, the former navy minister, became governor general of Korea in 1919 and prime minister in 1932. Yamamoto Jōtarō made a fortune during the boom economy of World War I and was elected to a Diet seat in 1920. A few years later he was appointed president of the South Manchurian Railway. Hayashida Kametarō, the former chief secretary of the House of Representatives, returned as a house member in the election of 1920. Of the big fish only Ōura did not stage a comeback, but that happened not only because he was discredited by the scandal but because there was not enough time for a political recovery: he died in 1918.

These early-twentieth-century bribery cases propelled the Justice Ministry, especially the procuracy, into a position of political influence. Beginning with the sugar bribery incident, the procuracy enlarged its investigative powers, and by the time the Ōura case was completed it had demonstrated the importance of suspension of indictment.[131] This wide discretionary power possessed by the procuracy, which could drop any case on grounds of lack of evidence, inappropriateness, or undesirability, became a sharp political sword in the hands of the Hiranuma clique, which could prosecute or not prosecute as it saw fit.[132] However, one must not view Hiranuma as merely another cynical bureaucrat, masking political ambition behind a facade of moral rectitude; Hiranuma believed what he said about public morality. Throughout his long career he aimed at preserving traditional moral values and cleaning up corruption in society. Commenting on Ōura, Hiranuma noted that the home minister had not bribed for personal gain; nevertheless, his political career had been corrupt, with many illegal and immoral acts. Thus he had to be removed from office.[133]

Political bribery scandals such as those in 1914 and 1915 stimulated liberals to debate social problems, including the matter of official corruption. Outstanding among these crusaders for a higher morality in politics was Professor Yoshino Sakuzō, Tokyo Imperial University, whose "On the Meaning of Constitutional Government and the Method by Which It Can Be Perfected" was published in the *Chūō kōron* in January 1916.[134] To stop political corruption, he wrote, voters must be taught "election ethics." Each voter must understand that his vote "is of great consequence to the fate of the nation. It is too sacred to be subject to influence by bribes or intimidation. . . . When legislators manipulate the people, invariably corruption and bad government flourish. . . . Therefore, it is especially important to impose strict penalties on the corrupt practices. . . . In this respect, a rather strict election law has been adopted in Japan; the only thing to be regretted is that it has not been rigorously enough enforced. . . ." Moreover, he wrote, when suffrage is restricted, "corrupt practices are carried on unreservedly. When the suffrage is extended to the limit, there can be absolutely no distribution of bribes and the like." Furthermore, he thought it was important to raise the moral conscience of politicians. "We must not only by means of law sternly punish any representatives who defile their offices; we must also resolve to employ the power of public opinion to bury them in political oblivion." After pointing out that government service was an exalted profession, he wrote, that "in Western Countries . . . men about whose character there is some doubt are never accepted as politicians in the first place. . . . The frequent occurrence of corrupt behavior among legislators is probably a peculiarity of Japan."[135] In general, liberals blamed vote buying and other forms of political bribery on "feudal" remnants, and they contended "that perverted loyalty which had linked feudal lord and retainer still poisoned personal relations in society, with corruption the result. Vote buying and other abuses occurred . . . because the weight of centuries of feudal, despotic rule still pressed heavily on the minds of the Japanese people, making them unable to grasp the fundamental principles of political morality."[136]

Several questions come to mind after this review of twenty-five

years of parliamentary government: How common was political bribery? What caused it? What effect did it have on political development? Regarding the first question, this chapter illustrates in the
Nittō and Ōura scandals that bribery to sway votes was commonplace. That civil and military bureaucrats were not immune to bribes
is illustrated in the Textbook and Siemens scandals. There is no
doubt in these cases that bribery occurred: it is well documented
in the court records. Additional evidence is supplied in this chapter
by Hayashida Kametarō, Hara Kei, Ōkuma Shigenobu, Toyabe Shuntei, Izawa Takio, and Yamagata Aritomo. Except for the social critic
Toyabe, these men were insiders in the political game, so their views
came from firsthand knowledge about political bribery. The evidence, then, is overwhelming: political bribery was a common affair.
This conclusion must be considered when the politics of this era is
viewed as a process of compromise between the oligarchs and the
party men. As was noted earlier, George Akita is correct; nevertheless, political bribery played an important role in smoothing the way
for the many compromises. Politicians were susceptible to bribery for
varied and complex reasons, but the basic reason in most cases was
the need for funds to run a political career. It was pointed out earlier
in this chapter that a sharp rise in expenses occurred as the size of
the electorate expanded. Moreover, candidates were forced to
depend upon local bosses who collected votes, and from about 1908,
money needs pushed politicians into the arms of businessmen. Two
hundred yen was the base salary for a lower house member in 1890;
this amount gradually moved up to two thousand yen. A Japanese
scholar who published in 1910 noted that "[a]n election in Japan
usually costs a successful candidate about 3000 *yen*. This is a very
heavy burden, if we consider the resources of most of our parliamentary candidates. In fact, some of them sell their estates in order to
obtain an election fund. . . . The worst part of the bargain, however,
is the uncertain length of their parliamentary existence, [because]
. . . the House may be dissolved at the fiat of the bureaucratic statesmen in power."[137] Besides the financial needs of elected politicians,
there is another obvious reason for political bribery: the needs of the
oligarchs who dominated the cabinets to get bills through the lower
house. Yamagata Aritomo admitted that both he and Itō Hirobumi
used bribery for this very purpose. Taken together, these situations
produced a symbiotic relationship: the financial needs of politicians
meshed with the government needs for votes. The result was a pattern of political bribery throughout the first twenty-five years of the
Diet. The effect of bribery upon political development is a slippery
topic to evaluate, but several results are clear. Exposure of corrup-

tion again and again hurt the reputation of elected politicians. One journalist, discussing the Nittō scandal, noted, "It goes without saying that this incident has given a severe shock to public respect for the Lower House of the Diet, and to public confidence in the integrity of Japanese business enterprise. . . . [T]he reputation of the House of Representatives is effectually smirched, and there will certainly accrue a marked increase of credit to Conservative politicians who oppose party Cabinets, and to the House of Peers as an incorruptible guardian of national interests [italics dropped]."[138] As each of the later scandals developed, newspapers attacked the purveyors of corruption, but because many newspapers aimed mainly at increasing circulation, they are not a good gauge of public opinion. We can only guess, then, that exposure of bribery among politicians and bureaucrats caused the public to hold them in lower esteem. Of one thing, however, we can be certain: these corruption cases stimulated the growth of the political power of the Justice Ministry, especially of the procuracy.

3. The Era of Party Government

THE TRANSITION from cabinets led by elder statesmen or their protégés to cabinets formed by party leaders brought neither political stability nor a lessening of political bribery. Indeed, during the era of party government, politicians engaged in an orgy of mutual vilification, with opposition politicians who schemed to destroy a cabinet trying to discredit cabinet officers and their Diet supporters by charging them with indictable offenses. This excessive spirit of partisan competitiveness reinforced a public perception that the parties were corrupt.[1] One newspaper editorialized, "In Japan the political parties are hostile groups, and they make it their first business to injure the interests of each other. They do not concern themselves much about the announcement of their respective policies for the interest of the nation. . . . Their antagonism often goes to the extremity of endangering the general tranquillity, causing serious fear and apprehension of thinking men."[2] Among those watching the political battles of the era were conservative bureaucrats some of whom despised party politicians and were eager to discredit them. Bribery charges were a favorite method to accomplish this end.

With the establishment of the Hara cabinet (September 1918–November 1921), for the first time a prime minister held a seat in the House of Representatives. Also, for the first time all cabinet officers, except for the service ministers, were members of the majority Seiyūkai. Prime Minister Hara was a master of politics who knew how to acquire influence and operate the political system.[3] As part of a campaign to secure and maintain Seiyūkai dominance, Hara began a massive railway-building program together with an expansion of public works projects. These programs were tied to the party's pork-barrel politics. Moreover, Hara opened a number of higher bureaucratic posts to patronage and established a working arrangement with the largest political clique in the House of Peers.[4]

41

Hara exploited all possible avenues to expand Seiyūkai power. Consequently, charges of political corruption were common in the Diet and in the press. In February 1920, for example, lower house member Inukai Tsuyoshi accused the cabinet of giving bribes to expand its influence: "Were any of the Sat-Chō cabinets in the past as corrupt as this one? Certainly not!"[5] In July, Shimada Saburō attacked the cabinet, charging that three ministers had used their positions to profit on the stock market. In the face of little proof, however, the issue disappeared.[6] This was the same Shimada who had spear-headed the anticorruption campaign against Hoshi Tōru and de-manded that the Diet investigate the Siemens and Vickers bribery case. When allegations were made about corruption in a Tokyo con-struction contract, the Justice Ministry was told to play down the case and not to make arrests.[7] Asked about the propriety of these orders, Hara wrote in his diary,

> Of course, they are quite proper. In such a case, as with electoral infringements, the more thoroughly it is investigated, the more criminals are turned up. Criminals are not, of course, to be con-doned; but from another angle, I cannot help feeling that such cases make a bad impression on people. In this recent case, it seems that quite a few men affiliated with the Seiyūkai are in-volved. . . . While it is necessary to dispose of the case fairly and properly, to widen it excessively would, on the contrary, have nega-tive repercussions on the public and cause opposition. That is why those instructions are quite in line.[8]

Discussing the notorious vote-buying frenzy at election time with a confidant, who suggested that one solution would be to create a sys-tem that did not require financing, Hara replied, "What a stupid thing to say! Doesn't everyone want money? First create a society with no desire for money. Then you will have a political system that doesn't need funding."[9]

A. Morgan Young, editor of the *Japan Chronicle* in Kobe, entitled one chapter of his book on Taisho "A Crop of Scandals." The year in question was 1921. Many distinguished government officials, former government officials, and businessmen were caught up in these brib-ery scandals.[10]

One of these scandals involved Nakanishi Seiichi, vice-president of the South Manchurian Railway. This case came to public attention via the *Osaka Mainichi Newspaper*, which published a letter in mid-1920 from Yamada Junji, chief, General Affairs Office, South Man-churian Railway, accusing Nakanishi of financial incompetence. Opposition parties in the Diet picked up this issue: Nakanishi was accused of purchasing a coal mine for more than three times its worth, of buying a ship from Uchida Nobunari for an exhorbitant price, of paying the Tanaka Trading Company three hundred thousand yen for a breach of contract, and of overpaying for a nearly defunct company. When Nakanishi was also charged with taking kickbacks on these transactions and passing the money on to the Seiyūkai, the case threw suspicion upon Hara and the party's top leadership.[11] Although the Seiyūkai rejected a vote of no confidence, the uproar forced the case into the courts. In late 1923, Nakanishi and others were found not guilty. Playing tit for tat, in March 1921 Hirooka Uichirō of the Seiyūkai attacked Katō Kōmei, president of the Kenseikai, for taking a 50,000-yen bribe from Uchida Nobunari. It was alleged that Katō had promised to oppose universal suffrage legislation; Katō countered by saying that this was a normal political contribution and that no such pledge was made.[12]

The most sensational corruption case, however, was centered on Koga Renzō, head of the Colonization Bureau. Because Koga and Hara were friends from student days, this scandal was especially embarrassing. Moreover, Koga was head of the Seiyūkai support group in the House of Peers. As this case was debated in the press and on the Diet floor, the public was treated to a wide display of alleged illegal activities in Manchuria: sale of seized opium to Chinese, overpayment for land, and taking bribes. The bribery charge was for permitting the creation of the Dairen Stock Exchange, for which Koga was alleged to have received a reward of a thousand shares of stock. Because procurators thought that some of the profit from opium sales went into the Seiyūkai political war chest, they urged the court to call the prime minister as a witness; this was not done. At the end of the trial in July 1922, Koga was acquitted on all charges except bribery; for that he received a six-month sentence, but with a stay of execution.[13] Procurator General Hiranuma Kiichirō, pondering how so many important people got caught up in the Koga and other corruption scandals, ascribed it to "the degeneracy of the upper classes."[14]

The combined effect of these corruption cases damaged political parties in general and the Seiyūkai in particular. Outstanding among the attacks on Hara's party was the speech by Kenseikai member Nagai Ryūtarō: "It is patent that the Hara Cabinet is bent upon furthering the interests of the minority at the sacrifice of the interests of the masses of the people. The fact that a few Ministers gained illegal profits in collusion with merchants under the Government's patronage is most reprehensive and such conduct on the part of the Ministers will have a most serious effect on national ideas."[15] Nagai demanded that Hara apologize for not stopping such corruption. Hara refused.[16] The exact effect of Nagai's speech on public opinion is unknown, but some people must have reflected that Kenseikai members also subscribed to the vices associated with a corrupt political machine and that the party had strong ties to the upper classes.[17] As for Nagai, he became famous for his rectitude and refusal to offer bribes or lavish "gifts" for votes. Nevertheless, like other politicians he offered pork-barrel promises to constituents.[18] His biographer notes, "As Nagai's career progressed he became proficient in collecting money. It was not that he really solicited—rather it was given to him from fans, as it would be given to actresses or to sumo wrestlers."[19]

That some people took seriously the financial scandals and the allegations of links between corrupt politicians and big business is reflected in the September 28, 1921, killing of Yasuda Zenjirō, head of one of the four great *zaibatsu* (big business concerns) and the nation's richest man, by Asahi Heigo, who was protesting inequality and corruption.[20] On November 4, Prime Minister Hara was assassinated by Nakaoka Kon'ichi, a railway switchman. Among the various reasons Nakaoka gave for the murder was that Hara had not led a crusade to punish government officials involved in bribery cases.[21]

On March 29, 1925, the Diet approved universal male suffrage. This was a long-pending piece of legislation, which Prime Minister Katō Kōmei (June 1924–January 1926) considered the most important law passed during his term of office. All males over the age of twenty-five who had lived in their electoral district for at least one year and who were not receiving poor relief were given the right to vote. Hence, the electorate increased from about three million to about twelve and a half million.[22]

In addition to universal suffrage, 1925 saw new election regulations. The amendments that had been made in 1900 and 1919 placed few restrictions on campaign practices. The 1900 election regulations had been changed to meet the demands of the manufacturing and mercantile interests. The existing system of small electoral districts was replaced by a system of independent urban districts (cities above 30,000) and prefectural rural districts. The new system favored the urban areas inasmuch as one lower house member could represent only 30,000 people (in a country area it could be 130,000).[23] Although candidates were prohibited from approaching voters at the polling places, there were no restrictions on electioneering elsewhere or on expenditures. Buying votes, of course, was illegal as before. The new House of Representatives Election Law of 1925 contained detailed regulations: restrictions were placed on campaign expenses, limitations were placed on the number of campaign workers, house-to-house canvassing was forbidden, restric-

tions were placed on the distribution of pictures and election literature, and so on. Heavier penalties for bribery were imposed: a fine
up to two thousand yen (old law was five hundred yen) and imprisonment up to three years (old law was up to one year).[24] Ostensibly,
the detailed restrictions in the new law were aimed at preventing
political bribery and other illegal activities. There was, however,
another reason for these highly restrictive regulations: "It . . . [was]
more generally understood that the anti-personal-canvassing-clause
was covertly meant by the lawmakers to keep lower class voters away
from actively participating in the electoral process in fear of the infil-
tration of socialism by the activities of socialist workers who were
then uprising."[25]

Under the 1925 multimember district system each voter cast one
vote; each party had the right to field multiple candidates. The new
law presented special problems for candidates: "[A] popular candidate may attract an unnecessary surplus of votes, or may lose
through the diversion of votes to less popular men in the belief that
the popular man is safe. There is the possibility that a majority party
in a district will fail to win a single seat if it presents too many candidates. Thus a candidate's colleagues may be more dangerous to him
than to his opponents."[26] Although it was important for candidates'
personalities to please voters, the important figures in election districts were the political bosses. These men, who never stopped campaigning, spent every day expanding a web of personal relationships
on which to draw at election times.[27]

Those who supported universal suffrage argued that it would,
among other things, decrease the amount of electoral corruption.
They reasoned that if all adult males could vote, bribery of voters
and other abuses would become prohibitively expensive.[28] One reformer wrote, "[T]he so-called political parties are bound together
by personal ties and connections, emotions, or individuals personalities. . . . If the right to vote is extended broadly . . . the foundations
of the existing political parties will be destroyed. . . . The organization of each party will reform itself . . . [and] it will become impossible to fight elections as previously by means of personal ties, connections, or bribery."[29] Another reformer thought that the 1925 law
would destroy the bribery system as politics entered a new phase.[30]
These rosy dreams of an era of clean politics were shattered in the
February 1928 election, the first national election under the 1925
law. Home Minister Suzuki Kisaburō supervised this election (Tanaka
Giichi cabinet, April 1927–July 1929), in which traditional dirty
tricks were employed to achieve a Seiyūkai majority. Afterwards this
election was condemned as the most corrupt since the 1915 election

supervised by Home Minister Ōura. Furthermore, election reforms notwithstanding, political leaders required money to hold factions together, so the old pattern of corruption between businessmen and politicians continued.[31] Reflecting on general elections held from 1928 onward, one Justice Ministry researcher concluded that the branch offices of political parties had become the headquarters for bribery; the political parties in their fierce struggle did not know how to restrain themselves.[32]

General Tanaka Giichi, former army minister, went on the reserve list in 1925 and entered the Seiyūkai. Crucial to Tanaka's success was the ability to raise large sums of money. Kuhara Fusanosuke, an old friend and a wealthy businessman, was brought into the party. Using his own wealth and his contacts in the business world, Kuhara became the party paymaster.[33] When Tanaka became president of the Seiyūkai on April 13, 1925, Kuhara contributed three million yen. This gift refocused public attention on earlier accusations that Tanaka, while army minister in 1920, had misappropriated secret service funds used during the Siberian expedition. Moreover, the contribution to the party stimulated allegations that Tanaka got the money in exchange for promises to businessmen of favors to come. A Kenseikai politician brought the matter to the Diet floor on March 4, 1926, and a motion to investigate these charges passed. The next day Mihei Toshiharu, a former finance officer in the Army Ministry, asked Tokyo District Court procurators to investigate Tanaka and his deputy, General Yamanashi Hanzō, for misappropriation of army funds. Some time later, however, Mihei withdrew the complaint. In the end, though rumors continued to circulate, nothing was found to implicate Tanaka.[34]

Simultaneously, an especially ugly corruption scandal, which touched famous politicians in the three major parties, caught public attention. This case centered on the Matsushima Brothels in Osaka and is regarded as the most scandalous of the political corruption cases of the late 1920s.[35] Among the politicians whose reputations were soiled by charges of bribery and fraud were Minoura Katsundo, Tokonami Takejirō, and Wakatsuki Reijirō. Minoura's involvement in this sensational case really caught the public's attention, because he had held a seat in the lower house from 1890 and because no political scandal had been attached to his record.[36] Tokonami was leader of the Seiyūhontō, and Wakatsuki was prime minister (Kenseikai). The involvement of high-ranking people stimulated public interest to the point that a record number of spectators showed up for the trial.[37] Besides the unfavorable publicity generated by this scandal, the Wakatsuki cabinet (January 30, 1926–April 20, 1927) was also under attack in the Diet for the handling of the case of Pak Yŏl (Boku Retsu), a Korean anarchist accused of plotting to kill the emperor and his son. The Seiyūkai, eager to embarrass the cabinet, seized upon a trivial mistake by a preliminary judge (he took a picture of Pak and his Japanese wife), charging that this underminded public trust in the judiciary and was an affront to the imperial family.[38]

When real estate companies in Osaka learned that the city might move the Matsushima Brothels, they vied with each other to control land at the new site. The Daitō Tochi Kabushikigaisha in early 1924 requested help from Seiyūkai members Yokota Sennosuke and Iwasaki Isao. Another company, the Shibatani Tochi Tatemono Kabushikigaisha, asked for help from Kenseikai member Tomita Kōjirō. A third company, Toyokuni Tochi Kabushikigaisha, also entered the contest. Its president, Tatsuki Masajirō, put two men in charge of getting this financial plum: Kokubo Shintarō and Nakamura Manjirō. Kokubo was president of Mansei Shintaku Kabushikigaisha; Nakamura was his executive assistant. In November 1924 they talked with lawyer Hirato Shin, who promised to act as a go-between with Seiyūkai member Iwasaki Isao. Taking no chances, the two on February 1925 used Andō Tooru as a go-between to get help from Kenseikai member Minoura Katsundo. Later others joined in Toyokuni's efforts: businessman Kawahara Giroku and Seiyūhontō member Takami Koremichi, who was chairman of the Party Affairs Committee (lawyer Hirato made this contact). At this point, Toyokuni had contacts with the three major parties.[39]

The final authority on moving the Matsushima Brothels lay with Home Minister Wakatsuki Reijirō. Normally, a home minister would approve the move of a public facility if the governor made a formal request. Nevertherless, Minoura, who had a long political history as a lower house member, a vice-minister, and a minister, went to Tokyo to sound out contacts in the Home Ministry while Takami worked on members of the Seiyūhontō and Iwasaki approached the Osaka governor's office. By October 1925, this lobbying had cost several hundred thousand yen. These activities did not go unnoticed. On January 11, 1925, pamphlets were distributed widely in Tokyo and Osaka in which the cabinet, real estate companies, and politicians were accused of profiting from the planned move of the brothels. Ōno Masatoshi, a member of the Osaka Municipal Council and a businessman with connections to the brothels, complained to district court procurators after his name appeared in the pamphlets. Procurators investigated the case for suspected libel and a violation of the Publication Law. Another case developed, however, when one of the suspects, Sanekawa Tokujirō, convinced procurators that they should investigate Toyokuni's Tatsuki and another person for bribery.[40]

Between March 25 and June 19, 1926, procurators indicted Iwasaki Isao, Hirato Shin, Masuda Iwao, Andō Tooru, Minoura Katsundo, Takami Koremichi, and Imakita Harusaku. The public, although used to allegations of financial corruption, was shocked by headlines about Minoura's arrest and detention at Osaka Prison because he was a respected senior politician who was regarded as comparatively clean. The trial at the Osaka District Court, which began on July 11, 1927, went through twenty-three sessions. Highly placed people in the dock and rumours of 560,000 yen in bribes made it high drama; people eager for a seat arrived as early as 4:00 A.M. for court sessions. Former home minister Wakatsuki did not testify, but in a deposition his recollection of the meeting with Minoura was quite different from that of the defendant. Wakatsuki swore that he said he would not permit the brothels to be moved; Minoura swore that the home minister said that he would approve the move if Governor Nakagawa Nozomi made a formal request. The depositions of Tokonami Takejirō and Governor Nakagawa also greatly differed from the statements of other defendants. For instance, Takami claimed that thirty thousand yen was handed to Mrs. Tokonami. She denied this in court.[41]

Unlike Prime Minister Wakatsuki, Vice-Minister Kawasaki Takukichi (formerly head of the Police Bureau, Home Ministry) submitted two depositions and attended the trial. According to the deposition of November 8, 1926, Kawasaki met Minoura and discussed the Matsushima Brothels in April 1925; several other meetings followed until October. Basically, stated Kawasaki, Minoura was told that a move of the brothels required a request from the governor and then an investigation by the Home Ministry to establish the need for a move. Kawasaki claimed that he neither told Minoura that the move could be made nor discussed such a move with his superior, the vice-minister. Asked what he knew about Governor Nakagawa's views on moving the brothels, Kawasaki said that he heard from the governor that this effort to move the brothels was causing trouble. Moreover, the governor noted that Vice-Minister Yuasa Kurahei told him that inasmuch as the ministry would not permit the move it would be best not to be involved in this dirty affair. Kawasaki was asked if he knew that Governor Nakagawa had sent a message to the Home Ministry on June 19, 1925, asking how to handle a committee charged with discussing a move of the brothels and that the ministry had replied on August 13. About this reply by the head of the City Planning Section, Kawasaki claimed no knowledge at the time.[42]

At the trial in Osaka District Court, Kawasaki told the judges that he did not tell Minoura that the brothel transfer could be carried out. In fact, his opinion given to Minoura was that the move could not be made. The judges asked if he had inspected the brothel site or had had someone go in his place. Kawasaki replied that no inspection had been made. Moreover, shortly after his first meeting with Minoura, Governor Nakagawa was in Tokyo for a conference. The governor mentioned the problem centered on the brothels, but noted that a move would not be permitted.[43]

Lawyer Hirato together with his assistant Masuda Iwao were seen as the main culprits in this case. The prosecution noted that Minoura and Takami were persuaded to lobby for the project by Hirato, even though Hirato was not certain that the brothels would be moved. Moreover, even though he had no firm agreement with government officials, he told clients that he had reached an understanding with authorities. Thus, he misled Kokubo and Kawahara while squeezing them for money. Furthermore, money supposedly paid to others was pocketed by Hirato. This was fraud, said the prosecution. Sentences were issued on October 13, 1927: Minoura (not guilty); Takami (not guilty); Hirato (eighteen months in prison); Imakita (not guilty); Masuda (six months in prison); Iwasaki (charges dropped because of his death); Andō (removed from the trial because of illness). Thus, this bribery trial concluded with no one convicted for bribery. The Osaka Appeals Court upheld the lower court decision. After recovering from illness, Andō went on trial on June 24, 1931; he was sentenced to a year in prison. On January 26, 1933, the Osaka Appeals Court upheld the sentence but added a stay of execution.[44]

Although the two court decisions must have pleased some defendants, remarks by Chief Judge Maezawa Kojirō on July 31, 1928, at the appeals court must have shocked them. Maezawa said that leaving aside the matter of guilty or not guilty their behavior was disappointing, especially because most of the defendants were from the upper social strata and some were important politically. People, he said, looked up to them as role models. Unfortunately, the defendants' terrible behavior would have a bad influence. The judge concluded by urging the defendants to act properly.[45]

On October 2, 1927, Shiono Suehiko, one of Hiranuma Kiichirō's most loyal followers, was appointed head of the procuratorial bureau of the Tokyo District Court. One of Shiono's first acts was to make Matsuzaka Hiromasa his deputy because he liked Matsuzaka's character and because Matsuzaka, who was at the Tokyo Appeals Court, knew the situation in Tokyo. Together they carried out an administrative house cleaning, purging the bureau of fifteen incompetent people and reorganizing the bureau's sections. Shiono, who was an innovative reformer, took his new position very seriously because he believed that the actions of the Tokyo bureau set the pace of the procuracy around the nation. Believing that procurators had a special mission to protect the nation from harm, Shiono ordered his subordinates to strive mightily to promote *seigi* (justice or righteousness). Moreover, he encouraged his men to pursue each investigation with vigor and to be willing to resign rather than to compromise their convictions. During Shiono's tenure (until September 20, 1930), the Tokyo bureau began a zealous prosecution of a number of sensational bribery cases involving high-ranking government officials.

Some scholars regard the Hiranuma-Suzuki clique as mainly pro-Seiyūkai.[46] There is some truth in this viewpoint. When Suzuki left the Justice Ministry, he joined the Seiyūkai, and he was home minister in the Tanaka cabinet, which was formed six months before Shiono took over the Tokyo bureau. Furthermore, Justice Minister Hara Yoshimichi (Tanaka cabinet) was selected by Hiranuma. Later Suzuki became president of the Seiyūkai. Nevertherless, Shiono's zeal to root out corruption knew no political boundaries; his bureau pursued politicians from all parties, including Ogawa Heikichi, the vice-president of the Seiyūkai and a former justice minister.

Shiono's bureau focused not only on corruption cases but also upon ideological crimes. After crushing the first Japanese Communist Party in the early 1920s, the state was preparing a massive blow aimed at the renewed Communist Party. Shiono's men were on the cutting edge of this effort to extirpate the party. The sledgehammer blow fell on the party on March 15, 1928, as nationwide about sixteen hundred communist suspects were arrested. This mass arrest was followed by others until the party was crushed in the early 1930s.[47] Although ideological criminal suspects were processed in a special section of the Tokyo bureau, procurators dealing with these crimes associated with colleagues who handled political bribery cases. It is not surprising that out of this association some of them concluded that the corruption of politicians and businessmen was somehow connected to the so-called bad thought of communist suspects.

Among the bribery cases handled by the Tokyo procurators that of General Yamanashi Hanzō, a three-time war minister and governor general of Korea from December 1927, aroused great public interest. A protégé of General Tanaka Giichi, Yamanashi acted as his deputy war minister in the Hara cabinet and then as minister. When Tanaka entered the political world via the presidency of the Seiyūkai, Yamanashi also moved into a leadership position in the party.[48] The fact that some people regarded Yamanashi, who was a member of the House of Peers, as a candidate for prime minister sharpened public attention.

Yamanashi was alleged to have accepted a bribe of fifty thousand yen from Kawasaki Tokunosuke, a rice wholesaler who wanted to expand his business into Korea. Police and procurators moved against Yamanashi shortly after the fall of the Tanaka cabinet (July 2, 1929) by arresting Hida Rikichi, the general's secretary, on July 29. Yamanashi resigned as governor general in August and was prosecuted on December 28.[49]

Somehow rice dealer Kawasaki communicated with secretary Hida. Hida's friend Gotō Chōei, a mine owner, and a publisher, Namitsu Kyūken, met with Kawasaki as well, and the group made plans for a Korean business venture. Kawasaki was told that to do business in Korea he and the others had to submit a group application covering rice, mining, and publishing to Governor General Yamanashi. A memorandum was drawn up and in return Kawasaki agreed to pay fifty thousand yen. He also gave Hida twenty thousand yen as expense money to work out some of the business details. Kawasaki had one meeting with the governor general in Tokyo: Hida introduced him as a businessman interested in Korea. Kawasaki gave the fifty thousand yen with the explanation that it was a political contribution. After receiving the money, Yamanashi asked if there was anything he could do in return for the gift. The group's business venture, however, was not discussed. Nevertheless, Kawasaki left the meeting certain that the deal had been consummated. A fourth person was present at the meeting: lawyer Ōi Shizuo.[50]

At the trial, the key point in connection with Governor General Yamanashi was whether or not he realized that he had accepted a bribe. The prosecution noted that when the scandal became public the money was returned to Kawasaki with the comment that the governor general did not know it was dirty money. On February 22, 1931, Yamanashi was found not guilty. Secretary Hida was given eight months' imprisonment for bribery and instigation; Gotō was sentenced to three months in prison for bribery and instigation; Namitsu got three months for bribery and instigation; Ōi was sentenced for abetting bribery and fined 150 yen. Kawasaki was judged guilty of bribery; he was sentenced to five months in prison and fined fifty thousand yen but was given a two-year stay of execution.[51]

The summer of 1929 was a busy time for Tokyo procurators. Hard on the heels of the Yamanashi case an even more sensational political bribery case burst into public view. Arrests in the Five Private Railway Companies Bribery incident began in late August 1929. Among the many influential people in the political and financial worlds who were caught in procurator Shiono's net was Seiyūkai vice-president Ogawa Heikichi. Besides being justice minister (first Katō cabinet), Ogawa was railway minister in the Tanaka cabinet (resigned July 2, 1929). Ogawa was prosecuted on September 26. Together with others he was accused of accepting bribes totaling six hundred thousand yen. Ogawa's high status did not protect him from being kept under detention in Ichigaya Prison while he was being interrogated by procurators (he was released on January 17, 1929).[52]

The trial of Ogawa and his codefendants held public interest from November 1930 until its conclusion on May 16, 1933. After 139 court sessions, the verdict was not guilty; the prosecution appealed the case, and at the second trial the verdict was reversed. Five people who gave bribes and Ogawa and others who took them were found guilty. After being sentenced on November 17, 1934, Ogawa and the others appealed to the Supreme Court on September 28, 1935. The Supreme Court upheld the lower court decision. Ogawa was given two years' imprisonment and fined 192,220 yen.[53] Minister Ogawa's defense team tried to save their distinguished client the embarass-ment of imprisonment by pleading for a stay of execution in consid-eration of Ogawa's long service to the nation.[54] The prosecution replied, "For a Railway Minister to receive money, or to enter into an understanding to receive it as a mark of appreciation for permission given for the building of a railway line, is a serious crime. It was also unprecedented that such a huge sum should have been involved."[55]

The Supreme Court upheld Ogawa's sentence on September 19, 1936; the following month he entered prison, where he stayed until June 10, 1937. Serving less than half of the sentence was the result of an amnesty. Then, in February 1940, he regained his civil rights via a pardon.[56] "The September 19 verdict was truly unexpected," wrote Ogawa in his diary.[57] The main reason for this verdict, he thought, was that the court bent to outside political and administrative pres-sures. Ogawa was hardly contrite in his final courtroom scene as he asserted innocence and attacked the court for debasing judiciary power.[58]

This dramatic case was difficult to prosecute because of Ogawa's political power and the fact that he never touched the money directly. Ogawa tried to conceal the bribes by having people who were not on the government's payroll pick up the money from the private railway companies; the money was further camouflaged by designating it as political contributions to the Seiyūkai. Although this defense worked at the first trial, it did not save the minister from prison.[59]

The retired Tanaka cabinet was hit by another bribery scandal in the late summer of 1929. This case involved the Decorations Bureau, which had awarded meritorious service medals in exchange for bribes. Because these decorations were given in the emperor's name, the affair was quickly politicized. A great uproar in the press and much public anger added to the already black picture of party politicians in general and the Tanaka cabinet in particular.

The key suspect in this case was Amaoka Naoyoshi, appointed by the Tanaka government to head the Decorations Bureau. A codefendant was businessman Kamohara Ryōyō. Amaoka, who married one of Prime Minister Katsura Tarō's daughters, was a former cabinet secretary. Amaoka together with Kamohara planned the medal sale scheme to pay off creditors. At least six people paid for medals: five businessmen and Fujita Ken'ichi, a financier and member of the House of Peers. The size of the bribes appears to reflect whatever the buyer could afford to give. For instance, one businessman paid about 27,000 yen but two others paid only 1,000 yen. Fujita paid 5,000 yen. Amaoka was arrested on September 11, 1929. On May 16, 1933, the Tokyo District Court sentenced Amaoka to two years in prison and a fine of 17,250 yen; Kamohara got eighteen months and a fine of 5,250 yen. The sentences remained unchanged at the Tokyo Appeals Court. The Supreme Court refused to hear the case.[60]

This expanding pool of corruption also touched the new Hamaguchi Osachi cabinet (July 1929–April 1931). Education Minister Kobashi Ichita was implicated in a bribery scandal involving the Echigo Railway; he resigned from the cabinet on November 29, 1929, and was arrested on March 7, 1930. Kobashi was another big fish netted by Shiono's aggressive procurators. Prior to 1920, when he entered the lower house as a Seiyūkai representative, Kobashi was a Home Ministry bureaucrat who rose to the position of vice-minister in 1918. Under the Kiyoura Keigo cabinet (January–June 1924) he was chief cabinet secretary. Kobashi moved from the Seiyūkai to the Seiyūhontō and in 1927 helped establish the Rikken Minseitō, which became the main opposition party to the Seiyūkai.[61]

This case grew out of the efforts of Kusumi Tōma, president of the Echigo Railway, to sell the railway to the government. In February 1927, he asked help from Satake Sango, vice-minister in the Railway Ministry. Using Satake as a go-between, he also approached Kobashi to get help from the Seiyūhontō. Kusumi promised a large payment if the sale bill passed the Diet. After the railroad was sold to the government for 12,410,000 yen, in May 1927, Kobashi was given ten thousand yen via Satake. To get this bill through the Diet, Satake handed out about two million yen in bribes. At the Tokyo District Court on December 20, 1930, Kobashi was given a ten-month prison

sentence and fined ten thousand yen; Satake got eight months. Both
defendants, however, were kept out of prison by a two-year stay of
execution. Kusumi was fined two hundred yen.[62] Kusumi told procurators investigating this case that former prime minister Wakatsuki
received a hundred thousand yen. When asked about this, Wakatsuki
replied that it was merely a campaign contribution.[63]

During the late 1920s, political bribery scandals were not limited
to Tokyo. One scholar notes, "There were so many cases that it was
like peak time of the flower blossoms. It went on all over Japan and it
involved civilians and the military."[64]

In 1930 Hosono Nagamori published a book about the deteriora-
tion of society. The primary source for this interesting work was articles that had appeared in thirty-nine newspapers beginning in late
1926. Hosono's comments on political and financial immorality
therefore reflect the content of these newspaper articles. Bribery
and other corruption scandals, wrote Hosono, have a bad influence
upon public morality. Evaluating the actions of bureaucrats, politicians, and businessmen, Hosono found them corrupt: bureaucrats
pray for money and are unprincipled; politicians are attached to
money and sell everything they can to businessmen; businessmen
will do anything at any cost to carry on business.[65] His harshest criticism was aimed at politicians: "They have no will and no principles.
They take these off like shoes. They believe only in money and the
benefits that come with their positions."[66] When politicians take bribes
and betray the people's trust, their actions have a negative influence
on public thought. Unfortunately, Hosono notes, most of the corruption among politicians, businessmen, and bureaucrats escapes
detention. Even in unusual cases of exposure, he concludes, the big
fish are seldom caught.[67] Hosono reproduced several newspaper cartoons. One published on November 17, 1926, in the *Kokumin Newspaper* shows Procurator General Koyama Matsukichi, dressed in judicial attire, examining the tongue of Prime Minister Wakatsuki. This
cartoon appeared after Minoura sued Wakatsuki for perjury. The
prime minister says, "I believe I have only one tongue." Koyama
replies, "Yes, it is one tongue." Wakatsuki says, "Well then, quickly
certify it!" Koyama answers, "Yes sir! Right away. I am going to stamp
it with a seal of approval."[68] A very nasty cartoon, published in the
Osaka Mainichi Newspaper of June 8, 1927, criticizes the irresponsible
and corrupt policies of the Seiyūkai. Two politicians, dressed like
sushi-shop employees, are depicted dropping people into a meat
grinder (called a "squeeze machine"). The characters written next to
the people being dropped into this machine read "the people's
blood." One of the shop employees is holding high a tray on which

sit a steam engine and a bridge labeled Sumida River. This savage cartoon refers to the various railway corruption scandals and to kickbacks from construction companies.[69]

Reflecting upon corruption scandals during his tenure as chief procurator at the Tokyo District Court, Shiono said that the rotten parties, in need of money to control their men, took bribes from businessmen. Because investigating these cases was difficult and dangerous, Shiono's men tried to play the parties against each other by concentrating on the major party out of power. This scheme did not always work, however; investigations often took strange twists and turns. Nevertheless, most of these cases were successful, he noted, with convictions in some instances of cabinet ministers. Another important point about these cases was that the procurators took the lead in investigations, a change from the normal practice of the Metropolitan Police Board starting investigations. Procurators heading investigations prevented police from knowing exactly where each case was going, thereby slowing the leakage of secret information. It was Shiono's opinion that these bribery cases increased the prestige of the Justice Ministry among the public and increased the pride of justice officials.[70]

Imamura Rikisaburō, a distinguished attorney, held a different view. For example, he viewed the indictment and trial of Education Minister Kobashi Ichita (Hamaguchi cabinet) as part of a plot to destroy the cabinet. Moreover, the publication in newspapers, in November 1929, of a letter written in December 1926 by Wakatsuki Reijirō was another part of the same plot. This was the letter in which Wakatsuki requested a donation from Kusumi Tōma for the party; it was found at Kusumi's home when authorities were investigating the Kobashi bribery case. Inasmuch as this sort of material was confidential, Imamura saw a political purpose behind its release. The headquarters for this plot to destroy the cabinet, Imamura thought, was the procurators' bureau at the Tokyo District Court. And behind Shiono, Imamura could feel the presence of Hiranuma Kiichirō, vice-president of the Privy Council.[71]

Prime Minister Hamaguchi, faced with a spreading domestic and world depression, boldly pushed a comprehensive economic recovery plan that included a return to the gold standard. This was accomplished on January 11, 1930. The Hamaguchi cabinet also created a House of Representatives Election Reform Study Commission. This reform idea carried over into the February 20 national election: the Minseitō's draft campaign platform called for clean politics and the promotion of public morals.[72] Nevertheless, the great Minseitō election victory "was not unaffected by the use of methods which the

party had itself previously condemned, for Home Minister Adachi
[Kenzō] had replaced 28 pro-Seiyūkai prefectural governors and
also made 118 other changes."[73] During the election campaign, candidates chasing voters used bribery in a traditional manner: vote buying remained the key to victory.[74] A confidential Justice Ministry
report on the 1930 election states that bribery was as widespread as
during the infamous 1928 campaign and that in some places election broker clubs were organized.[75]

One observer wrote in 1930,

> The fact is that, in order to secure a majority in the Diet . . . ample
> funds are essential. The shrewd business man, being well aware of
> this, is only too willing to supply these "sinews of war," for he knows
> that people in power can confer a great deal of advantage on their
> capitalist friends by means of subsidies, protection, purchases, and
> concessions of various kinds. . . . The need for the Government to
> have wealthy and generous friends, and its ability to put wealth in
> the way of those friends so that they can continue their generosity,
> serve, in fact, to create a vicious circle, which must be broken if
> Japanese politics are ever to be purified.[76]

Ikeda Seihin, a senior Mitsui executive, recalled some years later
that Mitsui had grown so big that "we had no need to borrow
strength from the government. . . . Military men seeing only that the
zaibatsu were giving money thought that the zaibatsu must be doing
improper things, but I certainly never did anything improper. . . .
Small zaibatsu may have tried to make money in this way, but big
zaibatsu such as Mitsui . . . did not use such sordid business methods.
I do not know about early Meiji, but when we had expanded there
was no need for such petty stuff."[77] In another postwar interview,
Ikeda said, "However, it would have been troublesome to have been
interfered with or obstructed. Consequently, after the rise of party
cabinets . . . [we desired to] avoid having party government regard
us with a jaundiced eye, and this became the origin of what has been
called the improper relation between the zaibatsu and the political
parties."[78] Ikeda, in a third postwar interview, stated that before he
became head of Mitsui Gōmei (September 1933) "the funds for
general elections had been handled exclusively by Dan Takuma,
Ariga Chōbun, and Fukui Kikusaburō, but they never told him anything about these matters and no records were kept in the company
files."[79] Ikeda's third account about contributions to politicians under-
mines the first two accounts. If we accept this denial of the nature
and extent of Mitsui's contributions as truthful, then Ikeda, at least
before September 1933, is a very poor source of information because

other people handled political contributions and they told him nothing about these activities.

Richard Sims, commenting about the *zaibatsu*–political party connection, states, "One writer, while recognising the importance of financial contributions from the major *zaibatsu*, has argued that these were not made in return for specific favours (as were some gifts from individual businessmen) but were based on historic ties; and he compares them with the backing by fans of a baseball team. A closer analogy might be with the patronage of *kabuki* actors, for funding rarely, if ever, went to the party as such, and often not to the party leader, but to particular politicians with whom business leaders had personal ties." Therefore, writes Sims, "[S]uch politicians, like the wealthy businessmen who entered politics directly, were in a position to earn the party president's gratitude or to build up their own influence by bestowing 'pocket-money' on less well-endowed Diet members. . . . [T]here can be no doubt that the provision of financial largesse opened the way to membership of the party directorate *(kambu)*, and this gave the *zaibatsu* indirect control of the parties."[80]

By 1931 the failure of Minseitō economic policies was apparent. The world depression doomed exports to a steep slump and stimulated unemployment. Many financial leaders concluded that Japan would be forced to reverse its policy and go off the gold standard, and in anticipation of a devaluation of the yen they purchased foreign currencies, especially dollars. In the face of an expanding depression, Finance Minister Inoue Junnosuke, on November 6, 1931, expressed total faith in the government's economic policies. Meanwhile, newspapers published articles about Mitsui Bank's and other banks' speculation in foreign currencies, thereby convincing many people that bankers were more interested in balance sheets than in national welfare. Failure of its economic policies plus the army's seizure of Manchuria in September brought about the collapse of the Wakatsuki cabinet on December 13, 1931 (Hamaguchi resigned in April and died in August as a result of a gunshot wound). Inukai Tsuyoshi (Seiyūkai) formed a new cabinet the same day. By the next day free trade in gold was halted. Gold speculators made fortunes; many people accused Mitsui in concert with the Seiyūkai of endangering the nation to turn a profit.[81] One reason for the public tendency to concentrate its anti-*zaibatsu* feeling on Mitsui rather than on other large companies was that the traditional sharp business practices of Mitsui were firmly fixed in the mind of the average person, who saw the company as greedy for profits at any cost.[82]

Former finance minister Inoue (Hamaguchi cabinet) was murdered on February 9, and Dan Takuma (Mitsui official and president of the Japan Industrial Club) was killed on March 5, 1932. Both murders were carried out by members of the Blood Pact Group (Ketsumeidan) led by Inoue Nisshō, a Buddhist priest. The arrest of Inoue uncovered a plot to kill about a dozen more prominent politicians and businessmen.[83] At the trial of those indicted for the murders, Inoue claimed "to have high regard for the constitution and parliamentary government; the only thing to which I object is the corrupt state of to-day's party government. To relieve the country from it, I thought it was necessary to deal with those who had predominant power over it."[84]

A month after taking office, Prime Minister Inukai dissolved the Diet to prepare for a general election. Unlike many of his contemporaries, Inukai was viewed by the public as a clean politician who sincerely wished to remove political corruption. Upon taking control of the Seiyūkai, Inukai prohibited the use of unfair political tactics and ordered members to strive for clean politics. His political platform for the Seiyūkai included a plank for election reform. In the general election of February 20, 1932, Inukai's party won a victory of unprecedented proportions—(303 seats against the Minseitō's 146), a majority even larger than that won by Hara in 1920. Although the Minseitō claimed that Inukai won because of vote buying and official interference, this appears to have been a comparatively clean campaign.[85] On May 15, 1932, naval officers and army cadets, some of whom were tied to the Blood Pact Group, murdered Inukai. They were motivated in part by the political corruption of the ruling elite.[86] Thus ended the era of prewar party government.

Although statistics are open to various interpretations, and although some scholars dismiss them as irrelevant, they do bring the subject of political bribery into a sharper focus. The following list shows the number of prosecuted bribery cases in violation of the election laws.[87]

1908	1,338	1924	13,986
1912	3,329	1928	8,745
1915	7,278	1930	17,124
1917	22,932	1932	6,426
1920	5,266		

Procurator Hirata Naratarō, who did a confidential study on political bribery, thought that the dramatic drop in the number of bribery cases in 1928, despite the fact that the electorate was nearly four times larger than in 1924, was due to the government's well-publicized information about the harsher penalties for violating the Election Law plus the fact that there were so many new voters, which temporarily disrupted the old vote buying system. The dramatic drop is especially interesting in light of the fact that the 1928 election is often condemned as one of the dirtiest.[88] The reason for the precipitous drop in 1932, according to Hirata, was twofold: the sensational Shanghai incident distracted the public, and the police were more lax in making arrests.[89]

Table 1. Position of Those Prosecuted for Election Bribery

	Diet candidates	Election managers	Election committee members	Workers at election offices
1928	10	16	444	51
1930	19	30	944	41
1932	1	9	363	21

Table 1 shows the positions held by some of those prosecuted for the crime of election bribery during the final three elections of the party cabinet era.[90] These figures reinforce Hirata's view that the public was distracted and that police surveillance was more lax during 1932. Moreover, the drop in violations of all provisions of the Election Law from 18,010 (1930) to 9,869 (1932) also supports his conclusion.[91]

Procurator Hirata viewed the 1932 drop in criminal cases as an aberration unlikely to be repeated. Indeed, he saw bribery so deeply imbedded in the political soil as to make it nearly impossible to root out. The only certain solution to the problem would be the elimination of political parties.[92]

This chapter illustrates that political bribery was widespread. Politicians appear to have accepted vote buying and other violations of election regulations as part of the normal political process. Money exchanged for votes on bills before the House of Representatives also was viewed by participants as part of the usual political process. When asked about the legality of funds received, politicians masked political bribery by saying that the money represented campaign contributions. Thus, campaign platforms notwithstanding, political bribery flourished during the era of party cabinets much as it had during earlier years. Liberal reformer Yoshino Sakuzō, who in 1916 wrote optimistically about the future of parliamentary government,

later became extremely pessimistic. Universal suffrage did not produce a better political system as Yoshino had hoped; instead it raised
corrupt practices to a higher level.[93] Yoshino thought that politicians
were

> enmeshed . . . so thoroughly in "connections of interest" that it
> had become virtually impossible for them to be critical about the
> institutions within which they operated. In their use of economic
> and political coercion to cultivate electoral bases they had made
> the Diet system perpetuate a corrupt majority and the inequities of
> bourgeois culture. . . . Yoshino then concluded that politicians in
> general could not be expected to transform a Diet system from
> within because their main concern was, through "contrivances," to
> build organized bases of power and select the best policy alterna-
> tives that existed at a given moment.[94]

Although political bribery flourished during this era, the zealous
prosecution of bribery cases by Shiono's Tokyo bureau signaled to
the political world that laws could not be ignored with impunity.
Shiono's justice sword cut both major parties: Minister Kobashi
(Minseitō) and Minister Ogawa (Seiyūkai). Table 2 shows the dis-
position of the cases of seven important government officials discussed in this chapter. Governor General Yamanashi, who was a
former army minister, is counted as a minister.

Table 2. Disposition of Cases Involving Government Officials

	Officials prosecuted	Convicted	Stay of execution	Not guilty	Imprisoned
Minister	4	2	1	2	1
Vice-minister	1	1	1		
Bureau head	1	1			1
Secretary	1	1			1
Total	7	5	2	2	3

The most interesting of these seven cases is that of Ogawa, who
was the only minister imprisoned. The following comment, by
Harada Kumao, who gathered political intelligence for Prince Saionji Kinmochi, indicates that Ogawa saw his indictment and trial for
bribery as a political frame-up. Harada wrote, "I understood, incidentally, that Ogawa had recently [November 1930] visited Konoe
[Fumimaro] to say he felt sure it was Suzuki [Kisaburō] who had

caused his arrest to keep him from a chance to become president of the Seiyūkai."[95] Without doubt Ogawa's legal problems and prison time hurt his political career, but they did not propel him into political limbo. During the trial he was reelected to the lower house (1932) and kept his seat until defeated in 1936. His supporters remained loyal and his reputation as a China expert was undiminished. Upon his release from prison he became a close consultant to Prime Minister Konoe Fumimaro. Afterwards he went to Hong Kong on an unofficial trip to stop the war between China and Japan.[96] Former Minister Kobashi Ichita, too, discovered that a sentence of guilt (but with a stay of execution) did not end a political career: in 1937 he became the mayor of Tokyo.[97]

By the late 1920s, various corruption scandals involving bribery and electoral interference filled newspaper front pages and kept the courts busy. These incessant corruption charges plus conviction of high-ranking politicians discredited members of the Diet and weakened the political grip of party government. Opponents of party government, delighted at the spectacle of party self-destruction, were happy to add to party woes by charging politicians with ideological deviation. In this matter, politicians had for some years been unwittingly aiding their enemies. Ishida Takeshi notes,

> The increase of voters which resulted from universal manhood suffrage, together with the general trend toward urbanization, compelled political parties to adopt new strategy for election campaigns. Not only the quantitative increase of voters, but also the qualitative difference of new voters made it disadvantageous for parties to depend solely on the traditional influences of local notables . . . in rural communities. Instead, parties had to appeal more directly to voters, using emotional slogans, mass pamphlets and posters. . . . [According to Ishida, the most potent weapon used] in campaigns was to accuse the other party of corruption and ideological deviation; one party could castigate another by saying that its opponent was not "carrying out the proper conduct as subjects of the Emperor." This kind of *exposé* and accusation adopted by all the major parties against each other undermined people's confidence in the party system in general. Thus the parties dug their own graves.[98]

One of the most influential of the groups that attacked parties for corruption and ideological deviation was the National Foundation Society (Kokuhonsha), of which Hiranuma Kiichirō was president. The creation of this group by Hiranuma and others was a reaction to the attempt by self-proclaimed communist Nanba Daisuke to kill the

crown prince in December 1923 (while Hiranuma was justice minister in the Yamamoto Gonnohyōe cabinet). The new organization's
main purpose was to enlighten the public about dangerous foreign
ideologies. From the beginning in 1924, this group combined a broad
cross section of important civil and military bureaucrats with a group
of justice officials who were the guiding force. By late 1926 nearly
half the association officers were connected with the Justice Ministry.
Much of their energy was devoted to the extirpation of communist
ideology. The organization expanded nationwide and reached a membership of eighty thousand.[99] As this organization matured, its anti–
political party attitude began to appear in its publication *Kokuhon*.

Hiranuma viewed political parties with mixed feelings. On the
one hand, the party battles and business-party corruption of the
1920s disgusted him; on the other hand, as a powerful bureaucrat
with plans to reform the government he sometimes cooperated with
parties. Although the Hiranuma-Suzuki clique sometimes aided the
Kenseikai or Minseitō, it more often supported the Seiyūkai (indeed,
Suzuki joined the Seiyūkai in 1926). Despite this political activity,
Hiranuma was increasingly dissatisfied with the parties. Nevertheless,
Hiranuma had political ambitions and some of his supporters were
eager to see him achieve the prime ministership.[100] During the polit-
ical battles of the late Taisho and early Showa period, the Hiranuma-
Suzuki clique aided Tanaka in overthrowing the Wakatsuki cabinet;
this same clique was very active in attacking the Minseitō cabinet of
Hamaguchi over the issue of the ratification of the London Naval
Treaty.[101]

Hiranuma and other contributors to *Kokuhon* maintained a steady
drumbeat of charges of corruption and ideological deviation against
the political parties. Writing in the New Year issue for 1925, Hiranuma pointed out that politicians were preoccupied with power
struggles and lacked concern for national affairs. In the April issue
Nagai Zenzō argued that universal suffrage would not flush out the
scandal-ridden Diet. As for the Peace Preservation Law of 1925,
which was designed to crush communists, writers for *Kokuhon* viewed
the law as useful to prevent political corruption and to aid in sending political parties to an early grave. The lawyer Takeuchi Kakuji, a
close associate of Hiranuma's, seized upon the scandal involving the
anarchist Pak Yŏl (which involved a photograph of Pak and his wife
taken by a judge), writing that this picture proved that prisons were
hotbeds of immorality and that accused assassins were receiving special treatment. It appears that Kokuhonsha supporters in the Justice
Ministry not only supplied this damaging photo but also leaked
information in connection with the Matsushima Brothels scandal,

hoping to push Wakatsuki out of office.[102] Mitsui Kōshi, in an article published in July 1927, attacked the newly formed Minseitō, claiming that *"minsei"* was a synonym for *"demokurashii"* (democracy), " 'a pretty name to conceal the despotism' of a parliamentary majority." This was an evil foreign concept. Thus, the new party name in fact was a "collaboration from within with the bolshevizing aggression of communism!"[103] Instead of working for the nation, wrote Hiranuma in January 1930, politicians produced ugly scandals, which resulted in the spread of dangerous thought.[104]

4. Purifying Politics

THE DECLINE of party rule after 1932 opened the way for the emergence of "revisionist bureaucrats." Revisionists advocated either ideological purification, state control of the economy, or both to increase the nation's military and spiritual strength. Home Ministry revisionist bureaucrats, who wanted to destroy the alliance between Diet members and local elites, targeted electoral corruption, which the public viewed as widespread and which politicians could not defend.[1] On June 23, 1934, the Reformed House of Representatives Members Election Law, which gave prefectural governors more control over the election process, went into effect. The maximum penalty for vote buying was four years' imprisonment and a fine of up to three thousand yen; election brokers were subject to imprisonment for up to five years.[2] This law also prohibited preelection campaigning, provided for government printing of campaign material, extended government control of speech at meetings, and severely limited election expenses.[3] Writing several years after the passage of this law, one scholar noted, "By providing a limited degree of proportional representation and curtailing the advantages of wealth in election campaigns, the revised election law has been primarily responsible for the increased number of proletarian and independent members in the Diet."[4]

Home Minister Gotō Fumio (Okada Keisuke cabinet, July 1934–March 1936), a leader of the revisionists, guided the Election Purification Movement, which was inaugurated via imperial ordinance in May 1935. By the following month election purification committees headed by governors and with police officials among the members had been established in every prefecture. These committees aimed to educate voters about proper election practices.[5] Prefectural police chiefs at an August conference in Tokyo were ordered by Gotō and

Justice Minister Ohara Naoshi to see that the September prefectural elections were conducted justly and fairly. The police chiefs were instructed to arrest all purchasers of votes and all election brokers.[6] It appears that police followed this order with a vengeance. Aikawa Katsuroku, the official in the Police Bureau, Home Ministry, who was in charge of supervising the elections during the early purification movement, stated in his memoirs that the police arrested "without mercy anyone who committed an election violation regardless of his reasons and without considering which party would become the majority party."[7]

Strict law enforcement helped make the September prefectural elections comparatively clean.[8] There was, however, a down side to the drive for election purity. On December 16, 1935, Justice Minister Ohara congratulated police officials assembled in Tokyo because there had been few complaints of infringement of personal rights in the recent prefectural elections. Nevertheless, the minister urged police leaders to take special care not to arrest people for trivial offenses.[9] What Ohara had in mind as "trivial offenses" is illustrated by another article on the same page of the newspaper in which his speech was reported: "Under the new Election Law, all except those whose names have been duly reported to the police are forbidden to give the candidates any service whatever. . . . When a motor-car carrying a certain candidate fell into a ditch, passers-by attempted to help [but] . . . the police interfered and ordered them to desist, saying that it was giving the candidate service." Another ridiculous example of police overenforcement involved a glass of water upset at the speakers' table, which was cleaned up by someone in the audience. "This was regarded by the police in attendance as an illegal act of offering the candidate service."[10]

Sassa Hiroo, a member of the Showa Research Association, commented on the election in the October 1935 issue of *Kaizō:* "The purification movement creates a premise for the cleansing of the political world and for the reconstruction of political parties. . . . The state would be an ally of the people against the corruption of the established political parties."[11] Rōyama Masamichi, a leading figure in the Showa Research Association and the first director of the Election Purification Movement, was a strong supporter of the purification movement, seeing in it the only hope of rooting out political corruption in election campaigns. Rōyama hoped that as the purification movement spread throughout the nation, Diet candidates could escape the need for party endorsements and could instead depend upon occupational groups for support. His goal, like Sassa's, was to eradicate the corruption of regular political party politics.[12]

The real test for the purification movement was the general election of February 20, 1936. Purification committees promoted the idea of clean elections through lectures, pamphlets, movies, and radio talks.[13] One scholar argues that the Home Ministry viewed this election as a victory for the purification movement. Officials were disappointed, however, by a 7.4 percent decrease (76.7 percent voted) in number of voters compared to the 1932 general election.[14] Despite the decrease, some 15,000 people were arrested for election law violations (bribery and other violations), suggesting an upsurge in illegal practices (it can also suggest stricter enforcement).[15] At any rate, violations numbered 10,401 in 1928; 18,010 in 1930; 9,869 in 1932.[16] The number of Diet candidates arrested (sixty-two) also suggests an upsurge in violations (or more enforcement of the law). By mid-May of the following year, six of these candidates had been convicted; the cases of the others were still in the appeal process.[17] Figures from the general election of April 20, 1937, however, suggest that the purification movement was influencing the behavior of voters and politicians. By about three weeks after the election, the police had handled only 1,950 people suspected of violating the Election Law, of which 221 were involved in bribing voters. Twenty Diet candidates were also under investigation.[18] Justice Ministry officials announced that "104 people had been prosecuted for election violations. . . . This shows a remarkable decline compared with the previous general election, in which some 600 people had been indicted at the corresponding date." Although justice authorities expected more indictments, they hoped that the number of prosecutions would be less than half those in the previous election.[19]

It should be noted, however, that behind the facade of election purification the "political merchants" continued to dispense money. For example, Sakomizu Hisatsune, who was Prime Minister Okada's secretary, acted as a go-between for one million yen from the Sumitomo *zaibatsu* to the Minseitō for use in the 1936 general election.[20] Election reform in the early 1930s did not solve the basic problem: money. Former home minister Mizuno Rentarō, writing in the Home Ministry organ *Shimin* in 1935, noted that a candidate spent from 20,000 to 200,000 yen. A newspaper source stated that the expenses of several politicians in the 1936 general election were about 150,000 yen each. Few candidates had deep enough pockets to finance an election campaign.[21] General Ugaki Kazushige noted in his diary in January 1935 that the president of a major party needed 100,000–150,000 yen per year; of this amount, 120,000–130,000 yen had to be be given to the party. During a general election year, about 2,500,000 yen would be required, for the support of about four hun-

dred candidates. Of this sum, the president would contribute
1,000,000 yen and the party members 1,500,000.[22]

A mid-August 1935 newspaper article indicates that at least some
Home Ministry officials feared that the police might be overzealous
in carrying out the purification movement: "The Home Office authorities fear that if the police, in their eagerness over the purification of elections, proceed to arrest all offenders, there will soon be
complaints of the infringement of personal rights. They will, therefore, give instructions to the local police to refrain from such action
as may be construed as infringement of personal rights."[23] A month
before the February 1936 general election Justice Minister Hayashi
Raizaburō said that "[e]lection offences are particularly deleterious
to the maintenance of the sanctity of the law, and must, therefore, be
punished with special severity."[24] Thus, policemen and procurators
were given a mixed message: do not violate personal rights and
sternly enforce the election laws. It appears that most policemen and
procurators acted on the latter part of this message. One response to
the government's crackdown came from Makino Ryōzō (Seiyūkai) at
the meeting of the budget committee on February 22, 1937. Makino
decried the abuse of authority by procurators and policemen, calling
attention to the fact that during the general election in 1936 between four hundred thousand and five hundred thousand people
were investigated by police on the basis of complaint letters. Daughters and wives of some candidates were even tortured, he claimed.
Authorities should, he argued, ignore such anonymous letters. Justice Minister Shiono Suehiko expressed his regret and said that guilty
officials would be punished. A week earlier Kokubo Ki'ichi (House
of Peers) had charged that in the prefectural elections of 1935 and
the general election of 1936 many cases of police torture were
reported. Home Minister Kawarada Kakichi replied that such cases
were under investigation and that some offending officials were
already on trial.[25] In the aftermath of the 1937 general election, the
Seiyūkai created a committee to look into cases of overzealous
actions by police and procurators. A spokesman stated, "[I]nforma-
tion received by the party headquarters from all parts of the country
shows that in many places local junior officials were guilty of en-
croaching on personal rights. Acting on false information given by
interested individuals, they arrested election managers and voters.
There are also cases where slight offences were punished with special rigour."[26] That there was substance to charges of police torture
to wring confessions from those suspected of Election Law violations
is substantiated by a "confidential" report done by Judge Kawakami
Kan in February 1938. One case discussed by Kawakami involved

Kawaguchi Yoshihisa, a Seiyūkai Diet candidate in the February 20, 1936, general election, who together with supporters was arrested for suspected bribery. Interrogations for this case were carried out by the Kanagawa Prefectural Police. The first supporter tortured was Hishinuma Shunkichi, who was accused of offering money to voters. Hishinuma and other suspects were subjected to one or more of the following: being beaten with a bamboo sword, kicked in the head and body, forced to inhale smoke, made to kneel on wooden rods, forced to inhale water, and thrown onto a hard floor.[27] House of Peers member Kokubo Ki'ichi viewed violations by police in Kanagawa as exceptionally bad: "Such cases occurred in Kanagawa, Kagoshima, Yamaguchi, Iwate and Okayama prefectures, and the forms of torture resorted to by the Kanagawa police were most shocking."[28] The Election Purification Movement, it appears, did decrease the amount of vote buying and other Election Law violations, but the price paid was high. The police, who had a long history of lawless practices and who were by the 1930s operating by their own special standards of conduct, became even more ruthless in their mistreatment of criminal suspects.[29]

New bureaucrats were not the only people eager to purify politics. At the end of September 1930, a group of two dozen army officers in Tokyo formed what was later referred to as the Cherry Society. This group aimed at a national reorganization that included the abolition of political parties.[30] A statement of purpose by these political reformers read in part, "[Politicians] . . . lack the courage to carry out state policies. . . . [T]hey are wholly preoccupied with their selfish pursuit of political power and material wealth. . . . Now, the poisonous sword of the thoroughly degenerate party politicians is being pointed at the military. . . . [W]e who constitute the mainstay of the army must . . . arouse ourselves and wash out the bowels of the completely decadent politicians."[31] The activities of radical army officers culminated in an attempted coup d'état in Tokyo on February 26, 1936. About fourteen hundred troops led by junior officers killed or wounded a number of senior politicians, bureaucrats, and military men. Only a stroke of good fortune saved Prime Minister Okada from death. Included in the rebel officers' manifesto was an attack upon financial magnates, politicians, and bureaucrats, all of whom were leading the nation to ruin. Unfortunately for the rebels, the emperor moved decisively to crush the rebellion.[32]

The Mitsui Company, which for generations bent like bamboo before prevailing political winds, adjusted its bribery payments to include radical army and civilian elements. As early as the spring of 1931, Ariga Nagabumi, the managing director of Mitsui, made a contribution of two hundred thousand yen to a representative of the Cherry Society. At the end of that year Ariga met Kita Ikki, a famous rightist known for a radical plan to reconstruct society. Asking Kita's help to protect Mitsui, Ariga bribed Kita with a payment of between twenty thousand and thirty thousand yen; Ikeda Seihin, after taking over Mitsui in 1934, continued to make 10,000-yen payments to Kita every June and December. Some of this money found its way to radical army officers. This protection money was well spent: Kita had Ikeda's name removed from an assassination list drawn up by the plotters of the February 26, 1936, army rebellion. Later, when Ikeda's name appeared on another list, he was warned in advance. Besides bribing rightist terrorists, Mitsui under Ikeda's urging began to bribe the public, trying to change the public's image of Mitsui as a company greedy for profits at any cost. In mid-1933 the company donated three million yen for unemployment relief, and in October 1933 it established the Mitsui Repayment of Kindness Society, a charitable foundation with a capital of thirty million yen. Following the February 26, 1936, army revolt, Mitsui adopted Ikeda's plan to remove most executives past fifty years of age. Thus, the old management group, of which the public had such a bad impression, was swept away. As for political parties, which Mitsui had subsidized for generations, Ikeda decided that ties must be cut to improve Mitsui's public image. Thereafter, the company refused requests for election campaign funds from the Minseitō, the Seiyūkai, and other parties.[33] "However, though he [Ikeda] did not give aid to any party as such, he did give money to individuals. '. . . I had to extend some amount of help to certain upright individual party members who, irrespective of their party affiliation, had a special relation with Mitsui. . . . I could not suddenly cut them.' "[34]

Another leading political merchant, Kuhara Fusanosuke, also bribed his way into the good graces of the rightist army officers. In the late 1920s, Kuhara was Tanaka Giichi's important source of political funds from the business community. Kuhara's company, Nippon Sangyō (Nissan), prospered during the 1930s as one of the so-called new *zaibatsu*; it was the first large firm to move a major part of its operations into Manchuria. Like Mitsui, Kuhara paid bribes to Kita Ikki and rightist army officers. Another business leader who gave financial support to rightist army officers was Ishihara Kōichirō, who headed Ishihara Industries and Marine Transportation Company. Ishihara gave 11,500 yen to Lieutenant Kurihara Yasuhide, one of the officers involved in the February 26 army revolt. During the period from October 1933 to October 1935, Ishihara supplied 260,000 yen to various rightist organizations.[35]

New bureaucrats and army rightists were not the only ones with a mission to purify politics. Procurators at the Tokyo District Court were at war with corrupt business practices throughout the late 1920s and early 1930s. Under Chief Procurator Shiono Suehiko (see chapter 3) the Tokyo bureau zealously prosecuted a number of important bribery cases regardless of the political affiliation of the suspects.

In 1934 Tokyo procurators investigated the most sensational bribery case of the interwar years, the so-called Teijin incident. Kuroda Etsurō, the leading procurator in the investigative phase of this case, told a defendant on May 2, 1934, that society, including the Finance Ministry, was rotten. Therefore, it was up to procurators to create an ideal society.[36] One scholar writes, "The main aim of the procurators seems to have been to demonstrate the utter corruption of the business world and the political parties. In many ways the handling of the case appears to have been designed to play the same role in disciplining the business world that the Minobe [Tatsukichi] case did in silencing the academicians."[37]

Teijin refers to the Teikoku Jinzō Kenshi Kabushiki Kaisha (Imperial Rayon Company), a subsidiary of the Suzuki Trading Company. After the trading company went bankrupt in 1927, the Bank of Taiwan took title to about 225,000 shares of Teijin stock. Most of these shares, however, were moved to the Bank of Japan in return for a government loan to the Bank of Taiwan. Because the government guaranteed the loan to the Bank of Taiwan, the shares could be negotiated only with the permission of the Finance Ministry. Over time the value of the stocks rose, and speculators tried to purchase them. In June 1933 a group of financiers purchased 100,000 shares. Although this purchase appeared to be a straightforward business transaction, rumors of bribery and manipulation of the stock market caught the attention of the media, the foes of the Saitō Makoto cabinet (May 1932–July 1934), and the procuracy. By the spring of 1934, well-known business leaders and important government officials were one after another charged with misfeasance and bribery. The arrest of two cabinet ministers plus the confession of the vice-minister of finance brought down the Saitō cabinet on July 3. After a lengthy investigation by procurators and a preliminary examination trial, sixteen businessmen, bureaucrats, and politicians faced the public in a dramatic trial of 265 sessions (June 22, 1935–October 5, 1937). Although all the defendants were pronounced not guilty on December 16, the long trial reinforced a negative public image of politicians and businessmen sharing a common cesspool of corruption. Perhaps most shocking was the procuracy's charge of bribery among high officials in the Finance Ministry. This trial held many surprises not the least of which was that although twelve of the defendants confessed to various crimes at the preliminary court examination they successfully repudiated these confessions in court. In this process of repudiation, the procuracy became a target of defendant and public anger, with courtroom, Diet floor, and newspaper charges of torture, forced confessions, and infringement of personal rights. This unprecedented attack upon the administration of justice further eroded public confidence in a procuracy already charged with "fascism."[38]

In early 1932, Fujita Ken'ichi, president of the Tokyo Chamber of Commerce and Industry and a member of the House of Peers, asked Mori Kaku, an influential Seiyūkai politician and Inukai's chief cabinet secretary, to act as a go-between in buying Teijin stocks. Mori in turn introduced him to Count Itō Miyoji, a member of the Privy Council. Through this route Fujita approached Finance Minister Takahashi Korekiyo. This approach, however, was unsuccessful. Perhaps Fujita's growing notoriety acted as a damper on this transaction. Fujita was on trial at the Tokyo District Court charged with embezzlement and misfeasance in the Gōdō Wool Weaving case (he was convicted on May 16, 1933, and sentenced to a year and a half in prison, but with a three-year stay of execution). Fujita had also been caught buying a decoration in the sensational Decoration Bureau scandal. Besides these possible reasons for the deal's failure, Itō Miyoji was much hated because of his long career of blackmailing businessmen and government officials. At any rate, Fujita tried again, hoping to use Baron Gō Seinosuke, a member of the House of Peers and a director of large companies. This approach, too, failed, because Gō informed Fujita that he would have to put up at least a third of the purchase price.[39]

The next attempt to gain access to the Teijin shares was made by Nagano Mamoru, who had been assisting Fujita. First he approached Shōriki Matsutarō, president of the *Yomiuri Newspaper* and a former Home Ministry police official. Shōriki in turn sought help from Education Minister Hatoyama Ichirō, asking that he talk with people at the Finance Ministry and the Bank of Japan about a sale of stock.[40] Other financiers and businessmen entered the picture in late 1932 or early 1933: Kawai Yoshinari, Kobayashi Ataru, Okazaki Akira, and Nagasaki Eizō. In February 1933, Kawai and Kobayashi discussed buying Teijin shares with Takagi Naomichi, a director of the Bank of Taiwan. Although bank president Shimada Shigeru was kept informed, Takagi was the key bank official involved in these discussions. On May 6, Kawai's group offered 117 yen per share plus a dividend for the first 100,000 shares and 122 yen per share plus a dividend if the sale took place immediately. On a second unit of 100,000, however, the buyers were to have the option of waiting a month to make a final purchase decision. The buyers, Kawai said, were life insurance companies and cotton dealers; each group would absorb half the shares. The insurance people were willing to pay immediately, but the cotton dealers would pay 30 percent in cash and the balance within three months. Kawai noted that Minister of Commerce and Industry Nakajima Kumakichi would decide how to divide the stocks among the insurance companies. Director Takagi replied that the price was too low: the Teijin Company was making a good profit and the stock would be paying a good return. Finally, by May 25 it was agreed that the buyers would take 100,000 shares at 125 yen each. Contracts to seal the agreement were exchanged on May 30. The Tokyo life insurance companies ended up with 60 percent of the stock and the Osaka cotton dealers with 40 percent. The next month the Bank of Taiwan used the money from this transaction to pay off the Bank of Japan loan. The stock sale caused little comment at the time.[41]

After the transaction various commissions and gifts were exchanged. Kawai, who played a leading role, got a commission of one yen per share from both the seller and the buyers (i.e., he received 200,000 yen). The Bank of Taiwan gave Nagano 60,000 yen, and Murachi Kyūjirō, an Osaka stockbroker, received 40,000 yen for services rendered. Kawai gave away his entire commission: 170,000 yen to Shōriki (105,000 of this was passed on to Fujita and Hatoyama); 15,000 to Nagano; 15,000 to Murachi. Nagano and four others also made a "political contribution" to Nakajima in the sum of 10,000 yen. Besides these rewards, at the June 26, 1933, Teijin Company shareholder meeting, Kawai was elected controller and Nagano became a director. They were able to use these inside positions to profit from the sale of Teijin stocks. Bank director Takagi was rewarded as well: he became president of Teijin.[42]

The year before the Teijin stock sale the Finance Ministry and Tokyo procurators locked horns over a tax evasion case. Procurators did not forget their humiliation in this conflict. The company suspected of tax evasion was Meiji Seitō Datsuzei, which imported and refined sugar. Police arrested and interrogated the head of Meitō, Sōma Hanji, but after Nakajima Teppei, head of the Tax Bureau, decided that the company was not hiding money owed the government, Sōma was released on May 11, 1932. This was a happy outcome for the company president, but it caused Nakajima some difficult minutes in the Diet, where members grilled him on this case. This incident, however, was quickly overshadowed by the killing of Inukai on May 15, the collapse of the Seiyūkai cabinet a few days later, and the creation of a national unity cabinet under Admiral Saitō. Unfortunately for Finance Ministry officials, however, a lawyer from Meitō went to Nakajima's office and offered to pay unreported back taxes. The Tokyo District Court's procurators reacted on June 22 by sending Procurator Kuroda Etsurō to discuss the case with Nakajima. Kuroda argued that Meitō might attempt to destroy evidence; Nakajima should bring the procurators into the case by sending them a complaint. Nakajima, thinking that more investigation was unwarranted, rejected Kuroda's advice. On June 24 Kuroda's suggestion arrived at the Tax Bureau in written form. Evening newspaper editions carried sensational stories about the Finance Ministry's permitting Meitō to escape taxes and about collusion between government officials and the financial world. Later, procurators urged a heavy fine of 34,430,000 yen plus 7,420,000 in back taxes. Nevertheless, the Tax Bureau decided to settle for a fine of 600,000 yen and back taxes of 120,000 yen. Although this settlement left Kuroda and other procurators dissatisfied, it was accepted by the Saitō cabinet, which announced that the tax and fine had been paid and that the case was closed.[43]

Late in 1933 the Saitō cabinet was criticized by Seiyūkai and Minseitō politicians who were angry that a nonparty cabinet was in power. Newspapers joined the baying pack, which succeeded in driving Minister of Commerce and Industry Nakajima Kumakichi out of office in February 1934. All the noise in the streets and in the Diet centered on a reprinted article about Ashikaga Takauji written by Nakajima in 1921.[44] Newspaper publisher A. Morgan Young wrote, "Presently there was a hue and cry after Baron Nakashima. . . . Many years before he had written an essay in praise of Ashikaga Takauji, a great man in his day several centuries before, but one who backed the wrong horse when there were rival claimants to the throne. The exigencies of loyalty had become so great that it was now disloyal to admire the fine qualities of this fourteenth-century dictator."[45] Unfortunately for the Saitō cabinet, a few days before Nakajima resigned, Education Minister Hatoyama Ichirō was charged with bribery by Okamoto Kazumi (Seiyūkai) in the Diet. Although an investigative committee cleared Hatoyama of this charge, the minister chose to resign.[46] Commenting on the Diet session, the *Asahi Newspaper* wrote, "[w]hen the session was halfway over, the customary mud-flinging contest started, culminating in the resignation of Mr. Hatoyama. . . . Altogether, the tone of discussion fell even lower than in former sessions, and the credit of political parties among the people has suffered further. . . . They are past praying for now as much as they were before."[47] Mixed in with the attacks on Nakajima and Hatoyama were questions in both houses of the Diet about the Teijin stock deal.[48]

This renewed interest in an eight-month-old stock transaction re-sulted from a series of articles in the *Jiji shinpō* (a newspaper) on the financial dealings and illegal stock manipulations of the Banchō Kai, including the Teijin stock transfer. This two-month-long exposé, which began in January 1934, was the brainstorm of Mutō Sanji, the newspaper president. Mutō, who had an unsullied business reputa-tion, aimed at cleaning up the capitalistic system by exposing rotten parts of the business world. A printed statement by Mutō that he took full responsibility for the articles lent them extra credibility. A public disgusted by a seemingly never-ending parade of bribery scan-dals was quick to accept the veracity of these articles. Mutō, who was a former president of the Kanegafuchi Spinning Company, formed a small reformist political party in 1923 and in 1924 was elected to the lower house, where he strongly condemned illegal collusion between businessmen and politicians. He left politics in 1932 to take over the *Jiji shinpō*.[49] The Banchō Kai was an informal but exclusive group of businessmen who formed a club in 1923 centered on Baron Gō Sei-nosuke, a member of the House of Peers and a director of several large firms. This group favored Hatoyama Ichirō and Nakajima Kumakichi with political contributions.[50]

In the meantime, procurators received complaints in Osaka (one) and in Tokyo (two) charging various people with crimes in connec-tion with the Teijin stock transfer. The complaint in Osaka, written by one of Mutō's supporters, charged that Takagi Naomichi (presi-dent of Teijin), Nagano, Kawai, and others were guilty of misfea-sance, embezzlement, and violations of business law. One of the complaints in Tokyo, written by Katō Noboru, accused President Shi-mada Shigeru of the Bank of Taiwan of receiving a bribe, misfea-sance, and making fake documents. The third complaint, written by Hasui Keitarō, an executive committee officer of the Dai Nippon Kikusui Minshū Tō (a rightist group) was directed at Shimada, Kawai, Nagano, and Shōriki. Tokyo District Court Chief Procurator Miyagi Chōgorō received these complaints in February. Procurator Kuroda, who had investigated the Meitō tax case, was the logical choice to head the investigative team; actually, he was the only choice, because the other procurators knew very little about the stock market. Procurator Biwada Gensuke was named co-head of the team. Once they decided that misfeasance had been committed, three other procurators joined the effort. By early April the team was ready for the search and seizure stage of the investigation.[51]

The savage attack upon the Banchō Kai by the *Jiji shinpō* created a public sensation and generated discussion in the Diet; it also alerted procurators at the Tokyo District Court. Angry over these attacks, some members of the group urged a libel suit, but Kawai argued that a published reply would be more effective. Kawai's statement, signed by Gotō Kunihiko (as an officer of the club), was published in *Keizai ōrai*'s March issue (out in February). Kawai explained that the Banchō Kai was a social organization centered on Baron Gō; it met once each month to discuss current issues; money-making deals were not a topic of discussion. Moreover, newspaper reports that Baron Nakajima had a deep connection with the group were grossly untrue. However, because the two barons were friends, they did socialize at affairs like the Banchō Kai's New Year party. Newspapers, Kawai concluded, that claimed that three members of the group were connected with the Teijin and the Kobe Seikōjo (this was a steel company) affairs were mistaken. On March 9, Mutō Sanji was shot dead. The *Jiji shinpō*'s response was to ask if the Banchō Kai, especially Kawai Yoshinari, was behind this. Given the disturbed nature of society in 1935, many people must have made this mistaken connection. In fact, Mutō's murder had no connection with the Banchō Kai. The tubercular young man who killed Mutō was trying to extort money.[52]

As the Tokyo procurators expanded the investigation of the Teijin stock transaction, they issued a press ban on this subject on March 25, 1934.[53] A few days later Chief Procurator Miyagi was ordered to report to a new position at the Nagasaki Appeals Court; he was replaced by Iwamura Michiyo, who was at the Nagoya District Court. Before Miyagi departed, however, he instructed procurators to limit the Teijin investigation by not involving personnel at the Bank of Japan. On April 3, Procurators Biwada and Nagao Takeo, who were on their way to Osaka to begin the search, seizure, and interrogation phase of the investigation, stopped off in Nagoya to see Iwamura. After hearing a report on the case, Iwamura said that they would not win a conviction if misfeasance was the only crime; they must add the crime of bribery to the charges. The two procurators took this suggestion to heart.[54]

On April 5 simultaneous investigations began in Osaka and Tokyo: officials raided offices of the Bank of Taiwan, offices of the Teijin Company, and private residences. Indeed, so many documents were seized at the Osaka headquarters of Teijin that a truck was required to transport the material. Takagi, the president of Teijin, was arrested in Tokyo and taken to Osaka. During the following days other people were detained: Okazaki Akira, a Teijin director (April 11); Kawai, Nagano, and Nagasaki Eizō (April 18); and so on. By mid-May the arrests spread to the Finance Ministry: Vice-Minister Kuroda Hideo (May 19); Ōno Ryūta, head of the Special Bank Section; Aida Iwao, bank inspector; Shidomoto Jirō, assistant bank inspector (May 20); Ōkubo Teiji, head of the Bank Bureau (May 21). At least two large newspapers, the *Asahi* and the *Nichinichi,* violated the press ban by publishing special editions on this sensational story.[55]

The key event in this early phase of the criminal case was President Takagi's confession, which implicated other people. Takagi confessed that Nagasaki gave thirteen hundred Teijin shares to Bank of Taiwan directors and that from these shares the directors in turn gave shares to Vice-Minister Kuroda, Bank Bureau Director Ōkubo, Railways Minister Mitsuchi Chūzō, and Commerce and Industry Minister Nakajima Kumakichi. Some shares were converted to cash and given to Finance Ministry personnel Ōno, Aida, and Shidomoto. Bank of Taiwan Directors Yanagida Naokichi, Koshifuji Tsunekichi, Okazaki, and Takagi pocketed the leftover cash. The second key event in this investigation was a petition to Chief Procurator Iwamura from Vice-Minister Kuroda written about a month after his arrest in which Kuroda explained what he did with the money he received from Nagasaki: ten thousand yen went to a political friend in the Diet (Ōyama Hisamaro), ten thousand yen went to Mitsuchi, and ten thousand or twenty thousand yen was donated to the Seiyū-kai; the balance was given to Ōta Osamu, a financier at the Yamaichi Shōken, to invest. Kuroda also said that upon hearing from a friend that Finance Minister Takahashi's son needed money, he loaned him thirty thousand yen.[56]

At a meeting of the Saitō cabinet on June 29, Justice Minister Koyama Matsukichi said that there was enough evidence to prosecute Finance Ministry personnel for bribery. He added, without mentioning names, that a former minister and a current minister were also involved. Newspapers picked up this sensational news on June 30; the cabinet resigned on July 3, 1934. The following day former minister Nakajima was detained (Shōriki was arrested as well). From the procurators' perspective, the investigation was following a smooth course. Because, they believed, the Teijin shares had been sold at less than fair market value, the sellers could be charged with misfeasance. As for Nakajima and the Finance Ministry personnel, they could be charged with bribery in connection with the stock transfer. Finally, they thought that Minister Mitsuchi, who was called in as a witness, had lied, so he could be charged with perjury. These decisions were reached between April 28 and September 13, 1934. Out of seventeen criminal suspects twelve confessed to various crimes during the investigation by procurators. Kuroda's unexpected death at age forty-three on July 23 is suggestive of the intense strain this investigation was putting on the procurators. The next step for prosecution was presentation of evidence to a preliminary court. Not unexpectedly, the preliminary court accepted the procurators' view of the case. The only exception was the dismissal of suspect Takanashi Hiroji, an inspector with the Kawasaki Daihyaku Bank.[57]

The public, which was hardened to news about law-breaking politicians and businessmen, nevertheless was shocked profoundly by the revelation that five Finance Ministry officials were accused of taking bribes. Aoki Kazuo, who was chief of the Foreign Currency Section of the Finance Ministry, noted that there had never been a bribery case in the ministry—hence, the disbelief among ministry personnel and the public shock.[58]

At the opening of the Imperial Diet on November 31, 1934, Iwata Chūzō, House of Peers, interpellated the government on the treatment of suspects in the Teijin case. He asked why suspects were detained when there was no danger of flight. Was a long period of detention used as a threat to extract confessions? Why were some of the accused kept manacled for several days at a time and thus unable to defend themselves from mosquitoes? Why were some kept in extremely small waiting rooms (i.e., waiting to be questioned) for entire days without being interrogated? Was this another tactic to wear down the defenses of suspects? In short, Iwata saw an infringement of personal rights. The next day Justice Minister Ohara Naoshi denied accusations that the procurators mistreated defendants. The reason for using handcuffs, said Ohara, was the fear that the man in custody would attempt suicide: treatment of suspects was not designed to force confessions.[59] Newspapers in Osaka and Tokyo published disturbing articles that probably undermined public confidence in the Justice Ministry's handling of the case. For example, one Osaka paper suggested that the preliminary judges found the procurators' evidence very weak. Procurator General Hayashi Raisaburō thought it necessary to refute this charge. A Tokyo paper noted that rumors were circulating that defendants had been forced to make groundless confessions.[60] On January 23, Minobe Tatsukichi (House of Peers), professor emeritus of Tokyo Imperial Unversity, questioned Justice Minister Ohara about infringement of personal rights of criminal suspects. Article 194 of the Penal Code, Minobe pointed out, made it a crime for government officials to force confessions and in other ways mistreat criminal suspects. Up to now, Minobe said, rumors he had heard about mistreatment of criminal suspects had been discounted, but in the Teijin case it appeared as if some of the rumors about violations of suspects' rights were true. For example, Okazaki "voluntarily" appeared at the Osaka City Police Station, where he was put in a small room with seven other people and kept there despite illness. A week later he was sent to Tokyo, again in the form of a "voluntary" appearance. Because no formal writ was served, Minobe considered this illegal detention. Who would "voluntarily" stay in such a filthy place? he asked. Minobe also asked Justice Minister Ohara to explain the use of handcuffs. Was this done to give the accused physical pain? And what about Nagano's cell, which was infested with bugs? Justice Minister Ohara replied that procurators acted properly, but that he would investigate the case of Okazaki. Any charges of "torture" applied to suspects, the minister believed, were mistaken. Replying to Minobe's charge that the Teijin Company documents had been illegally seized and that the method used to take Okazaki to Tokyo was not proper, Ohara claimed that the procurators had merely borrowed the company's documents (i.e., "provisional holding") and that Okazaki had "voluntarily" accompanied the procurators.[61]

On February 6, Iwata (House of Peers) again took up the question of infringement of suspects' rights. According to the memoirs by suspects, he said, the procurators who examined them charged that businessmen were responsible for corrupt politicians and that the Finance Ministry's actions taken in the Meitō tax case were wrong.[62] The procurators said the following: "We hold you, accused, of no account. It is the bigger ones, lurking in the background we want to bring to justice. Our object is to carry out a bloodless *coup d'etat* in order to purify society."[63] During this period, the *Kobe Newspaper* published excerpts from the memoir of Nagano. The procurators

> never allowed him to say anything except the words admitting the charge that he had given 1,300 shares as bribes. The instant he attempted to deny the charge, they thundered out, "Don't talk nonsense!" They rushed at him, ordering him to stand up, and ...forced his face up with their fists. He was pushed to the wall behind, and his forehead and jaw were then pushed so that the back of his head was knocked against the wall.... [One procurator later said,] "A fellow like you had better die. But, then, perhaps you lack sufficient pluck to take your own life. If you do not know how to kill yourself, I will tell you. Knock your head against the wall, that's the way. Come on do it!"[64]

The newspaper report continued, "He was then handcuffed [leather manacles]. As he could not use his hands ... he could not keep off the mosquitoes or fleas. He could scarcely sleep at night. . . . A jailer told him that it was by way of penalizing him that he was hand-cuffed. . . . Some time afterwards, a procurator, while examining him, uttered the threat that if he was obstinate he would have to be handcuffed again." Because Nagano refused to confess, he was trans-ferred on July 10 to another cell. This cell "was virtually a nest of bugs. Once he was inside it, he was attacked by a swarm of vermin . . . and he had to put up an all-night fight with them. This state of things lasted for about a month."[65] The *Japan Weekly Chronicle* edito-rialized that although some of the alleged mistreatment of suspects might be exaggerated, the charges made by the defense lawyers, some of whom had Diet seats, did appear true: some suspects had indeed been subjected to the third degree. "The charges are quite plain, and in certain important respects are not disputed. Defen-dants have been kept manacled for as long as 48 hours at a time; others have been confined in verminous cells and all—at one period or another—have been subject to little refinements of treatment that—designedly or not—were calculated to break down their resis-tance and produce the much needed confession which is so peculiar a feature of Japanese criminal procedure."[66]

The open trial began on June 22, 1935; Fujii Goichirō, who had recently been in charge of the trial of the Blood Pact Group, was the chief judge of the three-man court. Procurators Biwada, Hirata Susu-mu, and several colleagues faced a reinforced platoon of defense lawyers presided over by Imamura Rikisaburō, a distinguished lawyer with more than fifty years' experience. Among the sixteen defen-dants were four who had not signed confessions: former Minister Mitsuchi, Ōno, Aida, and Shidomoto (from the Finance Ministry); they steadfastly denied giving or receiving bribes. Shimada, former president of the Bank of Taiwan, repudiated his confession as forced and denied knowing about thirteen hundred shares given to various people. Other defendants also repudiated confessions given to pro-curators. Baron Nakashima, however, did admit to receiving ten thousand yen, but claimed that the money was for a political fund and had no connection with the Teijin case.[67]

The open trial went on for 265 sessions, excluding December 16, 1937, the day the verdict was given.[68] A main task for Judge Fujii was to determine if the Teijin shares were sold for a fair price. Takagi argued that they were and that it was not possible to predict the future value of stock shares. It was also proper, he said, to sell a hun-dred thousand shares to the life insurance–cotton business group because it was doubtful that anyone else could raise such a large sum (12,500,000 yen). Moreover, the Bank of Japan had put pressure on the Bank of Taiwan to repay the loan. Because proving misfeasance on the part of the sellers depended upon whether or not Takagi and other bank officials could have predicted the rapid postsale rise in value of Teijin shares, Judge Fujii grilled Takagi in one hearing after another. When Fujii pointed out that Takagi had confessed, Takagi replied that Procurator Kuroda had terrorized him. Kuroda, said the defendant, kept pounding away on the theme that plutocrats were in collusion with politicians and that even the Finance Ministry was corrupt. Kuroda cited, he said, the Meitō tax-dodging case as an example. Besides the continual browbeating, Takagi claimed that he was handcuffed for three days and nights. Finally, to escape this physical and mental agony, he agreed to whatever Kuroda said. The number of thirteen hundred stocks, he noted, was provided by one of the procurators. Fujii asked why Takagi did not correct his statements at the preliminary examination. Takagi replied that the judge had refused to listen.[69]

Suzuki Yoshio, Takagi's chief lawyer, told the court that his client was mistreated at the Osaka City Jail. On the morning of April 7, for instance, a guard threw him to the pavement and kicked him, and the procurator called him corrupt. Police treated him like a common pickpocket or robber, keeping him in a small cell with more than ten lice-ridden vagrants. Takagi, said the lawyer, was not psychologically equipped to take this kind of treatment. Because of such physical and mental abuse, Takagi confessed to whatever the procurators said. Takagi's stupidity, said Suzuki, was to think that by cooperating he could go home. Instead he was transferred to a prison in Tokyo. Suzuki noted that other people had also confessed, but pointed out that all of them had spent between a hundred and two hundred days in detention. When they did not give proper replies, they were punished by being handcuffed.[70]

Early in the trial the defendants turned the tables on the procurators and put them in the dock. At one hearing, for example, "Takagi turned on Procurator Biwada and thundered out that he would never forget the treatment he had received at his hands in Osaka. As he kept thundering, the Court admonished the accused. . . . Mr. Takagi told the Court that his manner of delivery was as nothing compared with the abuses heaped upon him by the Procurator." Takagi insisted that they had forced him to say "what he knew to be untrue." At another session, Shimada scathingly denounced the procurators. Asked why he used such harsh words, Shimada replied that procurators abused him during interrogations by yelling, hitting the table, stomping on the floor, and calling him a traitor.[71]

Throughout the trial Shimada backed up Takagi's contention that the sale price of the stocks was proper and that it was impossible to predict the future movement of share prices. Moreover, he pointed out that as early as 1931 the government was pushing the Bank of Taiwan to sell the stocks.[72]

And so this scandal-ridden trial dragged on, with one defendant after another repudiating confessions and heaping abuse upon the procurators. Scathing attacks upon the procuracy came from the Diet as well. Makino Ryōzō (Seiyūkai), for instance, charged procurators in general with "abuse of public authority. . . . The period of detention is very long. . . . Nowadays most cases take 100 to 200 days. There is a tendency to prolong the period of detention when the suspects are those of public standing."[73] Makino continued by pointing out that suspects held for long periods will give the replies procurators demand. He pointed to reports that a high official of the Railways Ministry, arrested a year earlier, was still being interrogated because he refused to confess.[74] The *Japan Weekly Chronicle,* stimulated by Makino's interpellation, editorialized as follows: "Here Mr. Makino was touching on the commonest abuse of all. . . . Once arrested a suspect has no chance at all of regaining his liberty until both the police and the procurator are convinced that examination has extracted from him everything he knows about the crime. . . . The Teijin scandal . . . is providing an outstanding example." The suspects in this case, noted the newspaper, "were kept in police cells, without being allowed to see their lawyers, for long periods. . . . Finally they were released on bail after having signed statements." In court the defendants explained that "only by signing confessions could they secure a respite in an examination which threatened to break their health."[75]

Among the many strange twists and turns of this trial one of the strangest was the appearance of Preliminary Judge Morozumi Seiei as a witness. This was the first time in Japanese judicial history that a preliminary judge took the oath as a witness. Chief Judge Fujii summoned Morozumi in an effort to clear up a question about a note passed between Nakajima and Nagano. This was an important legal point, because an exchange of information between suspects during the preliminary examination was illegal.

Judge Fujii asked, "On about July 22nd, 1934, when you were in charge of the present case, did you receive a request from the procurator in charge to consent to an exchange of notes between the two accused, that is to say the handing of a letter written by Baron Nakashima to Nagano urging the latter to confirm his statement to the procurator that he had the 200 Teijin shares (received from the Bank as gifts) realized by him?"[76] Morozumi replied that it would be

best to submit a written reply. Repeated requests by Judge Fujii did
not pry an answer to the question from Morozumi. This pattern was
repeated at a second court session, with Morozumi arguing that he
was not legally qualified to give evidence. To solve this problem,
Judge Fujii requested and received from the head of the Tokyo
Criminal Court Morozumi's preliminary examination record. Fujii
read this report into the trial record. According to the report, Morozumi stated that he refused Procurator Kuroda's request to show a
statement written by one of the accused to another. Kuroda could
not be asked, for he was dead, but Procurators Biwada and Hirata
insisted that Morozumi had given permission, adding that perhaps
he had forgotten. Finally, Morozumi appeared in court for a third
time; again he denied giving permission for the exchange of notes.
This in-house fighting among justice officials was an embarrassment
for the Justice Ministry and a considerable benefit for the defense
team.[77] A newspaper editorialized, "The dispute presents one of the
most serious legal questions in the Court history of this country.
Holding that the attitude taken by the witness is against the provisions of the Criminal Procedure Law, Counsel for the accused urges
the Court to take drastic action against him."[78] The Imperial Bar
Association supported the defense team, presenting a grievance resolution to Justice Minister Shiono.[79]

At a later stage of the trial, Procurator Hirata declared that the
charge of torture was "absolutely groundless. It is not unusual for the
accused to deny the facts of prosecution . . . but it is almost unprecedented that all the accused have hurled criticism and abuse at the
procurators in charge throughout the hearings. But these accusations are all groundless, and the procuratorial authorities did not
extort any of the confessions."[80]

At the final hearing the prosecution asked for the following sentences: Mitsuchi, perjury, six months; Nakajima, accepting a bribe,
one year; Kuroda, accepting a bribe, two years; Ōkubo, accepting a
bribe, ten months; Ono, accepting a bribe, eight months; Aida,
accepting a bribe, eight months; Shidomoto, accepting a bribe, six
months; Shimada, misfeasance and bribery, two years; Takagi, misfeasance and bribery, two years; Nagano, misfeasance and bribery,
two years; Yanagida, misfeasance and bribery, one year; Nagasaki,
misfeasance and bribery, ten months; Koshifuji, misfeasance and
bribery, six months; Okazaki, misfeasance and bribery, six months;
Kobayashi, misfeasance and bribery, six months; Kawai, misfeasance,
fourteen months.[81]

The Teijin trial of 265 hearings (plus a last session for the decision) set a court record.[82] Judge Fujii read the verdict, which was like

a hard slap in the procurators' faces, on December 16, 1937. Fujii criticized their evidence by likening it to "an attempt to scoop up the reflection of the moon from the water."[83] Most people in the court-room understood that the judge was referring to a well-known paint-ing in which a monkey was depicted on a tree branch, trying to scoop up the moon's reflection from the water.[84] At a press confer-ence Judge Fujii stated that the judgment had to be not guilty, be-cause "no criminal facts existed" *(hanzai no jijitsu ga sonzai shinai).* "Especially," he said, "I hope that you do not make a mistake on this point."[85]

According to the memoirs of Matsuzaka Hiromasa (chief of the Criminal Affairs Bureau) the court's verdict dealt the procuracy a terrible blow, and procurators were therefore eager to appeal the verdict. Justice Minister Shiono Suehiko (February 1937–August 1939) ordered Matsuzaka to make a close study of the case and to present a recommendation by December 23, the last day on which an appeal for a new trial could be made. On December 22, however, Shiono told Matsuzaka that he would not appeal because he felt that the case could not be won. Matsuzaka's next job was to calm down Tokyo District Court procurators. The following day Shiono held a meeting at which Tokunaga Eikichi (chief procurator at the Tokyo District Court), Procurator General Motoji Shinkuma, and several others were present. One official said that all the procurators thought that the defendants were guilty and that an appeal should be made. Tokunaga, who was particularly galled by the verdict (perhaps he was thinking about procurators being compared to a monkey!), urged an appeal. Motoji thought that with weak points in the indictment removed and other points strengthened the case might be won on appeal. No one in the room, however, could guarantee a victory. Shiono decided not to appeal.[86]

Former Justice Minister Ohara (in the Okada Keisuke cabinet, July 1934–March 1936) wrote in his memoirs that the Teijin case called for reflection by justice officials. On the one hand, he admit-ted the many faults in the procurators' investigation; on the other hand, he thought that the court gave the wrong verdict. Unfortu-nately, the court was too much influenced by the defendants' state-ments and published accounts. Absolutely, Ohara wrote, the case should have been appealed.[87] In addition, Ohara wrote, "Thinking back on the handling of Mr. Mitsuchi, I wonder if there was not a better way to handle that matter."[88] In fact, Ohara was in a position to do something about the matter of Mitsuchi. Before the open trial, Prime Minister Okada tried to save Mitsuchi embarrassment by ask-ing Ohara if something could not be done about his indictment.

Ohara understood that the prime minister was thinking along the lines of a suspension of indictment (the device used to soften the humiliation of Home Minister Ōura Kanetake in 1915), but Ohara either was unable to stop the prosecution or did not wish to do so.[89] Perhaps Ohara did not have the stomach for a fight with aggressive procurators and their supporters in high Justice Ministry positions.

The editor of Ohara's memoirs (this appears to be Kaji Kōichi, who as a journalist covered the Teijin incident) notes that procurators at that time knew little about stocks and bonds and consequently made many mistakes. However, there was enough evidence to illustrate that money moved in connection with the Teijin case. Nakajima, he points out, confessed even before he was arrested. It is unbelievable, wrote Kaji, that a worldly-wise businessman and politician like Nakajima would confess unless there was something to the charge. Moreover, the procurators should have concentrated upon the charge of misfeasance instead of bribery. Kaji concludes that the actions of both procurators and defendants blurred the truth.[90]

Justice Minister Shiono's memoirs on the Teijin case begin with the comment that although he was a complete outsider, a four-day review of the paperwork convinced him that the arrest and indictment of the suspects was correct. Nevertheless, Shiono's "sixth sense" told him that the charges were half true and half imagination. In deciding not to appeal the verdict, Shiono considered the war with China (from July 1937) and the damage already done to the reputation of procurators. Therefore, he thought it would be best for the Justice Ministry and the nation to put this difficult incident behind them. Shiono's account agrees with Matsuzaka's in that they both believed that some of the suspects had committed crimes. On December 23, Shiono announced that the Teijin trial was over.[91]

In a postwar interview Chief Judge Fujii was asked about errors made by justice officials. He replied that the procurators were not properly prepared and lacked a unity of purpose. Preliminary judges, too, added to the confusion by making mistakes. In some cases evidence about suspects meeting each other was incorrect. All in all, Fujii thought that the many problems grew out of an inadequate investigation. Moreover, it was obvious that the procurators did not understand the crucial item in the trial: the sale of stock. The two associates judges, Fujii noted, fully agreed that the evidence did not support the prosecution's case. Therefore, the not guilty verdict was easy to agree upon. Asked about the famous monkey and the moon statement, Fujii said that it was written by Judge Ishida Kazuto. Inasmuch as the three judges evenly divided the work of writing the opinion, this statement did come as a bit of a surprise, but the justices decided not to remove it, even though they realized that the procurators might be offended.[92]

Chief Preliminary Judge Morozumi, who was also interviewed after the war, repeated his trial testimony: it was improper for him to reply to Judge Fujii's questions. Therefore Fujii should read the report. Asked about Procurator Kuroda's request for permission of a note exchange between suspects, Morozumi replied that he said no. He concluded that he had acted correctly.[93]

Imamura Rikisaburō, the senior lawyer at the trial, pointed out in a lecture given at Minseitō headquarters in 1937 that procurators were more and more dominating political cases, pushing judges aside. This tendency to dominate went back as far as the High Treason incident (1910–1911) and was reflected fully in the Teijin trial. Imamura directed special attention to the procurators at the Tokyo District Court, saying that from about 1929 they aimed to destroy cabinets, using their prosecution power. The Teijin incident was the fruition of their campaign. This problem was solvable, he felt, by restoring the power of judges and by urging judges, procurators, and police to pay attention not only to the law but also to their moral responsibilities.[94] In *Discussion about the Teijin Incident (Teijin jiken benron)*, privately published by Imamura in December 1937, he continued to attack Tokyo procurators. Besides mentioning the Wakatsuki letter to Kusumi requesting a donation, which was leaked by someone, he also charged that in the Kobashi case the procurators pressured suspect Kusumi to change dates in his statement to implicate Kobashi. Furthermore, he recalled that Teijin suspects were told by procurators that businessmen and politicians were all corrupt and that it was the duty of incorruptible procurators to remove them from society.[95]

Defendant Kawai Yoshinari noted in his memoirs that procurators forced confessions from Takagi and Kuroda. Takagi signed a confession to escape the harsh jail conditions and the endless interrogations. All he could think of was returning home. Hospitalization for an ulcer was one indication of Takagi's stress. As for Kuroda, Kawai thought that for a heavy drinker like the vice-minister, a month without a drink combined with unpleasant jail conditions and interrogations put him in a mood to confess.[96]

Journalist Nonaka Moritaka, who closely followed the entire trial, blamed procurators for creating a serious political incident that was disturbing society. The government should, he wrote, investigate this incident to show the public who was responsible.[97]

The *Japan Weekly Chronicle* commented, "For the real importance of the trial, it seems to us, is not that a distinguished group of defen-

dants . . . happened to be in the dock . . . but that the Court believed
the oral testimony of the defendants as against their signed confessions. . . . The Court's refusal to believe the evidence of the preliminary examination . . . has finally proved the distinctive feature."
The paper continued, "There have been instances before in which
District Courts have shown some hesitation in accepting the statements of the prosecution, but never before with the decision and
publicity which has been the case in the Teijin trial. The protest that
false statements were made because certain officials refused to
believe other testimony, and because the defendants' treatment in
prison was so harsh . . . were investigated. . . ." Nevertheless, the paper
said, Judge Fujii did not "refer even indirectly to the defendants'
charges of harsh treatment during detention."[98] Instead, Fujii concentrated on the lack of evidence to prove misfeasance and bribery.

The end of the trial did not stop criticism of the Justice Ministry.
Politicians in both major parties attacked procurators for violations
of personal rights of defendants in the Teijin case and in other cases.
What was the government doing to reform this deplorable situation?
Who was going to take responsibility for mistakes made in the Teijin
case? They also asked why Chief Procurator Iwamura had been promoted to vice-minister instead of being forced to resign.[99] At a Diet
budget committee meeting on February 2, 1938, Shiono was attacked
for saying after the trial (in a press release) that he hoped that the
defendants had learned a lesson and would be better behaved in the
future.[100] Shiono replied that he had "always held that the judgment
pronounced . . . was right. At the time, the procurators concerned
were desirous of appealing against the judgment, but he caused
them to give up their idea. The Minister declared that he believed as
firmly as ever that the facts were as shown in the judgment. He dismissed as unfounded the newspaper reports which represent him as
expressing discontent with the judgment."[101] Although this statement took some heat off the Justice Ministry, it was a half-truth. As
Shiono's memoirs illustrate, he did not accept all the "facts" in Judge
Fujii's verdict; Shiono considered some of the accused guilty of criminal actions. On March 1, 1938, the Seiyūkai and Minseitō introduced a joint resolution urging the government to reform the
system of criminal prosecution. During the debate on the resolution,
which was adopted with a large majority, it was pointed out that no
justice official had taken responsibility for the Teijin case and
resigned.[102] Demands for judicial reform stimulated the Justice Ministry and several bar associations to form investigative committees,
but the expanding war with China diverted attention away from this
subject, and no changes were made in the justice system.[103]

It is difficult to weigh the harm done to defendants and justice officials by the Teijin incident, but it is obvious that some people fared much better than others. Baron Nakajima and former vice-minister Kuroda were reinstated as members of the House of Peers. Although Nakajima avoided politics and high finance after this brush with the law, he did become president of the postwar Japan Foreign Trade Association. On January 29, 1938, Mitsuchi was awarded the Order of the Rising Sun, First Class. This high decoration, which was to have been presented on April 29, 1935, was withheld until after the trial. Mitsuchi was a minister without portfolio in the first Konoe Fumimaro cabinet (June 1937–January 1939), and in 1940 he joined the Privy Council. After the war, Mitsuchi held two ministerships in the Shidehara Kijūrō cabinet (October 1945–May 1946). Former Teijin Company officials Kawai Yoshinari and Nagano Mamoru also held postwar cabinet seats. During the postwar era, Kobayashi became the first president of the Japan Development Bank and a powerful figure in the world where government and business overlapped. Nagano became a famous go-between in the shadowy world of political deal making. Shōriki held a ministership in the first Kishi Nobusuke cabinet (February 1957–June 1958). Lower-ranking Finance Ministry officials did not fare as well. For example, Ōno and Aida were reinstated, with Aida to act as a bank inspector and Ōno to act as financial commissioner to China. This latter post, however, had been vacant for many years, so it seems that Ōno was shunted into a dead-end job. As for justice officials, former justice minister Ohara was appointed to the House of Peers on September 2, 1936. Ohara did not receive the Order of the Rising Sun, First Class, until nearly thirty years after retirement; perhaps this honor was delayed because of the Teijin prosecution. He did serve briefly, however, as justice minister in 1954 (fifth Yoshida Shigeru cabinet). Former chief procurator Iwamura Michiyo's career was not derailed: he became justice minister in the Tōjō Hideki cabinet (October 1941–July 1944). During that time, he was awarded the order of the Sacred Treasure, First Class. Upon his death in 1965 the Order of the Rising Sun, First Class, was presented to his family. Former justice minister Shiono did not fare as well, receiving only the Order of the Sacred Treasure, Second Class, in March 1937.[104]

More than a year before the final verdict on the Teijin incident, the reading public was exposed to another sensational political bribery case, this one involving former railway minister Uchida Nobuya. Uchida, who was elected to the House of Representatives in every election from 1924, was a well-known entrepreneur. Politics was a second career; after he made a fortune in the shipping industry, Hara Kei recruited him into the Seiyūkai after World War I.[105] Uchida held the ministership in the Okada Keisuke cabinet, which was engaged in a massive effort to promote election purification and clean politics in general.

Long before Uchida became minister, "consultation corruption" *(dangō oshoku)* was present among construction firms submitting bids for Railway Ministry projects. Ironically, Uchida's attempt to purge the ministry of corruption led to his indictment for bribery. Soon after taking office he purged employees suspected of engaging in corrupt practices and tried to open up the bidding process to more firms. Among those hurt by this reform was Maeda Eijirō, who dominated the Dobokugyō, an association of authorized contractors. Cut off from sources of information in the Construction Bureau of the ministry, Maeda looked for a way to gain Uchida's cooperation.[106]

Picked for the job of gaining Uchida's goodwill was Tobishima Bunkichi, president of the Tobishima Group and former member of the House of Peers. Tobishima was one of a number of businessmen who sought Uchida's goodwill soon after his appointment as minister was announced. During Tobishima's visits to Uchida's private residence the conversations were on general topics; nothing was said about construction bids or contracts. After Tobishima learned that Uchida planned to establish a new political party, however, he raised fifty thousand yen from Maeda and others with a plan to offer the political donation to Uchida via Nanba Kiyohito, a member of the lower house and Uchida's right-hand man. Besides this payment to Uchida, the contractors also contributed several hundred thousand yen to candidates in the prefectural and general elections.[107]

Procurators charged that Tobishima gave the money to Nanba at a teahouse in Asakusa, requesting that Nanba urge Uchida to favor Maeda's group. Furthermore, said the procurators, after Uchida received the money, restrictions on Maeda's group were removed. A key point in the trial, which began on April 5, 1938, and lasted until the verdict on July 25, 1939, was whether Uchida actually got the money. The three judges chose to believe Nanba's testimony that he gave the money to Uchida. Therefore, the former minister was sentenced to eight months' imprisonment and a fine of fifty thousand yen. Nanba was given four months. Both men were given a one-year stay of execution. Uchida, who strongly denied the charge throughout the preliminary examination and the open trial, appealed the verdict.[108]

Judges in the higher court reversed the lower court ruling. In the verdict read on October 26, 1940, they noted that the defendant's long political career had never been touched by corruption and that he was well known as an incorruptible official who enforced government regulations. Moreover, in dealing with businessmen, he refused to discuss ministry business; his family was lectured not to accept gifts. The court concluded that it was unthinkable that the former minister had accepted a bribe.[109]

Uchida presents a view of these events in a postwar book. Tobishima offered the money and Uchida claims he refused to accept it. Then Tobishima discussed the matter with Nanba, who took the payment. Some of this money was given to prefectural officials and some was used to pay Nanba's bills at various Akasaka inns. During the police investigation, officers insisted that Nanba must have passed on the money, noting that if he had not done so he could be charged with fraud. Police officers emphasized that the penalty for fraud was higher than was the penalty for assisting in the crime of bribery. Under this sort of pressure Nanba changed his story. As Uchida wrote this book, a postwar bribery case was the center of newspaper attention. Procurator Baba Yoshitsugu, discussing the case with journalists, compared the case with a prewar political bribery case. In the old case, he said, they were frustrated because the money did not move, but in the current case it moved. Uchida well recalled Baba, who had led the prosecution team.[110] The procurator's comment in a nutshell explained why the higher court judges overturned the earlier conviction: the procurators did not prove that Uchida had received the money.

The government's effort to purify election campaigns, begun during the Saitō and Okada cabinets, was not tested for five years at the national level after the 1937 campaign. Then, in 1942, the only wartime election for the House of Representatives was held. Government agencies propagandized for a clean campaign and made a special effort to eliminate electoral abuses.[111] This was a strange election in which candidates ran for office with no party affiliation; indeed, there were no political parties! Under wartime pressures and calls for greater national unity all political parties had dissolved by mid-1940. On October 12, 1940, the Imperial Rule Assistance Association was founded by the government to replace the old political organizations. The godfather of this superorganization dedicated to complete national unity was Konoe Fumimaro. Although most old party leaders joined the IRAA, the House of Representatives continued to function. In the end, the IRAA failed as a mass political organization; the abolished political parties displayed a remarkable vitality, and old political patterns remained in place.[112] Indeed, leaders in the House of Representatives preserved their prerogative "to serve as the exclusive vehicle of popular political representation. As the chief brokers for the Lower House in debates with the government over legislation and budgetary proposals, they continued to wield sufficient political leverage to exact concessions from the cabinet."[113] The little-changed nature of politics is well illustrated in the April 30, 1942, House of Representatives election, the so-called Tōjō election.

Tōjō together with other army officers hoped to bury the old-line politicians in the 1942 election. Voters were urged to support only those candidates who received government nominations. Although the number of new faces elected was higher than in previous elections, only one major politician lost his seat. Thus, even in the midst of wartime emergency the effort to break the grip of politicians on their local support bases and to sweep away the old political leadership failed.[114] It appears that vote buying and other forms of corruption did decrease, but in many respects this election was typical. For example, the government used police to influence voters (police pressure was uneven because it depended upon the attitude of prefectural officials); illegal money played a role (a secret army fund of ten million yen was used to subsidize nominated candidates); and solid *jiban* support usually resulted in election.[115]

What was the result of the anticorruption movements of the 1930s? Did political bribery decrease or increase? Were old political patterns shattered by the emergency era of the 1930s and the war years after 1937? Because modern social scientists rely so heavily upon quotable numbers, a great temptation when dealing with the subject of political bribery is to quantify. Scholars using information about the number of suspects arrested and convicted can compile an index of corruption. This approach, however, has drawbacks. For example, the number of bribery suspects arrested per year depends upon the willingness of police to pursue bribery cases. The same applies to procurators and the rate of conviction. Japan during the late 1920s and early 1930s was caught up in a political war against domestic communists. Police and procurators, whose numbers were stretched thin before the anti-communist crusade, were under extreme pressure to crush the illegal party. Common sense suggests that these law enforcement officers were more concerned about the "Red Scare" than about cases of political bribery. It is true, of course, that the Special Higher Police (the elite unit created to handle ideological crimes) did not deal with bribery cases, but during the anti-communist campaign all other police units, including the Higher Police who did deal with election violation cases, were mobilized to aid the elite unit in the anti-Red crusade. For these reasons it is almost certain that the number of political bribery cases was underreported. With the above reservations in mind, the following figures are presented. These numbers represent public officials arrested for bribery under provisions of the Penal Code (arrests under provisions of the Election Law are excluded),[116] including civil servants at all governmental levels.

1933	1,664	1940	2,128
1934	3,885	1941	2,722
1935	3,089	1942	3,299
1936	4,471	1943	6,166
1937	2,469	1944	3,272
1938	2,365	1945	2,343
1939	1,774		

More important than annual statistics for the number of government officials arrested for bribery is a recognition that in many respects the period from 1933 to 1945 has a continuity with earlier years. That the number of bribery cases during elections decreased during these years appears to be correct. Nevertheless, the old-style politicians survived this stressful period, and their long-time political merchant supporters even flourished. In fact, politicians and the *zaibatsu* outlasted the new bureaucrats, the radical army reformers, and others who tried to purge political corruption from society. Old business and political customs even managed to score a spectacular victory over the elite procuracy in the Teijin trial. It is also of note that the Mitsui Company continued in 1941 to use its "research department" for "political maneuvering—with cabinet ministers, army and navy officials, bureaucrats, Diet members." There are no figures for bribes given, because no records were kept.[117]

During the 1930s the sensational Teijin incident and the trial of former minister Uchida spotlighted the dark side of party politics: the incessant search for funds. These corruption cases, although not the main reasons for party decline, were a contributing factor because facts coming out of the trials made it appear as though selfish politicians cared little for national welfare. Moreover, the Teijin case presented the public with an ugly picture of the interaction among politicians, businessmen, and bureaucrats. To a lesser extent, Uchida's trial illustrated the same unsavory dealings. Many newspaper readers, as they reflected upon these trials, must have decided that anti–political party forces produced superior national leaders.

5. Occupation Era

THE PRIMARY GOALS of SCAP (the Supreme Commander for the Allied Powers, i.e., Gen. Douglas MacArthur; but used here to refer to Allied authorities in general) were the demilitarization and democratization of Japan. Although the first goal was accomplished easily within a few months, the second task was more difficult and took much longer. The Occupation agency within General MacArthur's headquarters that directed political reforms was Government Section. This key agency was headed by Brigadier General Courtney Whitney (from December 1945), whose deputy was Colonel Charles Kades (from September 1946). Reformers in Government Section planned to democratize political parties and to revise the election regulations, but it is doubtful that they anticipated the problem of widespread political bribery. An exception among the reformers was Harry E. Wiles, whose books on pre-1945 Japan display a special interest in bribery and other forms of political corruption.

Determined to promote democratic self-government, SCAP began in January 1946 to purge undesirable organizations and people from public life. One consequence of this drastic action was a wholesale removal of politicians from the postwar political parties; this removal resulted in a "leadership vacuum that opened the way for a new generation of political leaders. Prominent among these new leaders were men who had risen to high positions in the national bureaucracy. Since the American Occupation was an indirect occupation that worked through the existing Japanese government structure, the bureaucracy was left relatively untouched by the purge."[1]

SCAP also promoted democratic self-government by pressuring officials to liberalize national election regulations. Although the enfranchisement of women was insisted upon, it appears that the Japanese were given a free hand in altering the law governing election to the House of Representatives. The Shidehara Kijūrō cabinet (October 9, 1945–May 22, 1946) lost no time in introducing a bill to reform the Election Law. The main points of the revision were voting rights for everyone over twenty and a minimum age for candidates of twenty-five, a limited plural balloting system and multimember electoral districts, and the removal of many restrictions on campaigning. The House of Representatives Election Law (Law Number 42) was passed by the Diet on December 15 and promulgated on the seventeenth. This law divided the nation into fifty-four districts. Except for the most populous prefectures, each prefecture constituted one district. From four to fourteen representatives were permitted to win lower house seats, depending upon population in a district. Each voter cast from two to three votes, depending upon the size of the district. At stake was a total of 466 lower house seats. The law was designed to stop corrupt election practices by reducing campaign restrictions and by furnishing aid to candidates. Under this law, for example, anyone could campaign, not just a campaign manager and an election committee; restrictions on the number of public meetings and speakers were removed, as was limitation on the number of advertising posters. Moreover, the new law attempted to offset the greatly increased election expenses stimulated by the adoption of an expanded suffrage by providing government aid. Each candidate was permitted to use designated public facilities; prefectural officials were ordered to inform voters about each candidate's political views; free radio time was mandated for party leaders; and the old penalty for spending more than the maximum on campaign expenses was abolished. To discourage traditional patterns of corruption, however, Article 12 stipulated that those who sold or purchased votes were liable to penal servitude for up to three years and a fine of up to twenty thousand yen.[2]

The first election based on an expanded suffrage was held on April 10, 1946. Three months earlier Government Section had ordered that "every step possible be taken looking toward a free and untrammelled expression of the people's will in this election. To such end you will give the fullest publicity to the penal provisions of the law, and will take such steps as may be necessary to ensure their vigorous enforcement."[3] Five major parties fielded candidates: Liberal, Progressive, Socialist, Cooperative, and Communist. The Liberal camp won 140 seats, the Progressive Party won 94, and the Cooperative group won 5. One publication summed up the election this way:

[I]t can be seen that those affiliated with the conservative camp account for an overwhelming majority. Against this, the strength of what is regarded as the progressive forces . . . does not reach 100. It is evident that in spite of the fact that the call for a democratic front has received the support of public opinion, it remains that the conservative forces still maintain a firm base . . . and one can perceive the fact that in particular the jiban fostered over the years by the old forces of the Seiyukai and the Minseito in the rural villages have yet to be shaken.[4]

Writing two years later Kenneth Colton, an Occupation research analyst, noted that the Progressive Party cultivated the old Minseitō spheres of local political influence, reaching into the ranks of local mayors and village headmen for support.[5] Despite this and other indications that party politics more or less followed the pre-1945 pattern, in the crucial area of party financing an important new element appeared. Before the war, parties depended upon contributions from big business and secret government funds, but defeat eliminated many of these traditional resources and forced parties to look elsewhere for money. Construction companies were one important new source; another source was the industrial loans controlled by the government.[6] Within a few weeks after this election the cabinet of Shidehara Kijūrō was replaced by that of Yoshida Shigeru (May 22, 1946–May 23, 1947), head of the Liberal Party.

Experiment with the large-district election system appears to have pleased few people in authority. Consequently, on March 31, 1947, the revised House of Representatives Election Law (Law Number 43) reintroduced the medium-sized multimember district and single-entry ballot that closely resembled the 1925 law. This system gave the nation 117 multimember districts. Each voter was to cast one ballot and, depending upon the district's size, a winning candidate was among the top three, four, or five.[7] Noteworthy is that campaign restrictions were increased. For example, election literature and posters were severely restricted. This trend continued during the following years, with a steady reimposition of pre-1945 controls on campaign activities.[8]

The motive of the conservative Yoshida cabinet in promoting the new law despite objections of the opposition was to hinder the growth of small parties, especially those on the left. Moreover, the small constituencies made it easier for conservative political bosses to use bribes and other illegal methods to capture votes. Although Government Section was unhappy with this development, it maintained a hands-off attitude. Despite the new electoral system, the election of April 25, 1947, resulted in surprise victory for the Japan Socialist Party, which under the leadership of Katayama Tetsu formed a coalition cabinet on May 24.[9]

A Government Section report on Election Law violations during the 1947 campaign listed 2,997 violations. By June 10, 1,028 people had been fined, 71 imprisoned, 1 given a remission of sentence, and 1 found not guilty. The balance were awaiting trial. Interestingly, the areas with the largest number of offenders were not big cities but places like Mito (208), Sendai (239), Fukushima (307), and Yamagata (337). Political bribery (i.e., vote buying or vote selling) was the charge in 2,610 cases.[10] Another SCAP document noted that even though five levels of government were involved in the 1947 general election, there were only 2,997 violations. This was viewed as a favorable outcome, because the 1946 election campaign, which had involved only one level of government (i.e., the lower house), resulted in 2,632 indictments. Furthermore, the report pointed out that election regulations were more stringent in the 1947 campaign than in 1946. The document concluded that political morality was greatly improved.[11]

Commenting on the number of electoral offenses, Russel Brines, Associated Press, wrote, "Under Japanese political mores this was inconsequential."[12] Mores aside, a comparison with Election Law violations during the prewar era supports Brines' view that the total number of violations was inconsequential: 10,401 in 1928; 18,010 in 1930; 9,869 in 1932 (see chapter 4). Moreover, his conclusion is reasonable given that the number of voters during the three prewar years was roughly between 12,400,000 and 13,100,000 and that in 1947 it was nearly 41,000,000.[13] As for the economic aspect of running for national office, Brines reported that 75,000 yen was the legal limit for each candidate's campaign expenditures. "No candidate officially reported exceeding that amount, for obvious reasons. But in political circles it was whispered freely that a prospective candidate with less than 500,000 yen at his disposal had no chance of winning."[14]

From early in the Occupation, rumors circulated about huge stocks of hidden military supplies. Repeated SCAP investigations aimed at uncovering hoarded materials found little more than the normal inventories of black-market operators. In 1947, however, before Katayama Tetsu formed a cabinet, the hoarded materials issue caught public attention when former vice-minister Sekō Kōichi (Home Ministry, former Yoshida cabinet), charged that at least a hundred billion yen worth of military stocks was held in secret by big-business concerns. Sekō's outcry resulted in the formation of a Hoarded Goods Committee (within the Economic Stabilization Board) to investigate the charges, with Sekō as the vice-chairman (February 24–April 11). Although people were uncertain about how seriously to take Sekō's disclosures about illegal transfers of government materials, he did catch public attention when he charged that several of Katayama's new ministers were involved in illegal schemes to profit from secretly hoarded goods. This was enough to trigger a response in the lower house, which on July 25 set up a Special Committee for the Investigation of Concealed and Hoarded Goods. This committee, the first of its kind to be created by the lower house, was headed by socialist Katō Kanju. The committee's report was released by the lower house on December 20, 1947. It confirmed that the Suzuki Kantarō cabinet (April 7–August 17, 1945) had ordered the release of military goods to unknown numbers of individuals and companies and that no payment for these goods went to the public treasury.[15]

Reports that large sums of money gained by the sale of illegal hoarded goods were being used to bribe politicians and other public officials and that these illegal funds were used to finance election campaigns in 1946 and 1947 brought swift action. Government Section saw this spreading pool of corruption as a threat to the SCAP program of political reform. Consequently, Brigadier General Whitney suggested that Procurator General Fukui Seita investigate the hoarded goods affair. Furthermore, Government Section pushed the Finance Ministry to increase the Justice Ministry's budget for additional procurators, an urging that led to the hiring of hundreds of new procurators; many were earmarked to investigate the hoarded goods scandal.[16] In early February 1948, Colonel Kades addressed a national conference of procurators:

> The United Nations are watching to see whether only the words of Japanese Society have changed but the melody remains the same. The world is watching to see whether it is true under the new Constitution, as it also was under the Meiji Constitution and as it was actually enforced by the Tokugawa Shoguns, that courtesy would not be extended to the "commoner" and punishment should not be administered to the "gentleman." Because democracy is rooted in equality under the law, the law in a democracy becomes the great leveler of society. The procurators, whose only client is the people can, therefore, render no greater service to Japanese democracy than by prosecuting vigorously and courageously, those hitherto privileged politicians and industrial barons who have flouted public decency and public morality by selling the economic heritage of the Japanese people for a mess of black-market profits.[17]

After Katō became labor minister in the Ashida Hitoshi cabinet (March 10–October 15, 1948) the hoarded goods committee, its name changed to the Illegal Property Transactions Investigative Committee, was taken over by Mutō Unjirō, another socialist. Equipped with the power to examine witnesses under oath, the Mutō committee examined former candidates for Diet seats and Diet members about sources of campaign funds. Soon it was obvious that some witnesses were committing perjury. In his first interim report Mutō pointed out the conflicting testimony and recommended a new law to make the use of secret funds illegal. Over the lifetime of the Mutō committee dozens of politicians were quizzed by procurators, and some were arrested for bribery. By far the biggest fish caught in the legal net was the socialist Nishio Suehiro, who was deputy prime minister in the Ashida cabinet. While testifying about political contributions made by construction company operators, he admitted that in April 1947 he had received a 500,000-yen political contribution and that he had not included it in the official party report on expenditures. Nishio argued that this was a personal donation to him as an individual and was not meant as a bribe to influence his political actions. Opposition politicians replied by seizing this issue to push for a no-confidence vote. Nishio had, they insisted, violated Cabinet Order 328, which made the reporting of campaign funds mandatory. Nishio resigned on July 6 and was arrested the next day. Indicted on charges of having committed perjury and of violating order 328, he was acquitted by the Tokyo District Court.[18]

Much more sensational than the Nishio affair, however, was the corruption exposed by the Mutō committee in connection with the Coal Mine State Control Bill. Although the Katayama cabinet was a coalition government, the prime minister was pledged to expand state ownership of businesses, especially key ones like coal, fertilizer, and banking. Unfortunately for Katayama and his supporters, more moderate socialists and conservatives rallied against this plan. From SCAP's viewpoint, the most pressing need was a dramatic increase in coal production, which was needed for economic recovery. General MacArthur agreed: the Japanese could reorganize the coal mining industry as long as reorganization did not conflict with SCAP policy and as long as production increased.[19]

Members of the Kyushu Coal Operators Association acted against the proposed nationalization bill by creating a lobbying fund based on a charge of ten yen per ton of coal mined by association members. This produced a war chest of many millions of yen, which were used to bribe lower house members. Fancy restaurants in the neighborhood of the Diet building did a booming business as rumors of big payoffs circulated.[20] Other means besides lavish entertainment and cash payments were employed to stop the bill: a five-man assassination squad was dispatched from Kyushu to kill Mizutani Chōzaburō, minister of commerce and industry, and Itō Ushiro, chairman of the committee considering the bill. Picking up rumors about the planned murders, the Metropolitan Police Board assigned body-guards to the politicians. Later it was revealed that the assassins got to Tokyo, entered the Diet building, and tried to get at Mizutani and Itō. Fortunately for the politicians, the assassins could not get close enough to use their daggers. Eventually, the conspirators ran out of funds and returned to Kyushu.[21]

The consideration of this bill turned the Diet into a hornets' nest. Not only did opponents of the bill use standard filibustering meth-ods, but they also used fists, with fights occurring one after another. Observers whose memories were long enough recalled noisy Diet sessions of the 1920s. In the end, however, the Katayama cabinet got a watered-down version of the bill through the Diet, to go into force in April 1948. One well-informed contemporary ob-server notes that the law had no real effect.[22]

Rumors about large sums of money being spread around in con-nection with the coal mine legislation attracted the attention of procurators at the Tokyo District Court, but they were too busy and too short of staff to take action. One reason for this situation was that procurators were involved in another corruption case touching the Ashida cabinet (see below). At this point SCAP officials, who read in newspapers that mine owners were misappropriating government funds earmarked for housing for the miners, stepped into the pic-ture, putting pressure on Chief Procurator Satō Hiroshi to investi-gate. As a result of this pressure, money, personel, and equipment were made available to Procurator Nakamura Nobutoshi and a thir-teen-member staff. On October 19, 1948, they began to investigate the coal mine case.[23]

An opening wedge into this case was supplied by Okabe Tokuzō (Democratic Party), who made a slip of the tongue on September 24, 1948, as he testified before the Mutō committee. Using Tsugo-kawa Shinzō as a go-between, he said, he gave 50,000 yen to Kawasaki Shūji, who was vice-head of the Party Affairs Investigation Section. The procurators viewed this as the start of the money trail. When Kawasaki was quizzed by the committee, however, he claimed that the money had been returned. Nevertheless, after comparing testi-mony from various people, the committee concluded that Okabe distributed 450,000 yen to several Democratic Party members. More-over, Takeuchi Reizo, who appeared to be in charge of the lobbying effort to stop the bill (he was sent from Kyushu by mine owners for this purpose), gave 500,000 yen to Uehara Etsujirō, who chaired the Liberal Party's Special Planning for Coal Committee. Uehara denied taking the money. Furthermore, mine owner Azabu Tagakichi, the committee noted, gave 1,300,000 yen to Yoshida Shigeru, who passed 700,000 of it to the Liberal Party; some people believed that part of this money went to Shidehara Kijūrō (former prime minister) and Tanaka Man'itsu (former minister without portfolio in the first Yoshida cabinet). Finally, the committee stated that 2,000,000 yen was given to Democratic Party member Nagao Tatsuo, who in turn passed it on to Chief Party Secretary Takeda Giichi (Democratic) and to Tanaka Man'itsu. The committee regarded these funds as bribe money used to defeat the bill to regulate coal mines.[24]

Tokyo procurators were not able to open up this case until they discovered material evidence in the form of canceled checks for several million yen drawn on Kyushu banks. This discovery plus interrogations resulted in the indictment of Kiso Shigeyoshi and Haraguchi Hideo for giving bribes. These men were key figures in the Kyushu group trying to stop passage of the bill. Tanaka Man'itsu, Takeda Giichi, Tanaka Kakuei, and Fukatsu Tamaichirō were among those indicted for taking bribes. On the eve of the Tokyo District Court trial, procurators were confident of convictions; as Procurator Asami Toshio pointed out, it was rare to find such solid evidence as the three checks each for a million yen. The prosecution's case, however, began to crumble at the first trial and continued to fall apart at the second one. Tanaka Man'itsu was found not guilty; Tanaka Kakuei got six months; Fukatsu and Kiso were judged guilty but with stays of execution. Takeda Giichi (a former minister of welfare) was tried in a different court and found not guilty. At the appeals court Tanaka Kakuei's sentence was reversed. Thus, both former ministers escaped punishment and only one politician among the above received a prison sentence—and it was not served.[25]

A charge of bribery was difficult to prove, as this case well illustrates. As we have seen, the procurator needed to prove not only that an official accepted money and was in a position to do the person who offered it a favor, but also that the official who accepted the money regarded it as a bribe. A look at how judges and lawyers viewed the cases of Fukatsu and the two Tanakas provides some insight into the process of how judges established whether or not bribery took place. The judges saw Fukatsu's case as open and shut: he got the money directly from Kiso and did something in return in his official capacity; they could see no other justification for Fukatsu's keeping the money. As for Tanaka Man'itsu, the chief judge at the first trial was unwilling to accept the procurator's argument that the money was a quid pro quo for a vote against the bill. Instead he accepted the argument that both the giver (Kiso) and the taker

(Tanaka) regarded the money as a political contribution for the establishment of a new party. Tanaka's leaving the Democratic Party and joining a new group influenced the judge's decision. Interviewed sometime after the trial, Tanaka's lawyer, Abiru Ken'ichi, said that everyone agreed that Tanaka got money, but he returned it just before the vote on the bill; this fact impressed the judge. Moreover, in their statements to the procurators and others, Kiso and Tanaka constantly stressed that the money was a political contribution and had no connection with the bill.[26] Abiru concluded, "In short, it is a peculiar law: if the suspect does not consider the money as a bribe, then the crime of bribery is not established. Thus, when suspects are making statements [i.e., to procurators and preliminary judges], only the stupid ones get caught."[27]

Tanaka Kakuei told procurators that he asked a fellow party member, Nagao Tatsuo, for contacts to expand his construction business. Nagao introduced him to Kiso, who gave him work constructing living quarters for miners. The million yen, Tanaka claimed, was upfront money for this building project. Naturally, he claimed that the money was not connected with the bill. Even though Tanaka could produce neither a written contract nor an account-book entry, the appeals court judge ruled that a contract existed because each man was president of a company. Two other facts helped Tanaka, according to lawyer Masaki Tōru: although some construction work was done by Tanaka's company at Kiso's mine, Kiso never used the term "Diet member" (*daigishi*) in referring to Tanaka; in the case of other members he always used this term. This helped convince the judge that Kiso regarded him as merely a contractor.[28]

A week before taking office the Ashida Hitoshi cabinet pledged to raise ethical standards and to pass an anti–political corruption law.[29] Ironically, rumors of political corruption dogged this cabinet from the beginning, and within a few months it was destroyed by the biggest bribery scandal of the Occupation era. Hard on the heels of Nishio's arrest (see above) the Showa Electric (Showa Denkō) Company scandal began to erode the cabinet's political foundation.[30] Although the attack on Ashida followed the traditional pattern of the opposition trying to destroy the cabinet, this affair had an added twist in that some officials within SCAP were defending while others were attacking him.[31] In addition, statements such as the following were commonplace: "Implicated in the Showa Denko Scandal, he [Ashida] was forced to resign."[32] This is incorrect. In fact, Ashida was prosecuted for taking money from construction companies; this affair had no direct connection with the Showa Denkō scandal. Nevertheless, procurators managed to include the former prime minister in the Showa Denkō trial (there were three groups of defendants).[33]

Let us, therefore, take a brief look at what should be termed the Ashida incident. Ashida, like any party president, was happy to accept political donations. Through a go-between (a politician, Kitaura Keitarō), Oka Naoki, president of a company that made floorboards for the Occupation forces, presented Ashida with a million yen as a political contribution. Umebayashi Tokio, president of a construction company, gave another million yen via politician Ayabe Kentarō.[34] Ashida claimed during the first trial that about ten days before his arrest a procurator told him that the investigation would be terminated if Ashida would resign from politics. Ashida rejected the offer, demanding an open investigation. According to former procurator Mitsuhiro Hiroshi, who handled the Showa Denkō case on appeal, the prosecution's case against Ashida was extremely weak, with insufficient evidence to prosecute a prime minister.[35] Former minister Nishio Suehiro, who discussed this case in a book published in 1968, received a letter from Nagawa Yasuo, the chief lawyer for Ashida. Nagawa pointed out that even though the public regarded Ashida and the Showa Denkō incident as synonymous, there was no connection between the money received from the company presidents and the other case. Why, then, was Ashida being prosecuted? Inasmuch as the cabinet had fallen after ministers were charged with taking Showa Denkō money, he dismissed the charge by some people that SCAP's General Headquarters (GHQ) had targeted Ashida to destroy the cabinet. In fact, Nagawa believed that Ashida was prosecuted because procurators were worried that GHQ would think that they were not doing their best if they neglected to charge the former prime minister.[36] "At that time," wrote Nagawa, "the younger procurators were overly energetic and too righteous. They were also concerned about selling their own names."[37] In light of Colonel Kades' dramatic pep talk to procurators in February 1948, Nagawa's conclusion makes good sense.

The political storm that hit Ashida began two months before the cabinet's formation, when Takahashi Eikichi (Liberal Party), a member of the Illegal Property Transactions Investigative Committee, charged that the president of Showa Electric Company, Hinohara Setsuzō, had colluded with Ashida and two others to take over various *zaibatsu* that were being dissolved by SCAP. Indeed, said Takahashi, Hinohara became head of Showa as a result of such illegal maneuvers. Although the public heard about this case only after Takahashi's speech, police authorities, following up numerous anonymous letters, already were investigating Hinohara. On May 25, the Metropolitan Police Board raided the Tokyo headquarters of Showa Electric, seizing documents. Among these documents was a notebook that contained a long list of persons to whom "gifts" had been given. Moreover, the police also discovered that to conceal the "gift" record, the company had been keeping a double set of books. Therefore, the police were certain that some of this money was used for political bribery.[38]

During this period, the Reconstruction Finance Bank made government loans to certain industries to promote economic recovery. Showa Electric, a giant chemical fertilizer manufacturer, had borrowed several billion yen in government money and was attempting to get more loans. The value of the money and goods that Hinohara spread among bureaucrats and politicians is estimated at between thirty million and a hundred million yen. Besides entertaining people in expensive restaurants, he handed out packages of a hundred thousand yen wrapped in newspaper.[39]

Although some aspects of this bribery scandal remain a mystery, at least one connection between Ashida and Hinohara is visible. In March 1947, the Democratic Party (built on the ruins of the Progressive Party) was founded; in May, Ashida became its president. Ashida's key supporter in the maneuvers that brought him the party presidency was Sugawara Michinari, whose brother-in-law was Hinohara Setsuzō. At a secret meeting with Sugawara, Ashida explained that he did not have enough funds to become party president and asked Sugawara to take care of this matter. Sugawara then agreed to "take care of all money matters, but there will be just one conduit. I will not hand over a single sen to anyone other than Chizaki [Usaburō]. . . . [Y]ou mustn't accept a single sen in construction contributions."[40] How much money Hinohara contributed to the Ashida campaign to gain the presidency and then to form a cabinet is unknown, but it was rumored that two hundred million yen changed hands at the time he was appointed prime minister.[41]

Arrests in the Showa Electric Company case began in June 1948 and continued until mid-December. Among the first group apprehended were Hinohara's private secretary Sunahara Tokiya; Satō Shūzō, another of Hinohara's aides; Tsuda Nobuhide, the official in charge of ammonium sulphate in the Commerce and Industry Ministry's Chemical Bureau; and Nimiyama Tsutomu, head of the First Section, Chemical Bureau, which dealt with fertilizer. Confident they had a strong case, police and procurators raided Hinohara's home on June 23; he and some employees were arrested. Next, on September 10, came the arrest of Shigemasa Seishi, formerly vice-minister of the Agricultural and Forestry Ministry, and Matsuoka Shōhei, the former chairman of the Executive Bureau, Liberal Party. Three days later Budget Bureau Chief Fukuda Takeo (Finance Ministry) was arrested. During the following weeks, Ōno Banboku (Liberal Party adviser), Ninomiya Yoshimoto (Industrial Bank vice-president), lower house member Ozawa Senshichirō (Liberal Party), former finance minister and director of the Economic Planning Board Kurusu Takeo, and Deputy Prime Minister Nishio Suehiro were arrested together with Mitsuki Tokihiko (Kurusu's secretary). Even after the Ashida cabinet resigned, the arrests continued: Shimokabe Mitsushi (Ashida's secretary and son-in-law) on November 3 and some days later Suehiro Kōjirō (a former Industrial Bank vice-president). In an unprecedented action, Tokyo procurators requested the arrest of former prime minister Ashida while the Diet was in session. The request was approved by a vote of 140 to 120 (the Socialist Party abstained). Ashida was questioned on December 7 and prosecuted on December 16 for accepting a bribe and for tax evasion. Forty-four of the sixty-four arrested in this case were prosecuted.[42]

Procurators believed that they had strong proof of bribery because Hinohara stated that the money and goods were given to various bureaucrats and politicians in exchange for a better deal for his company (i.e., a large loan). Furthermore, he said that because political donations produced only indirect results, he never gave them; instead, he always gave money for a specific purpose. Naturally, defendants insisted that the money received was not a quid pro quo for a specific favor. Former deputy prime minister Nishio, for example, who admitted getting a million yen, claimed that this money was merely a donation, which he accepted not as a politician but as a private individual. In his case, Hinohara had told the procurators that the money was given to silence criticism from the Socialist Party about the huge government loan. Ashida, who was accused of taking a bribe of two million yen, argued that he was not guilty of bribery because he exercised no control over the loan funds and thus was in no position to grant Hinohara's loan request. Ōno told the court that the two hundred thousand yen was not a bribe, but merely a "gift" from a friend. Matsuoka termed his hundred thousand yen a "loan." And so it went in a trial that for some people lasted until 1962 (this included appeals). Only three defendants were judged guilty: Hinohara, Kurusu, and Shigemasa. The company president was sentenced to one year in prison, the former finance minister to eight months, and the former vice-minister of agriculture to one year. The two former government officials were assessed fines as well. None of the men served prison time; each received a stay of execution.[43] Justin Williams, chief of the Parliamentary and Political Division of Government Section (from July 1949), commented as follows on the politicians' defense: "Each rested his case on the standard and previously successful defense used in political scandals, that the money was presented as political party donations and not as bribes to influence government officials or to hush up rumors of corruption in political circles."[44]

Nishio Suehiro, who was a defendant in the Showa Denkō trial, thought that one of the most important aspects of the case was the missing money. The trial documented payments of six million yen, but Hinohara spent eighty-five million yen. What happened to most of the money?[45] Although no foreign names appeared in trial documents, Masumi Junnosuke observes that it appears as though "the recipients of Hinohara's most extravagant bribes and lavish entertainment were members of the Government Section . . . and the contigent of foreign correspondents." Some of Colonel Kades' enemies in SCAP leaked this information to police and Japanese journalists and "it was published in the *New York Times* . . . and then reprinted in the Japanese papers, where it set the Japanese political world aflame."[46] Nishio agrees with this conclusion: the battle for control of SCAP policy spilled over into the Showa Denkō investigation. Colonel Kades, who was personally touched by the scandal, was unable to do much to defend the Ashida cabinet. Out of this political battle Major General Charles Willoughby, head of G-2, emerged the victor.[47]

Nishio also provides an enlightening account of how he received the million yen. About November 20, 1947, Watanabe Toshinosuke, an old friend from the prewar labor movement days and head of the Labor Bureau in the Katayama cabinet, visited Nishio's official office. Watanabe said that two friends, Satō Noboru and Fukuya Shūichi, wanted to introduce Nishio to a businessman. Nishio not only knew Fukuya but was under obligation to him for acting as a middleman in obtaining a 1,000,000-yen political donation from an Okayama businessman. He therefore agreed to the meeting. On November 23, at Satō's residence, he was introduced to Hinohara and Fujii Takashi. Fujii said that they wanted his help in silencing criticism in the Diet by Inamura Junzō about government loans being given to Showa Denkō. Fujii suggested that Inamura's sharp comments were inspired by the fact that a company in his district was not getting any of the money. Because of such critical questions, rumors were circulating, and they were hurting company business. Nishio replied that although he understood the problem he could not silence Inamura. Thus he could not accept their request. After this meeting, which lasted about ten minutes, Nishio told Fukuya that he was unable to help. Two days later, however, Fujii showed up at Nishio's official residence saying that he had a political donation. Nishio claims that he thought this was Fujii's way of saying thank you for attending the earlier meeting and therefore took the money; but he did not say again that he was unable to help them. Later he realized that he should have stated clearly to Fujii that the money was not to be viewed as payment for a favor.[48]

Nishio's account is probably true. Important politicians, especially state ministers, were targets of people who wanted political favors. For example, as soon as Uchida Nobuya's appointment as railway minister was announced, businessmen came to his private residence seeking influence for themselves or clients. As Uchida was to discover, saying no and refusing money were not enough. Tobishima boasted to others about his visits to Uchida and about how close he was to the minister. Eventually, Uchida's right-hand aide took money from Tobishima, setting off the 1936 scandal (see chapter 4).

Nishio provides us with an unusually frank comment on how it felt to be a suspect in a political bribery case: "[T]here is no way to measure the political and social damage done to me and many other defendants." Recalling that during the prewar era, in labor's fight with a repressive government, he had spent forty-five days in jail, he noted that it did not bother him because everyone knew that people in the labor struggle were suppressed. "Now, however, I was nearly sixty years old and had a social position. Yet I was imprisoned in Kosuge under suspicion for bribery!"[49]

The trials of those involved in the Showa Denkō and the coal mine bill scandals illustrate the great difficulty procurators faced in bribery prosecutions. The revised Penal Code of 1947, in which the bribery articles retained the same numbers as in the prewar code (i.e., Articles 197 and 198), reads (Article 197) as follows: "In case a public official or an arbitrator has received, demanded, or promised to receive a bribe in connection with his duty, he shall be punished with penal servitude not exceeding three years."[50] The key phrase in gaining a bribery conviction was "in connection with his duty." Thus procurators had to prove not only that money changed hands but that the official who took the money was in a position to carry out an illegal favor. Moreover, judges had to be convinced that the official understood that the money was a bribe. Besides these legal obstacles, procurators usually faced defendants who claimed that money received was merely a loan, a political contribution, or a gift. Readers will recall that prewar politicians used these excuses for bribes exposed to public view as well.

An interested observer of the Showa Denkō incident was Tsuji Kan'ichi, a lower house member from Aichi Prefecture from 1946. Tsuji saw the indictments and trial of the defendants who were found not guilty as very unfair because a corruption case hurt reputations.

As an example, he pointed at former vice-minister Shigemasa Seishi. A witness at the first trial told the court about a conversation with the defendant in which Shigemasa said,

> Yeh, I really lied about Mr. Ōno this time and put him in a lot of trouble. In fact the procurator's questioning was so severe that if I didn't agree that I'd given 200,000 yen to Mr. Ōno in connection with Shoden the procurator said that they would prosecute me for fraud and embezzlement. I was ill and worried about my health. I thought that once we got to the trial . . . I could tell the truth then. Also, I thought that no one would believe that Mr. Ōno would accept such a small amount of money as 200,000 yen. Thus, I lied.[51]

Just thinking about this case gave Tsuji a "cold chill." He concluded, "You don't know who will have the bad luck of being a victim."[52]

It is impossible to measure precisely the political and social effect of this scandal. Most obvious is that socialist politicians lost public favor after the fall of Ashida's cabinet. In the election of January 23, 1949, the electorate punished the former cabinet coalition and rewarded the Democratic Liberals (Yoshida Shigeru) with the first absolute majority since 1890.[53] Procurators may have risen in public esteem by indicting so many big shots, but conviction of only three defendants in this long series of trials probably dulled their image. As for the three convicts, Hinohara withdrew from the front ranks of the business world, but he did hold presidencies in two companies. Former finance minister Kurusu became president of the Economic Policy Association. Shigemasa, the former vice-minister, continued his Diet career and in 1962 headed the Agricultural and Forestry Ministry in the second Ikeda Hayato cabinet. The postscandal careers of important politicians who were not convicted is instructive: little stigma appears to have remained from the political bribery charges. Ashida, still in detention, was reelected in the January 23, 1949, election and remained in politics for many years; Nishio was reelected several times and in 1960 established the Democratic Socialist Party. Ōno, too, continued a lower house career, and in 1953 he entered the fifth Yoshida cabinet as a state minister. After being finance minister in three Satō Eisaku cabinets and in the second Tanaka Kakuei cabinet, Fukuda became prime minister in December 1976.[54]

The spreading pool of political corruption exposed by the lengthy investigation of the Illegal Property Transactions Investigative Committee and the Showa Electric Company scandal spurred the Diet to enact the Political Funds Regulation Law (Law Number 94, July 29,

1948). The purpose of this law was to oversee funds collected by political parties and other organizations connected with politics. Such organizations were required to provide periodic reports, which would be put in the public record. Penal provisions of this law provided imprisonment for up to five years and fines up to a hundred thousand yen. In some cases, an election could be voided.[55] Furthermore on April 15, 1950, the Diet enacted the Public Offices Election Law (Law Number 100). The purpose of the law was to consolidate all local and national election regulations in one law.[56] One expert on Japanese elections states that the law "incorporated many of the prewar restrictions on campaign practices, and revision of that Law in 1952 marked a return to the 1934 Law in terms of the limitations it places on campaign activities. A candidate for the Lower House campaigns within a legal strait jacket. His every campaign activity, from the number of speeches he may make to the size of the one-paper lantern he may hang outside his campaign headquarters, is regulated by law."[57]

The effect of anticorruption laws may be judged by looking at the October 1, 1952, election for the House of Representatives, which was held five months after the Occupation ended. During September, radio stations, newspapers, and public lectures urged voters to carry out a fair election; public response appears to have been receptive to this message. Nevertheless, some candidates violated the law by spending as much as twenty million yen each in bribing voters with money or entertainment (the average amount permitted for campaign use per candidate was 380,000 yen). Moreover, some candidates broke the law by campaigning too early. After the election, the five major parties reported monetary contributions of 272,052,000 yen. One political commentator said that this amount was only the tip of the iceberg and that the total was more likely ten billion yen. Authorities arrested more than ten thousand campaign promoters for violating various provisions of the Election Law. Many candidates, however, escaped arrest by hiding behind their election managers and other campaign officials. Obviously, the fair election movement coupled with the anticorruption laws failed to stop the old custom of using illegal funds and bribery to win elections.[58]

SCAP promoted democracy not only by reforming the nation's legal structure but also by trying to change basic political attitudes and values. Although the ultimate effect of SCAP's reforms is unknown, it appears that they did little during the Occupation years to change a political climate in which bribery flourished. Former Government Section official Harry Wildes (May 1946–May 1947) wrote in 1954, "While this [corruption], too, was in the Japanese tradition,

the era following surrender, supposedly one of spiritual regenera-
tion, broke all records for bribery and malpractice."[59]

Herbert Passin, another former Occupation official, believed in
1968 that the Occupation reform program contributed to an increase in the amount of corruption in government and a lowering of
public confidence in politicians. Unfortunately, he writes, "the can-
cerlike growth of elective positions, promoted by the Occupation,
has probably turned out to be on the harmful side. It leads to over-
politicization, a kind of overloading of the political communication
circuits. There are today several hundred thousand elective positions
to be filled in Japan. . . . And if we add the ill-fated local school
boards, we realize that the American reforms brought about an
enormous election inflation." Not only do all these election contests
keep voters busy, but they all cost money. Thus, Passin notes, "an
enormous number of people [are] electioneering, organizing support groups, and raising money. The opportunities, even the com-
pulsions, for corruption became very strong. . . . [T]he legal limits
fixed for permissible campaign expenditures were so stringent that
almost any elected representative could be charged with technical
violation of the election laws." These limits were so unrealistic that
they contributed to a growing feeling among the public that "if not
all politicians are corrupt, at the very least politics is a dirty business.
This attitude is not conducive to stable parliamentary democracy."
Finally, Passin notes that the old problem of extreme factionalism
survived the reform era. Indeed, he felt that "our political reforms
certainly reinforced it and perhaps made it worse. By inflating the
number of elective political positions and in general raising the level
of politicization of the country, we have made the problem of financing so difficult that the factional system has become entrenched as a
life-and-death matter for politicians."[60]

6. "New" Japan

On April 28, 1952, Japan became a sovereign nation dominated by conservative political and business forces. One of the outstanding traits of this synergism of politics and business was the frequent occurrence of political bribery cases. During the 1955–1993 period, for example, major newspapers focused on an average of slightly more than one political scandal per year.[1]

By 1952, important businessmen, who had traditionally supported the party in power, were eager to regulate the flow of political funds; they wished to lower the cost of political contributions and to prevent sensational corruption scandals, which focused public attention on illegal and unsavory activities. Therefore, key businessmen urged feuding conservative politicians to stabilize the political world by forming a united party. Attracted by the lure of big political contributions and fearful of the unification movement among socialist politicians, the Liberal and Japan Democratic Parties merged into the Liberal Democratic Party in November 1955. This was the beginning of the long-lasting "1955 System." At the beginning of that year, an Economic Reconstruction Council, set up by the business world, pledged to supply election funds to conservative politicians.[2] In the midst of the political maneuvering that resulted in the new conservative party, however, the business world's fears were realized when the fifth Yoshida cabinet (May 21, 1953–December 10, 1954) was hit by a major political bribery case that reminded the public of the Showa Electric Company scandal and the fall of the Ashida cabinet.

The Shipbuilding scandal, which caught public attention in the spring of 1954, originated in a lawsuit between three businessmen at the Tokyo District Court in August 1953. Procurators investigating this case discovered two very large commercial bills (each for 10,000,000 yen and bearing the name of the Yamashita Steamship

Company) in the safe of Inomata Osamu. Moreover, they discovered that Inomata had received a loan of 185,000,000 yen from the Yamashita Steamship Company. The steamship company's account books however, showed no entry for either the bills or the loan. Soon it was learned that Inomata had received a loan of 33,500,000 yen from Japan Sea Transport and 90,000,000 yen from Japan Transportation. Eventually, procurators determined that at least 100,000,000 yen was rebated to Yamashita Steamship Company by a shipbuilder and that this money was used to bribe politicians and bureaucrats.[3]

After the collapse of the Korean War economic boom, ship transportation and shipbuilding companies pressured the government for financial aid, citing the high cost of bank interest rates and exorbitant taxes. Representatives of these companies distributed money among key bureaucrats and politicians to obtain favorable loan terms. Money needed for bribery came from secret kickbacks from the shipbuilding companies to the shipping companies. Normally, the builder would return 3–5 percent of a ship's price to the ordering firm. Greasing the proper government officials paid off with the passage of a Law for the Subsidization of Interest and Insurance Against Losses in Oceangoing Shipbuilding in January 1953. Among other things this law permitted the borrowing of money at 7.5 percent (the normal bank interest rate was 11 percent), with the government pledged to pay the difference of 3.5 percent to banks. Shipping companies, however, wanted government support expanded, so the law was revised in August 1953. Under the new law the government pledged to pay off up to 30 percent of shipping companies' bank loans. It is estimated that 50,000,000 yen was spread among politicians and bureaucrats during the lobbying effort for the revision.[4]

In their investigation of Inomata Osamu, Tokyo District Court procurators had stumbled onto a go-between who was involved in the kickback and bribery schemes. Using evidence collected from Inomata's files, procurators arrested Yokota Aizaburō, president of Yamashita Steamship, and two other company officers. More evidence was seized, including the so-called Yokota memo, which listed more than thirty well-known politicians and bureaucrats. Yokota not only entered dates and names, but also included details about the purpose of each meeting. The memo was, of course, a list of those given "contributions" (i.e., bribes) for the passage of the January 1953 law. Among the names were Deputy Prime Minister Ogata Taketora; Liberal Party secretary-general Satō Eisaku; Ikeda Hayato, president of the Party Policy Affairs Research Council (Liberal Party); and Transportation Minister Ishii Mitsujirō. The amount of grease pumped into the political machinery, the procurators estimated, was about 100,000,000 yen; all major shipping companies contributed. Of this total, the Liberal Party got the largest amount (30,500,000 yen) for use during the general election in April 1953. Satō took another 20,000,000 yen for the Liberal Party fund and for his good work received another 2,000,000 yen.[5]

In this investigation procurators interrogated more than 150 people; before the case was over it expanded into the biggest political bribery scandal to date. Yokota of the Yamashita Steamship Company and three other company employees were charged with giving and receiving bribes. Other ship transport and shipbuilding presidents and employees were indicted as well. Among those indicted for receiving bribes were Tsuboi Genkō, head of the Secretariat of the Transportation Ministry; Kuniyasu Seiichi, chief of the Marine Coordination Division of the ministry; and fifteen other ministry employees. Lower house member and deputy secretary-general of the Liberal Party Arita Jirō was charged with both taking and giving bribes. Liberal Party Diet members Sekiya Katsutoshi and Okada Gorō were also indicted.[6]

During the investigation, procurators documented that both Satō Eisaku and Ikeda Hayato received 2,000,000-yen "contributions." The money was not a bribe, said Satō, who blamed improper bookkeeping in connection with collecting political donations for the Liberal Party. Moreover, he pointed out that he received no personal financial benefit. Procurators refused to accept this defense and argued that the money was given to influence the revision of the January 1953 law. Satō had, therefore, violated Section 4, Article 197 of the Penal Code. In Ikeda's case, procurators accepted the argument that the money was a going-away "gift" received before a trip to the United States. On April 21, 1954, Procurator General Satō Tōsuke requested via Justice Minister Inukai Takeru (also known as Inukai Ken) permission from the lower house to arrest Satō. Under extreme pressure by Prime Minister Yoshida and Deputy Prime Minister Ogata, Inukai refused to ask permission for the arrest, citing as his authority Article 14 of the Public Procurators' Office Law (Law Number 61, April 16, 1947). Inukai resigned the day following this unprecedented exercise of executive authority.[7]

Why did Inukai commit political suicide to save Satō? Inukai told the press that Satō's involvement in bills before the Diet was crucial, and because of this unusual circumstance, the arrest had to be delayed until the end of the session. In fact, Inukai owed Yoshida a heavy political debt and for that reason was willing to make this sacrifice. Several years earlier Yoshida had promised Inukai, who was not in the Liberal Party, a cabinet post; keeping this pledge was difficult, however, because some important members of the Liberal Party disliked Inukai. While this problem was being worked out, Inukai took a trip abroad paid for by Yoshida's financial supporters. Inukai finally got the justice slot in October 1952 and thus became indebted to Yoshida.[8]

Inukai's action not only caused a public outcry, but also demoralized Tokyo procurators. No doubt spirits improved when Justice Minister Katō Ryōgorō (April 22–June 19) notified Procurator General Satō that with the dissolution of the Diet on June 19 Satō Eisaku was no longer immune from arrest. By that time, however, procurators thought that the bribery charge against Satō would be impossible to prove because the delay had forced them to release more than seventy people who must have subsequently discussed what they told procurators. Nevertheless, procurators thought there was evidence that Satō had violated the Political Funds Regulation Law, so they indicted him. Satō's arrest triggered the resignation of Justice Minister Katō; he was replaced by former justice minister Ohara Naoshi. As Ohara was trying to calm down angry procurators, Prime Minister Yoshida announced that there was nothing wrong with the government's handling of the Shipbuilding scandal: the justice minister's use of executive authority was quite proper. Moreover, the prime minister said that Satō's imperfect bookkeeping was a natural thing; to arrest him because an account book was vague on where money went was the sort of action that destroys political party politics.[9]

In this bribery scandal, seventy-one businessmen and politicians were arrested (thirty-four were prosecuted) and thirty-four bureaucrats in the Transport Ministry were arrested (seventeen were prosecuted). Most of the big fish, however, escaped the legal net. Only Liberal Party politicians Arita, Sekiya, and Okada together with Transport Ministry bureaucrats Tsuboi, Kuniyasu, and three colleagues received prison terms. All eight, however, got stays of execution (the appeals court verdicts for the two trials were on January 28, 1960, and May 1, 1962). As for Satō Eisaku, who went to trial at the Tokyo District Court on December 18, 1954, fate was kind: he was saved by a general amnesty declared on December 19, 1956, when Japan joined the United Nations.[10] Thus, the conservative political establishment weathered the Shipbuilding scandal with no lasting damage: Satō and Ikeda Hayato moved on to prime ministerships in the early 1960s.

Although exposure of political bribery did not bring down the fifth Yoshida cabinet, it did contribute to the cabinet's collapse in

December 1954. Big-business leaders, who strongly supported the formation of this cabinet, were by the summer of 1954 ready to drop Yoshida. During the spring, newspapers carried front-page reports on dirty deals between businessmen and politicians. In an April 18 editorial, the *Asahi Newspaper* insisted that Yoshida's resignation was the only way to restore public trust in government.[11] An opinion poll taken on February 28 in the Tokyo metropolitan area asked, "Do you think the Yoshida Cabinet should take responsibility for the recent political bribery cases?" Nearly seventy percent of the respondents said "yes." A poll taken on March 18–19 in Tokyo, Osaka, and Yokohama asked, "Do you think the Yoshida Cabinet should assume the responsibility of the recent scandals involving government officials?" The "yes" percentage was the same.[12] An outraged public, as reflected in opinion polls, continued during the second half of the year to call for Yoshida's resignation.[13] Despite Yoshida's loss of popularity, however, the government showed no sign of resigning. One contemporary observer of this heated controversy wrote, "[Yoshida] and his followers in the Diet undoubtedly feel that, below the rip tides stirred up by the press, a hard core of their support remains only mildly disturbed by such irrelevant factors as pecuniary improprieties, since that support does not rest on such unstable bases as ideas about the integrity of politicians."[14] This writer was referring to the traditional *jiban* political system in which personal loyalties (reinforced by payoffs) shielded politicians from public criticism. Near total immunity from public criticism, however, did not protect Yoshida from an outraged big-business establishment. By the autumn of 1954, big-business leaders had decided that Yoshida must be retired to improve the political and economic situation. Faced with a cut-off of political contributions from big business and a revolt within the cabinet, Yoshida's government fell on December 10, 1954.

One result of the crisis year of 1954 was a decision on the part of the Federation of Economic Organizations (Keizai Dantai Rengōkai or Keidanren) to avoid another ugly scandal by finding a reliable source of money for the conservatives. On January 11, 1955, Keidanren vice-president Uemura Kogorō proposed to the executive committee of the board of directors that a new organization be created to collect political funds. An association called the Economic Reconstruction Council was the result. Its aim was to keep socialists from taking control of the government and to support a merger of conservative politicians. The new association, as a registered political organization, would not have to pay taxes. Political contributions by business would be tax free up to a certain amount.[15] "The aims of the new method of political financing . . . is thus fairly clear. The situation of business recalled that of 1931 when it was under attack by rightwing fanatics. . . . But, in 1955 business was faced with leftwing opponents in the trade unions and Socialist parties who were more intelligent and better organized and consequently more formidable in the long run."[16]

In an interview many years later, Hanamura Nihachirō, head of Keidanren's general affairs section, stated that after the Shipbuilding scandal he was told by Vice-President Uemura Kogorō that a source of "clean money" had to be created to support conservative politicians. What Uemura had in mind was "donations from businessmen who would not extract specific favours for their largesse. Small- and medium-sized firms could not be tapped because they always wanted immediate returns on their political investments. . . . Somehow, large companies must be convinced to contribute without seeking quid pro quos."[17] Over the following years big business came to see the wisdom of paying political insurance premiums and signed on to Hanamura's list. The new association regulated the flow of money, with the aim of giving to political parties and not to factions or individuals.[18]

Former prime minister Yoshida noted in his memoirs that the shipbuilding bribery case and the "wild charges" that arose at the time, remained one of the most disagreeable memories of his political career. "I have never been able to fathom the whole affair," he wrote, "but, from what I was able to learn concerning Sato's supposed complicity, I understood that a court of law might take up the question whether or not there had been a breach of the law concerning the Regulation of Political Funds and Expenditures, but never was an explanation advanced by the Procurator's Office why Mr. Sato had to be arrested." The bill to aid the shipping industry, he continued, "was one of national importance, and as such there could not have been—and never was—any question of its passage or rejection being influenced by money; contributions to Liberal Party funds were arranged by responsible men in financial circles and members of the shipping industry were by no means the only people who responded to the party's appeals." Next Yoshida charged that procurators, instead of collecting "objective evidence," employed "medieval" methods by pressuring confessions from criminal suspects. "The question of Mr. Sato's arrest came up," he went on, ". . . when proceedings in the House of Representatives had reached a crucial point. . . . [N]o reasons advanced were strong enough to authorize the serious interruption of Government business his arrest would have entailed." The decision to prevent Satō's arrest until after the

Diet session, Yoshida wrote, "was seen as an attempt by the Government to put illegal pressure on the investigation . . . and produced a storm of criticism from all sides, although, when the session ended . . . [procurators] refrained—for their own inscrutable reasons—from taking any action." Yoshida concluded that even more than the actions of procurators he was distressed by "the way in which some . . . politicians, who well knew the actual circumstances connected with the incident, chose to utilize the affair as a political weapon . . . and in doing so received the plaudits of the public."[19]

Complaints about nasty opponents who used this bribery scandal as an anti-Yoshida weapon ring false, coming from an experienced politician; Yoshida would have done the same to the socialists. As for the procuratorial camp, the political motives of those involved in this case are unknown, but within the Justice Ministry procurators had not only the legal right to pursue investigations as they saw fit but a proud tradition of independence.[20] The actions of some procurators in pre-1945 investigations (e.g., the Teijin incident), however, resulted in a public image of investigators who forced confessions. No doubt Yoshida gained some sympathy from readers by reminding them of past pressure tactics. Probably Yoshida's observation that procurators dropped the bribery case against Satō "for their own inscrutable reasons" found a receptive audience as well. This was a strange turn of events, inasmuch as the time lapse between the intervention of Justice Minister Inukai and the end of the Diet session was only a few weeks. Procurator General Satō's explanation, given on June 16, that all of the interrogated bribery suspects had been released, is weak.[21] Some of these suspects must have signed statements that could have been used. On the other hand, perhaps procurators simply did not have enough proof for a bribery indictment. Observers of this scandal might also have wondered why Procurator General Satō did not resign in the face of Justice Minister Inukai's intervention: resignation would have maintained some degree of honor for the procuratorial corps. Finally, speculation is in order about procurators' motives in investigating postwar bribery cases with such vigor. A partial answer is that conflict between police and procurators over who controlled investigations was a long-standing problem even before the Showa era, but by the 1930s procurators had gained the upper hand in this contest, especially in political cases. The 1948 Criminal Procedure Code, however, shifted control back to police. Procurators resisted this change and strove to regain lost power and prestige. Finally, a compromise with police placed procurators in command of investigations concerning serious brib-

ery cases.[22] If this struggle by procurators to regain pre-1945 emi-
nence is kept in mind, their bulldog determination in pursuing
corrupt politicians and businessmen is better understood.

Justice Minister Inukai's use of Article 14 provoked a heated legal
controversy among scholars. Several years later three justice officials
were interviewed and gave their opinions. Former justice minister
Ohara Naoshi recalled the heated arguments over the use of this
article but noted that it was not the first time that a justice minister
had exercised his right to command in connection with a specific
investigation. This right, noted Ohara, is based on the legal structure
that supports the Justice Ministry. Therefore, Inukai's action was not
legally wrong.[23] Former Procurator General Satō Tōsuke stated,
"Perhaps you could say that if I had resigned at the time it might
have taken care of the problem, but if I had done that the spirit of
the prosecution would have collapsed. It would have created chaos.
Besides that, it would have left behind a very bad precedent."[24]
Asked whether Article 14 should be deleted, Satō replied that it
should be kept as a check on overagressive procurators but should
not be used often. Hanai Tadashi, who was the head procurator at
the Tokyo Appeals Court, said that after Article 14 was used the statements of suspects changed. Without the use of that article, he felt,
the case would have expanded greatly and would have crushed the
Yoshida cabinet.[25]

The unification of conservative forces in November 1955 (Liberal
Democratic Party) marked the beginning of one-party political dominance that lasted for nearly four decades. Although members of the
new party agreed on unity to build a stable conservative government
and economy, their shotgun political marriage prevented neither
internecine political warfare nor the expansion of money-domi-
nated politics. The new party was from the start a collection of
factions, but factionalism was not institutionalized until the party
presidential election in 1956, in which party Secretary-General Kishi
Nobusuke lost by seven votes to Ishibashi Tanzan. At stake in this
election, besides the prime ministership, was the patronage controlled by the winner and the ability to attract large sums of money.
Moreover, the political faction in control of the government was
positioned to grow and dominate politics.[26] This party election, furthermore, "set the pattern for the flow of immense amounts of
money in presidential contests." It was estimated that "the Kishi faction spent 300 million yen for his election bid, that the Ishibashi faction spent 150 million yen, and that the Ishii Mitsujirō faction spent
80 million yen. These totals, representing huge sums for that period,
were passed from the candidates to the heads of factions." It was

therefore not surprising that the "presidential elections became known as 'money politics.'" By the time of the presidential election in 1964 (Ikeda Hayato won) even some conservative politicians "felt that the campaign had been an appalling pattern of bribes and expensive entertaining."[27]

Rapid industrialization during the 1950s weakened the old *jiban;* to cope with this problem some politicians organized *kōenkai* (permanent political support groups) designed to reinforce *jiban.* Besides this strengthening of *jiban,* politicians expanded their influence by peddling pork-barrel projects. Of special interest were civil engineering projects, which were stimulated by the Ikeda cabinet's economic policies during the early 1960s.[28] This spoils system had two aims: a flow of money into a politician's war chest and a flow of goodwill among voters.

Although this period produced no political bribery scandal to match either the Showa Electric or Shipbuilding affairs, corruption exposed during Prime Minister Satō's administration was sufficient to earn the name "black mist." The most serious bribery case involved the Kyōwa Sugar-Refining Company. In 1966 the public learned that Kyōwa officials had given large donations to Liberal Democratic politicians (later it was learned that Aizawa Shigeaki, a socialist, also received funds) to obtain a loan from the Central Cooperative Bank for Agriculture and Forestry. Among the recipients of "donations" was Shigemasa Seishi, who got about 22,000,000 yen funneled through a support group. Shigemasa, a former minister of agriculture and forestry, was chairman of Kyōwa before that appointment. During the investigation procurators discovered that about 120,000,000 yen had been used to grease the political machinery and that socialist Aizawa, a member of the House of Councillors Audit Committee, received 1,000,000 yen. After interrogating dozens of Diet members, procurators indicted only Aizawa. Found guilty, he was sentenced to two years in prison for taking a bribe and other crimes. Egged on by the press, socialists denounced the scandal and demanded a national election; Satō's factional opponents, too, hoped to use the scandal to unseat the party president. Despite attacks from without and within, the Liberal Democrats maintained control of the government after the January 1967 election, and Satō remained party president.[29]

Even though the Liberal Democratic Party was under fire by the socialists, who denounced the government as corrupt, and rent by civil war, as some party members campaigned on an anticorruption platform, the conservatives weathered the political storm.[30] The Liberal Democrats survived this crisis because "the nation's masses were mainly satisfied with the economic performance of the succession of conservative administrations." Farmers were happy with "the good prices of their staple product, rice, thanks largely to generous government subsidies." Many urban workers were pleased by steadily rising wages, which by 1970 were "an average of 2.3 times what they were in 1955." Thus, the conservative party won because voters were unwilling to throw out the politicians "behind the economic miracle."[31]

Tanaka Kakuei took the presidency of the Liberal Democratic Party in 1972 and formed a cabinet on July 7. Tanaka was a construction company owner who used civil engineering administration and public works to build a political power base in Niigata Prefecture. During the 1960s era of rapid economic growth induced in part by policies of the Ikeda cabinet (Tanaka was minister of finance twice during three cabinet changes), Tanaka "adapted himself to the boom with unsurpassed skill . . . and climbed to the apex of politics by doling out funds derived from land speculation, dummy companies, and the construction business. . . . He also extended his network to every part of the interest distribution structure, and boasted that his faction was a 'general hospital' capable of taking care of every need."[32] Like Prime Minister Hara Kei half a century earlier, Tanaka understood money's role in the political system. "Everybody needed money—for reelection campaigns, for his faction, for entertaining and cultivating the bureaucrats who made the vital decisions—and everybody needed more of it than was allowed under the various laws that controlled political funds. Tanaka had a lot of money, and he used it—not for himself . . . or even exclusively for the people of Niigata, but in order to get things done."[33]

A test for Tanaka's money politics came in the July 7, 1974, election for the House of Councillors. Many observers, reflecting on the gradual decline of support for the Liberal Democratic Party and the economic slump caused by the world oil crisis, predicted a conservative defeat.[34] Tanaka reacted to this prediction by pressuring big business to supply more money and other campaign support. According to Hanamura Nihachirō, a former vice-chairman of Keidanren who for thirty-four years acted as a middleman, passing out money to politicians, Tanaka used the specter of a radical socialist upsurge to wring more funds from businessmen.[35] As a result, nearly every conservative national candidate got a corporate backer. Although this practice was not new, the scale of support and its unconcealed nature were.[36] The election battle turned into what many considered the most expensive and the dirtiest in postwar politics.[37] Although from 1955 the Liberal Democratic Party had overcome numerous bribery scandals and charges of election corruption with vague promises of reform, this time was different. In an article ("A Study of Tanaka Kakuei—Basis of His Financial Power and Personal Networks") in the November 1974 *Bungei shunjū*, Tachibana Takashi, in muckraking detail, illustrated the money flow into and out of the Tanaka organization. Weekly magazines and newspapers followed up with enough information to sustain public interest. Among other things public attention was directed to Tanaka's extravagant use of money to win the party presidency and the spreading about of money in the July 1974 election. The prime minister's personal finances were also spotlighted. What set Tanaka apart from other politicians playing the "money game" was the excessive scale on which he gathered and dispensed huge sums of money. In handing out funds Tanaka not only supported his own faction and other Liberal Democrats, but gave money to bureaucrats and, it appears, to opposition politicians. Most political observers thought that Tanaka would somehow maintain his political balance, but the combination of the poor showing in the 1974 election and the rapidly rising inflation rate doomed his hold on the prime ministership. Other factors also helped push him out of office: no classmates from elite universities, no marriage ties with the business elite, and no close links to old established families.[38] Finally, Tanaka, claiming ill health, resigned as prime minister; his replacement was Miki Takeo, one of the rare conservatives with a "clean" political image. Miki, who had resigned as deputy prime minister in protest over 1974 election campaign excess, was seen by party leaders as the perfect symbolic choice.[39] Prime Minister Miki stated, "I will carry out fundamental reform in the matter of how political funds are collected and used."[40] Even cynical critics, aware of Miki's pure reputation, believed that real political reform was on the way.[41]

Prime Minister Miki and other reformers tried to impose radical reforms to curb money politics. In the end, however, as public interest turned to other topics, antireform politicians passed a watered-down reform bill, which became law on January 1, 1976. In fact, the reform of the Political Funds Regulation Law "essentially made legal and legitimate various practices that had received heavy criticism during the previous year. Financial conduits . . . created to collect and donate billions of yen . . . were now legalized, and each political party was allowed to designate one such organization to handle its fund-raising activities. Corporate contributions were completely legalized and thus legitimized, even de facto quotas were established."[42] Under the revised law, an organization could give funding groups or political parties a maximum of 7,500,000–100,000,000 yen annually (based on the size of an organization), and only half that amount could be donated to individuals or factions; an individual could donate no more than 20,000,000 yen to a funding group or a political party, half that to an individual or faction. Reports were required from recipients.[43] The main purpose of revising this law, and of revisions made in the Public Offices Election Law, was to shift the focus away from individual politicians who used personal connections to appeal to voters and to emphasize instead party principles. Furthermore, reformers wanted to redirect the normal money flow to factions toward parties and to encourage smaller individual contributions by the public.[44] These reforms, however, "did not bring about the kind of fundamental change that was ostensibly their objective. Japanese politicians rose to the challenge posed by these reforms by searching out every conceivable loophole in the law that might allow them to avoid having to change their time-tried ways of doing things."[45] Candidates made good use, for example, of the fact that the law did not require reporting names of contributors who gave less than a million yen per year. Furthermore, because the law did not restrict the number of organizations a single politician could establish, politicians could gather funds from a number of organizations. Finally, factions and individuals could turn to special fund raisers (usually buffet-style parties) because income from this source did not count as a political contribution.[46]

One close student of the Miki reform program concludes that it had little or no effect on money-power politics. Miki's program for party reform was based on three pillars: liberating the party from its dependence on big business, ridding the party of factionalism, and creating a mass membership to support the party. Reformers reasoned that with a mass membership qualified to vote for the party president, vote buying would be impossible. Membership dues would offset the loss of funds from big business and special interest groups.[47] It was hoped that, with the presidential selection moved away from party lower house members "to mass members who could not be bribed, factions organized and maintained primarily for the purpose of intraparty leadership struggle would decline and the party would become more policy-oriented."[48] The January 1977 reform, at least in the first stage, worked well, with a great jump in party membership to a million and a half within a year and a half. In the presidential contest in late autumn of 1978, however, the behavior of the new mass of voters showed no change when compared to the old system's restricted electorate. As usual, the party Dietmen divided into factions. Few of the mass members identified with the party; instead, the majority identified with a particular member of the Diet.[49] As one scholar put it, "Allegiance of its [local support group] members to the MP is personal, parochial, and particularistic." Because of this situation the Diet members were able "to discipline this enormously expanded mass party membership during the primary ballot. . . . The traditional factional struggle did not abate at all; instead, it intensified and expanded its scope to the mass membership at the grassroots level."[50] Thus, the first presidential election (Ōhira Masayoshi won) showed little difference in the way the president was chosen

> either in political content, electoral behavior, factional efficacy, candidate characteristic, pattern of inducement, or outcome. Instead, it highlighted the potency of the dynamic and the logic of factionalism. . . . The factional politics proved to be amazingly adaptable to the new rules . . . and displayed its enormous capacity to absorb a vastly expanded universe of participants. The party's internal relations as well as its ties with . . . large special interests remained intact in basic character.[51]

Tanaka Kakuei's resignation plus political reform measures enacted by the Diet might have pacified angry voters had not the Lockheed scandal surfaced in an early February 1976 congressional investigation in the United States, when A. Carl Kotchian, a Lockheed Aircraft Corporation vice-president, admitted that the company dispensed more than $22,000,000 in bribes to sell passenger jets in Japan. Tokyo procurators reacted to this news by beginning a criminal investigation in midmonth, looking for tax evaders. During the next several months the criminal cases implicated numerous big-business men, politicians, and the prime minister's office. On August 16 former prime minister Tanaka was indicted for accepting a bribe and for violating the Foreign Exchange Law; fifteen other people were indicted for bribery and other criminal acts.[52]

Kotchian's version of this affair was published in the *Asahi Evening News* during August 23–27, 1976. According to Kotchian, in August 1972 he suggested to Hiyama Hiro, an official of Marubeni Corporation, a trading company and Lockheed's sales agency, that the superior qualities of the Lockheed passenger jet should be brought to the attention of Prime Minister Tanaka. The following day Okubo Toshiharu, the company's managing director, said that a customary contribution in a transaction of this size was five hundred million yen. That same day Kotchian visited the headquarters of Kodama Yoshio, who had been a secret agent for Lockheed since 1958. Kodama, who was perhaps the most notorious operator in the underworld of business-politics wheeling and dealing, introduced Kotch-

ian to Osano Kenji, a powerful businessman and long-time confidant
of Tanaka's. If Lockheed was serious about selling jets, said Kodama,
it would be best to build a bridge to the prime minister via Osano.
Again Kotchian pledged to pay five hundred million yen. Thus, in a
single day Lockheed was committed to paying a billion yen. Eventually, payment was made and Lockheed got the jet contract.[53]

Procurators, who pushed hard for convictions, were rewarded
with confessions by most defendants. At the trials (there were four
different trials, based on the money routes determined by procurators) defendants repudiated these confessions, claiming that procurators fabricated them. Tanaka was an exception: he not only denied
knowing about the secret deal to sell jets but also insisted that he had
received no money. The trial judges, however, determined that
Tanaka was bribed and that as prime minister he was in a position to
influence the purchase of jets. On October 12, 1983, Tanaka was sentenced to four years in prison and fined five hundred million yen;
Ōkubo was given two years with four years' probation; Enomoto
Toshio (Tanaka's secretary) got one year with three years' probation;
Hiyama Hiro (a Lockheed contact with Marubeni Company) was
given two years and six months in prison; and Itō Hiroshi (a director
of Marubeni) received two years. These convictions were appealed
on May 29, 1985. Only Itō's sentence was modified, to two years with
four years' probation.[54] As for Tanaka, an appeal was before the
Supreme Court when he died on December 16, 1993.

Among those involved in the other trials were Hashimoto Tomi-
saburō, former minister of transport, and Satō Takayuki, former parliamentary vice-minister of the same ministry. Both were indicted for
taking bribes. Hashimoto was accused of accepting fifty million yen
paid via Marubeni; his defense team argued that no money had been
received and that their client was not involved in the jet decision.
Satō's defense was similar: no bribe taken and no involvement in the
jet sale decision. On June 8, 1982, Hashimoto was given two and a
half years in prison and three years' probation and fined fifty million
yen; Satō got two years with three years' probation and was fined
twenty million yen. This trial was completed for Satō in July 1986 (he
withdrew an appeal to the Supreme Court) and finished for Hashimoto in January 1990 (he died). Wakasa Tokuji, former president of
All Nippon Airways, was found guilty of bribing Hashimoto and Satō
and was sentenced to three years of prison with five years' probation.
Kodama and Osano were also prosecuted but for nonbribery violations (e.g., tax laws). Kodama died during the Tokyo District Court
trial and Osano died after the appeals court had reduced his sentence to ten months in prison with three years' probation.[55]

Former prime minister Tanaka concluded from the guilty verdict at the first trial "that he had been made a scapegoat by his political opponents and the left-tending journalistic establishment of Tokyo for practices that . . . [were] common in Japanese political life." Furthermore, he felt "that his political opponents changed the rules on him in this particular case."[56] Tanaka's frustration and anger are understandable; his view that political opponents were behind the prosecution is remarkably similar to that of Seiyūkai vice-president Ogawa Heikichi, the only cabinet minister convicted of bribery to enter prison in the pre-1945 era.

As in earlier political bribery scandals, measuring the effect on the public of the Lockheed case is difficult; a widespread feeling appears to have been that this was simply the latest ugly episode in an endless series and that the political system was bound to produce such results. Nevertheless, if election results are used as a measuring stick, the scandal caused an erosion of Liberal Democratic strength in the House of Representatives in the 1976 and 1979 elections. This declining trend was somewhat reversed in 1980, but after Tanaka's conviction in 1983 the party suffered a lower house defeat. Still, in the face of party setbacks, Tanaka, who had earlier withdrawn from the Liberal Democratic Party, maintained the strong support of Niigata voters; in the election of December 18, 1983, two months after conviction in the court of first instance, he won his greatest election victory. Furthermore, six of his followers entered the second Nakasone Yasuhiro cabinet.[57]

Although a decade passed before the public was treated to another major bribery case, Tanaka's ongoing legal battle and a dramatic faction split (Tanaka had a stroke and lost control) kept the public eye on the scandal. Furthermore, two other political bribery cases surfaced to stimulate public interest in this subject. First, in May 1979, at the Tokyo District Court, former vice-president Kaifu Hachirō of Nisshō-Iwai Trading Company went on trial for violation of the Foreign Exchange Law and for perjury. During the trial the name of Matsuno Raizō, former director of the Defense Agency, came up in connection with a 500,000,000-yen payment. It was charged that the McDonnell Douglas Company paid this sum through the trading company to gain Matsuno's aid in the sale of fighter planes to Japan. Matsuno admitted receiving the money between 1967 and 1971 but claimed that it was a political contribution. He was not indicted.[58] Second, in October 1979, newspapers broke the story that the public corporation for international telecommunications (Kokusai Denshin Denwa Kaisha) had lavished entertainment, gifts, and money on numerous politicians and bureaucrats. Although two bureaucrats were indicted for taking bribes, no politicans were charged.[59]

In 1989 another political earthquake hit: the Recruit scandal. Like the Teijin affair of more than half a century earlier, the new scandal involved the transfer of stocks and political bribery, and like the earlier incident it swept up businessmen, politicians, and bureaucrats. As the scandal unfolded, the public saw a picture not only of staggering amounts of money used to influence politicians but also of corruption among senior bureaucrats in central government agencies. So embarrassing were these revelations, which stained the reputations of former prime minister Nakasone and other senior Liberal Democrats, that Prime Minister Takeshita Noboru resigned in June 1989.

At the center of this scandal was Ezoe Hiromasa, chairman of the hugely successful Recruit Company, an information industry enterprise. Beginning in 1960 as a small concern that handled advertisements in university newspapers, Ezoe's company evolved into a nationwide organization that provided employment information for university students and a guide to colleges and universities for high school students. Recruit Cosmos, a real estate subsidiary, was established in 1964. By 1987, the Recruit business empire consisted of twenty-seven branches with more than six thousand employees.[60] Ezoe smoothed the way for company expansion by handing out "gifts" to politicians and bureaucrats. One payoff was to offer for sale (buyers were also offered loans for the purchase price) shares of the real estate subsidiary before open sale on the market: huge profits would be made when the shares were officially listed. Recruit's business methods caught public attention in June 1988, when the *Asahi Newspaper* carried an article about the deputy mayor of a city who had received unlisted Recruit stock shares. By July, what began as a minor scandal expanded into something more serious, as former prime ministers Nakasone and Takeshita were identified as recipients of Recruit shares. Finance Minister Miyazawa Kiichi was caught in the scandal's web in October and by December was forced to resign. Justice Minister Hasegawa Takashi and Harada Ken, director general of the Economic Planning Agency, soon followed Miyazawa's example. The scandal had reached major proportions.[61] Indeed, "[t]he impression conveyed by the media in mid-1989 was that everyone who was anyone was on the take, and there . . . [was] no reason to believe that Recruit was alone in filling the trough."[62]

On June 12, 1989, when the Justice Ministry's report on the Recruit scandal was submitted to the House of Representatives, virtually all top Liberal Democrats and even top opposition party leaders were tainted publicly by "gifts" from Ezoe. Nevertheless, no major politicians were indicted. Of the eleven politicians and bureaucrats put on trial three were found guilty of accepting bribes: Shinto Hisashi, former chairman of Nippon Telegraph and Telephone; Shikiba Ei, another NTT executive; and Katō Takashi, a vice-minister in the Labor Ministry.[63]

The Liberal Democratic Party responded to the Recruit episode by promising substantial reform of the political funding system and by selecting a prime minister untainted by the corruption scandal. Chosen to represent the party's new clean image was Foreign Minister Uno Sōsuke, whom the Recruit Company had considered unimportant to the point of not offering a stock bribe.[64] Addressing a plenary session of the Diet, Uno stated, "The Recruit scandal has triggered a widespread mistrust of politics and plunged our democracy into a serious crisis. The Uno Cabinet believes that grappling with political reform is the most important task of this government, in order to restore public faith in politics."[65] Although political commentators disagreed on whether the prime minister was Nakasone's or Takeshita's puppet, there was a consensus that his cabinet would be short lived. No one, however, predicted that it would fall in two months. Shortly after Uno took office his mistresses began to complain about his stinginess. Attacks on the prime minister's character, however, were ignored by the major newspapers until an article appeared in the *Washington Post.* Then the sex scandal became a hot topic not only for Japanese gossip magazines but for the mainstream press.[66]

As Uno was being humiliated by the media, the public went to the polls for the July 23, 1989, election for the House of Councillors and for the first time refused to give the Liberal Democratic Party its customary majority (the party ended up with 109 of 252 seats).[67] The Recruit scandal, however, was only one element in this election defeat, and probably a minor one at that. Even though the opposition parties focused on the sex scandal, as did the media, a new and unpopular value-added tax (VAT) passed on December 24, 1988 (effective April 1, 1989), was of more interest to voters.[68] "What seems to have heightened the public's intolerance for this new tax was the image of LDP Dietmen forcing new burdens on the people while at the same time illegally, or at least unscrupulously, receiving large sums of money under the table. . . . The negative ramifications of the Recruit scandal for the ruling party's image, however, went beyond the [political] morality issue and raised an unstated competency issue." Unlike the party's response to earlier scandals, the Recruit affair "threw the party into confusion, and the difficulty the

party had in coming up with a successor and the successor's relatively low previous status in the party did not inspire confidence. . . .
In the aftermath of the Recruit scandal, the perceived competency
gap between the LDP and its opposition decreased significantly."[69]

On August 9, 1989, Kaifu Toshiki became prime minister. The following October, as the party voted to extend Kaifu's presidency, the
prime minister said, "Furthermore, I think every politician must do
his or her best to push forward with drastic political reform by estab-
lishing lofty political ethics and by winning public office through
open and inexpensive campaign activities."[70] At the next general
election for the House of Representatives, on February 18, 1990, the
Liberal Democrats won 275 seats out of a total of 512 (eleven conservative independents later joined them).[71] Why had the voters reaf-
firmed faith in the scandal-ridden party? First of all, the old guard
worked hard to improve the party's image: Kaifu, an articulate member of a small, reform-minded faction, was chosen as party president;
other politically attractive relatively young men were chosen for key
party positions; two women were given cabinet posts. Second, the
party announced plans to revise the hated VAT. Third, the socialists,
after their 1989 election victory, appeared bogged down in factional
fighting and tightly stuck to obsolete policies. Last, as with earlier
political bribery scandals, the effect of the Recruit affair quickly dissi-
pated over the months between the 1989 and 1990 elections; all but
two of the sixteen candidates tainted by corruption were reelected,
with the victorious candidates claiming that the election restored
their public reputations.[72] In spite of the Liberal Democrats' miracu-
lous recovery from the Recruit scandal, however, some political commentators foresaw more corruption scandals because the party had
become decadent and lost its ability for self-cleansing.[73]

On January 24, 1991, at the Liberal Democratic Party's con-
vention, a political reform declaration was adopted. By August the
cabinet was ready to submit three political reform bills to the extra-
ordinary Diet session. Among other things the bills sought to introduce a single-seat district election system together with proportional
representation. During the session, however, the government and
the opposition were unable to agree upon a reform bill. Nevertheless, Prime Minister Miyazawa Kiichi, who had replaced Kaifu in
November 1990, continued to press for political reform. In the
spring of 1992, the party's Political Reform Headquarters submitted
a set of proposals to Miyazawa: Diet members would be required to
disclose their personal assets, imbalance in representation in the
Diet would be corrected, and efforts would be made to make political funds more transparent. It is unclear how much effect this
reform program had on voters, but it is clear that the party won a

sweeping victory in the House of Councillors' election on July 26, 1992: half the 252 seats were contested; the party won 70.[74]

Hard on the heels of the July election victory the Liberal Democrats were hit by another corruption scandal, this one involving the Tokyo Sagawa Express Company (a parcel delivery firm). In a manner reminiscent of the Recruit Company's tactics, Sagawa Express distributed political "donations" to about 130 Diet members. Among those investigated by Tokyo procurators was Kanemaru Shin, vice-president of the Liberal Democratic Party, who was regarded as the party's major power broker. Faced with evidence that he failed to report five hundred thousand yen received from Sagawa Express (a violation of the Political Funds Regulation Law), Kanemaru admitted guilt on August 27 and resigned from his party position and from his post as leader of the Takeshita faction (based on the old Tanaka Kakuei faction). This quick admission of guilt, plus the payment of a small fine, did not mollify public anger, which erupted in various forms of protest. Finally, Kanemaru resigned from the Diet on October 14.[75] Party secretary-general Watanuki Tamisuke stated that the Kanemaru affair was "extremely regrettable and our party regards this fact with all seriousness and gravity, and expresses its apology to the people. . . . The case has aroused strong public dissatisfaction with, and distrust in, politics. Our party takes this to heart and is determined to dedicate itself in unison to restore the public's confidence in politics."[76] Prime Minister Miyazawa, in a policy speech to the Diet on October 30, said, "It is most regrettable that public confidence in politicians has been badly shaken. . . . I strongly feel that public distrust in politics has never been so deep as today. . . . Our reform program would make political funds transparent, political activities less costly, and realize elections fought on policy proposals."[77]

Kanemaru was mistaken if he hoped that admitting guilt and resigning his official position would stop public protests. Procurators, perhaps stung by the public outcry, arrested Kanemaru on March 6, 1993, on charges of tax evasion, a crime easier to prove than political bribery. Searches of Kanemaru's home and office on March 8, witnessed by television cameras, turned up tens of millions of dollars in gold, cash, and bonds. Even to a public conditioned to the idea that politics was dirty business, this shocking exposé proved unsettling because Kanemaru's hoard seemed to be for personal rather than political use.[78] According to one scholar, this was probably the first time in which the private residence and political office of a major politician were searched by police and procurators. Kanemaru was indicted on March 13; his trial began on July 22, 1993.[79]

In the aftermath of Kanemaru's resignation, a bitter power struggle erupted in the Takeshita faction, which split into two groups. On December 18, one group formed the Reform Forum 21. This group, led by Hata Tsutomu, later founded the Shinseitō (Renaissance Party). Hata's faction called for major changes in election methods and a reform of the political donation system. Earlier in 1992 another political reform group, led by Hosokawa Morihiro, a former prefectural governor, launched the Nihon Shintō (Japan New Party). In June 1993, Takemura Masayoshi, once head of the Liberal Democrats' political reform committee, founded the Sakigake Shintō (Harbinger New Party).[80]

When Prime Minister Miyazawa presented a political reform plan during the spring of 1993, he was blocked not only by opposition politicians who disliked the plan's single-member district system, which they thought favored the Liberal Democrats, but also by some Liberal Democrats who seemed to think that this political storm, like earlier ones, would soon pass. They were mistaken. After the reform program was shelved temporarily, the opposition together with some Liberal Democrats won a no-confidence motion based on Miyazawa's failure to fulfill his public promise to carry out political reform. The prime minister dissolved the lower house.[81] On July 18, people spoke at the polls, removing the Liberal Democratic majority in the lower house for the first time (the party won 223 seats, 33 shy of a majority).[82] By the month's end, seven parties united to form a coalition government, with Hosokawa (Japan New Party) as prime minister.[83]

The new prime minister's political reform program, like Miyazawa's, met determined opposition from politicians who feared change in the political system. The Diet, however, passed a compromise political reform package (four legislative bills) on January 29, 1994. In brief, the new electoral system called for three hundred single-seat constituencies and two hundred seats based on proportional representation, tighter control on fund raising, and government subsidies to parties. The new electoral system would take effect after an independent commission redrew the boundary lines of the three hundred new units.[84] One journalist noted, "The new rules should gradually curb powerful blocs in the Diet composed of members who are indebted to special interest groups—such as the construction industry or agricultural lobby—by their acceptance of political contributions from them."[85] The *Economist* editorialized, "The new system reduces the temptations for candidates to bribe voters. At the same time, constituency boundaries are being redrawn. That is meant to weaken the power of constituency parties, which have grown expert at raising and distributing illegal campaign money.

White envelopes stuffed with cash will matter less; televised appeals to voters will count for more."[86] Journalists less optimistic about the effect of Hosokawa's reforms wrote, "According to one television poll, only 14% of the respondents said they thought the anticorruption measures went far enough."[87] The *Mainichi Newspaper* editorialized, "The bill doesn't answer at all public calls for an immediate end to the close ties between business and politics . . . that have become such a hotbed of corrupt money politics."[88]

Soon after passage of the political reform legislation, Hosokawa's government began to disintegrate over the issue of tax reform. Political enemies quickly brought up old corruption charges against the prime minister centered on a loan and a political donation from the notorious Tokyo Sagawa Express Company; this company was much on the public mind because of the trial of Kanemaru Shin.[89] Hata Tsutomu, another so-called reformer and a former Liberal Democrat, formed another coalition cabinet on April 25. Unfortunately for Hata, the continuing bitter debate over tax reform cracked the coalition; this left the prime minister in charge of a minority government (commanding only 182 votes in the lower house; 256 were needed to pass legislation); it lasted only fifty-nine days.[90]

The next coalition cabinet shocked political commentators: Murayama Tomiichi, leader of the Social Democratic Party, was picked as prime minister in a government backed by the Liberal Democrats. Not since the cabinet of Katayama Tetsu (May 1947– March 1948) had a socialist held the prime ministership. "The bizarre partnership between the Liberal Democratic Party and the Socialists," wrote one journalist, "stunned the country and prompted immediate fears that whatever halting progress had been made toward deregulating the economy and cleaning up a corruption-ridden political system could be halted or reversed."[91] The *New York Times* editorialized, "Only a political system in its death agony could produce a government like the one Japan's Parliament chose yesterday."[92] *U.S. News and World Report,* however, predicted that the coalition, guided "by veteran LDP politicians who know how to grease the wheels of government," might just confound pessimistic political commentators.[93] The Liberal Democrats dominated this new coalition, holding thirteen of twenty-one cabinet seats, including that of the deputy prime minister (Kōno Yōhei, president of the Liberal Democratic Party). Furthermore, they outnumbered the socialists nearly three to one in the lower house.[94]

Fragmentation of the Liberal Democratic Party and the rapid turnover of the prime ministership (Murayama was the seventh prime minister in seven years) stimulated the production of articles and books on political reform. *Blueprint for a New Japan (Nihon kaizō keikaku)* was published in 1993 (the English edition in 1994). Ozawa Ichirō, the author and former secretary-general of the Liberal Democrats, was early on one of Tanaka Kakuei's protégés and later one of Kanemaru Shin's chief disciples. Like most other senior Kanemaru faction leaders, Ozawa was tainted by the series of corruption scandals. Feelings about Ozawa's interest in reform were mixed, with analysts arguing that he was merely shielding himself from public criticism and possible indictment by procurators; others thought that genuine reform was truly his goal.[95] Robert C. Angel, a close student of Japanese politics, saw Ozawa's new interest in political reform as a "transmogrification that rivaled Saul of Tarsus' experience on the road to Damascus."[96]

Ozawa's book identifies a lack of leadership in the political field as a major problem: the major cause is the extreme diffusion of power within the Liberal Democratic Party and the rest of the state control apparatus as well.[97] "The LDP's Policy Affairs Research Council—which ostensibly directs party policy—is actually an assembly of diverse and special interests. . . . The government, meanwhile, is itself scattered among many institutions and interests. Its ministries and agencies are discrete entities. No overarching institution exists to coordinate and control the whole. The cabinet, of course, technically plays this role, but it has never actually been expected to do so." As for the prime minister, Ozawa notes that he "is nothing more than master of ceremonies for the ritual at hand."[98] To change this failed polity, Ozawa advocates a systemwide reform, from the prime minister's office downward. "Anything that does not absolutely require intervention from the central government should be transferred over to local governments. In addition, we must limit power by ensuring that the government periodically changes hands. . . . [W]e must have a government that takes responsibility for a fixed period of time, for clearly defined powers and policies."[99]

Among various reforms Ozawa emphasizes the need for a better system of political funding. The best way to avoid corruption scandals and to restore public trust is to make the money-flow transparent. Groups and companies should never give money to individuals but only to parties. Total disclosure with harsher penalties for violators should backstop this reform.[100]

Ozawa blames many of the nation's political problems on the aging of the "1955 System," during which politics became mainly secret negotiations between political factions that divided up the budget among themselves, other parties, bureaucrats, and business. There was little serious debate over policy as they cut up the economic pie. Those with a longer historical view know that the problems Ozawa outlines stem from more than the decay of the "1955 system" and the political distortions caused by the postwar U.S.-Japan agreement on defense and other issues. In fact, the political structure of the modern state was burdened with what Maruyama Masao terms "its 'original sin': the pluralism of political power."[101] During the early and middle Meiji years, strong leadership by the state's founding fathers obscured the weak political center, but by the 1930s and the early 1940s the flaws in the Meiji governmental system were obvious. War, defeat, occupation, and political reform did not eliminate the factional nature of the nation's political structure. Only a massive overhaul of the political system could bring about true reform. One Japanese scholar stated that only a combination of the reform power behind the Allied Occupation and the French Revolution would make a difference in politics.[102]

Talk about political reform among politicians and in the media was accompanied by a number of books published the same year as Ozawa's. For many people, political reform meant stricter control of money politics and reform of the electoral districts system. But as Hokkaido University Professor Yamaguchi Jirō points out, these are cosmetic changes; real political reform, one that rejuvenates democratic politics, requires reorganization of political parties and new attitudes among citizens. The "iron triangles" linking politicians, bureaucrats, and interest groups, formed to gain mutual benefits at the expense of taxpayers, have to be broken if there is to be genuine political reform. In short, the political world is in need of a complete realignment, which would not only lead to more openness of administrative processes, but would cut down the amount of widespread corruption. Yamaguchi thinks that a new generation of young politicians may be able to transcend the old factional boundaries, form new political groups, and create true reform.[103]

Certainly, winds of political change are blowing, but most reform proposals demand a decisive change in attitude among politicians, bureaucrats, and citizens. Because factions in politics date from the First Diet in 1890 and because factions permeate society (i.e., my group vs. your group), a rapid change in this aspect of politics is unlikely. Political analysts stress that the basic political problem is the undemocratic nature of the bureaucracy. They note that "since 1941 Japan has had a bureaucracy-led industrial cooperation system."[104] In late 1993, Ozawa Ichirō called for cutting the number of higher bureaucrats, upgrading the rank of politicians who acted as watchdogs in each ministry, and introducing politicians with the rank of bureau chief into selected key ministries. What Ozawa aimed at was a version of the U.S. system of presidential appointees. Bureaucrats strongly rejected this plan as an effort to politicize the civil service.[105] Thus, political reformers should expect hard fighting on the part of bureaucrats who want to preserve the status quo. As for citizens, who have a long history of accepting abuse at the hands of bureaucrats and politicians as long as the economy is expanding, reformers should not expect an overnight change in attitude. In conclusion, the required massive political reform effort is unlikely to occur in the near future. More modest changes, of course, can be expected.

7. Conclusion

From antiquity, the Japanese state promulgated statutes aimed at political bribery. Article 5 of the so-called Seventeen-Article Constitution (604), for example, commanded officials to handle law suits impartially and not to accept bribes. By 645, the central government's antibribery regulations promised punishment for those who disobeyed. Concern with political bribery reflected, in part, the effect of various Chinese legal compilations, including the T'ang Penal Code, which spelled out in detail sanctions for those who offered and those who received bribes. Penal provisions to deter bribery and to punish offenders were maintained by later regimes; the Ashikaga shogunate, for example, specified removal from office of officials taking small bribes and execution of those receiving large bribes. Bribery as a legal concept was maintained during the Tokugawa, with punishments ranging from deportation to execution. The Meiji state followed this tradition, and after basing antibribery laws on Chinese law, switched to a Western-style penal code, which contained a detailed section on official corruption. According to the Penal Code of 1908, any government employee convicted of taking a bribe in connection with official duties could be imprisoned for up to three years (Article 197); any person convicted of giving a bribe to an official could be imprisoned for up to three years (Article 198).

There was also an antibribery ethic outside legal boundaries. Tokugawa Confucianists stigmatized political bribery as an immoral act. The continuation of this ethic into the era of the modern state is exemplified by Hiranuma Kiichirō, who dedicated his life to upholding the Meiji legal structure and to promoting traditional morality (i.e., mainly Confucian morality). Reflecting on the case of Home Minister Ōura Kanetake, whom he drove from office in 1915, Hiranuma noted that not only did Ōura break laws but also that "his political morals were very bad."¹ Blended with this Confucian anti-bribery ethic was the Christian distaste for bribery. This ethic was represented by Shimada Saburō, politician and journalist, who, from the first session of the lower house in 1890, was outspoken in condemning political bribery. It was Christian reformer Shimada who denounced Hoshi Tōru in 1900 as a cancerous growth needing removal from the body politic.² Throughout the balance of the Meiji era and into the Taisho, politicians and businessmen felt the sting of Shimada's attack on political corruption. Another promoter of the antibribery ethic was the Christian businessman and politician Mutō Sanji. What Mutō regarded as immoral secret deals between businessmen and politicians prompted him to use the *Jiji shinpō* in an effort to clean up the business-political world. This effort precipitated the Teijin incident of the mid-1930s.

These antibribery currents, statutes, and morality were blended in the Imperial Rescript on Education, issued on October 30, 1890. An often quoted part of this brief document reads as follows: "should emergency arise, offer yourselves courageously to the State; and thus guard and maintain the prosperity of Our Imperial Throne coeval with heaven and earth." For our purpose, however, the part preceding this is more important: "always respect the Constitution and *observe the laws* [italics added]."³ Thus, in the document that provided the foundation for the modern state's morality and which was memorized by generations of students, obedience to law was not neglected. This rescript was issued by the emperor as a personal communication to the people (unlike other imperial rescripts it was not co-signed by state ministers). Thus, from 1890 onward, officials involved in political bribery not only were defying laws and moralists, but defying a divine emperor as well.

Understandably, in view of the power held by *hanbatsu* oligarchs, who dominated the early state, enforcement of antibribery statutes was not a prominent feature of the political world until the late Meiji period. There was, however, one exception to this general rule that those holding high political status were above the law: the Election Law was enforced. No doubt oligarchs, who were deeply suspicious of emerging political parties, were happy to see political opponents legally penalized and publicly shamed.

The sensational nationwide textbook bribery case exposed in late 1902 must have shocked Yamagata Aritomo, who was the champion defender of the superiority of the imperial bureaucracy; not only were officials of the prefectural bureaucracy indicted, but governors appointed by the Home Ministry as well. Not unexpectedly, however, the big fish escaped the legal net in a manner repeated during the following decades. Justice Minister Kiyoura Keigo, a close associate of Yamagata's, set a precedent by interfering in the prosecution of Governor Abe Hiroshi. Justice ministers in the later cabinets of Hara Kei and Yoshida Shigeru followed this example.

Procurators, as exemplified by Hiranuma Kiichirō, became more aggressive at the end of Meiji. The Greater Japan Sugar Refining Company scandal illustrates their expanding power. In this case, however, even Hiranuma, who was morally incorruptible and solely devoted to official duties, limited the scope of the investigation after Prime Minister Katsura Tarō threatened to interfere. Prosecution resulted in unprecedented convictions of numerous businessmen and politicians. This action set a pattern for later years, when procurators displayed vigor and tenacity in pursuing a number of high-profile political bribery cases. Another pattern that began with this case was the suspension of prison sentences. Over the following decades, the majority of those convicted for political bribery under Articles 197 and 198 of the Penal Code were not sent to prison. Fairly strict enforcement, then, was balanced by an extreme leniency in sentencing. The continuation of this sentencing pattern is illustrated by a Justice Ministry document published in 1980: "89.9 percent of bribery convictions [under the Penal Code] in 1978 resulted in suspended execution of sentences, a very high rate which has characterized this class of offense for some time."[4]

What the public thought about those who violated the antibribery provisions of the Penal Code and Election Law is difficult to pin down. Social critics, scholars, journalists, and other members of the elite public sometimes excoriated those who gave and those who accepted bribes, but even among this group there was a certain ambiguity toward violators. Yoshino Sakuzō, for example, who was a staunch foe of political corruption, understood that Diet politicians were in conflict with an entrenched oligarchy. "Yoshino despised Hara's pork-barrel politics, his bargaining for positions of power which he used to cultivate regional bases for the party. Yet he noted that Hara had surpassed all other party politicians in manipulating an essentially restrictive legal structure and bending it to favor party growth. As Yoshino grudgingly put it, 'Hara had overcome obstacles in a rather fine way.' "[5] As for the general public, from the time of the first national election to the time of Tanaka Kakuei's bribery conviction, voters were forgiving. They were happy to accept largesse from politicians, even those convicted of bribery, and return them to office. Most voters, it appears, accepted vote buying and other illegal activities as part of the normal political process. One observer of life in a *buraku* (hamlet) in the 1940s wrote, "After living in the *buraku* for a time, I realized that it thinks and feels differently from the State about crime. . . . [I]f a violation of the national law does not happen to cause any harm to the *buraku,* the *buraku* is little concerned with it. For instance, black marketing, gambling, hunting out of season, and tampering with the election process are all illegal, but the *buraku* makes no attempt to stop them . . . and the *buraku* will not cooperate with the police in their efforts to stop them." The essayist continued by noting that those seized by police for such crimes were, when they returned home, "still regarded just as highly as before. The society of the *buraku* simply does not classify such actions as criminal."[6] Voters, then, especially in rural areas, viewed indictment and conviction for bribery as unimportant; they were interested mainly in what a particular politician could do to help them. This viewpoint changed little over the decades. The following comments are based on a 1969 publication: "The village makes great demands. The elders want to purchase fire-fighting equipment. The village schools want either a piano or an organ. . . . Well-stuffed envelopes are expected at each festival, wedding and funeral. The shopkeeper expects a wreath when he opens a new store. Somebody must pay for the outings of the boy scouts. When the ladies of the village decide to visit the hot springs, somebody must hire a bus. For these and other expenses the Dietman is expected to pay handsomely."[7] Commenting on the insatiable demands of voters, a politician retired after fifty years in politics said, "They *force* the politicians to spend money on them. For instance, any time anything happens, they immediately demand a wreath. . . . When they come to Tokyo from the provinces, they demand a box lunch. . . . What's more, they act as if these demands were a natural right. They lead the politicians around by the nose."[8] During the postwar period, many Diet members reinforced the traditional *jiban* with a *kōenkai.* These organizations were very expensive to maintain.[9] A 1984 source notes that "the amounts of money or gifts given to any one constituent are rather small, but in the aggregate the funds needed to finance these activities are enormous. . . . Even in nonelection years . . . the day-to-day expenses of nurturing one's constituency are enormous."[10] In summary, as long as the flow of individual gifts kept coming and pork-barrel projects aided the larger community, voters were willing to overlook crimes like bribery. This willingness is well illustrated here by the many examples of politicians who were indicted or convicted for bribery and yet managed to continue with political careers. Although it appears that the political order is changing in the 1990s, the image one sees of the electorate, from the first party government until the recent past, is that of a "mildly apathetic, basically contented, noticeably materialistic" group.[11]

The public is less tolerant of corruption among bureaucrats, especially those in the central government's higher civil service, than among politicians. This heightened expectation of bureaucratic performance is based on bureaucrats' pre-1945 elite status as the emperor's men and their postwar elite consciousness derived from passing difficult competitive examinations.[12] As noted in this text, bribery charges against Finance Ministry personnel in the Teijin incident caused a great public stir. That the public continued to expect a strong antibribery ethic among higher civil servants is illustrated by the fact that when a section chief and a subsection chief were arrested on suspicion of accepting bribes from a company in March 1986, the story was the main item on the front pages of the *Asahi Newspaper*.[13] "The newspaper noted that this was the first time in twelve years that a leading official of a key ministry or agency . . . had been arrested on charges of corruption. The significance attached to the event was reflected in the prompt public apology by the chief government spokesman."[14] If judged on discovered cases of political bribery among higher civil servants, the postwar bureaucracy is remarkably free of corruption.[15] As for the postwar judiciary, there is not one known case of bribery. To uncover corruption among judges and justice bureaucrats a researcher would have to turn to the early years of Meiji, a time before the reformed legal structure was in place. In these early years, when there was no tradition of judicial independence, the newly emerging *hanbatsu* oligarchy was brazen in taking what it wanted and often acted as though it was above the law.[16] As for prefectual and city-level civil servants, political bribery appears to flourish much as it did during the prewar era. One author notes, "In local governments, bribery was particularly frequent in deals for securing offices such as speaker of prefectural or municipal assemblies or for obtaining public works contracts. . . . Of the 196 corruption cases detected in 1980 involving local government, 85 per cent concerned bribery or embezzlement. . . . Many of these cases were connected with construction projects."[17] A 1980 Justice Ministry report states that although bribery cases among higher civil servants decreased, local government officials were more frequently involved, especially in construction and civil engineering projects. Moreover, another trend illustrated in the report was that more mayors and governors were charged with bribery.[18] According to a February 1992 newspaper report, at least thirty-six governors, mayors, and construction-company executives were under investigation for rigging bids and bribery. Procurators in these cases claimed that they were eager to sweep away the traditional illegal system of secret deals among businessmen, politicians, and bureaucrats.[19] A leading procurator in this campaign, Yoshinaga Yūsuke, stated that the role of the procuracy was "to clean out the sewers."[20] Earlier, Yoshinaga had played an important role in the prosecution of Tanaka Kakuei and in the Recruit scandal investigation.

Most tolerant of political corruption were politicians and their bureaucratic allies. During the Meiji era, this contempt for state statutes probably was due to the former samurai ranks of many officials (i.e., they felt above the law). High-ranking people caught in the 1914 and 1915 bribery scandals were puzzled about being indicted. Home Minister Ōura excused bribery by saying that it was part of the normal political process. Yamagata Aritomo agreed: Ōura acted for the sake of the nation and did nothing wrong. Cabinet colleagues were equally puzzled about why Hiranuma and Suzuki wanted to impose a penalty; they saw nothing wrong with Ōura's actions: the political system had worked that way for decades.[21] Although party politicians in later years became more conscious of statutes and ethical norms, this fact did not stop the practice of accepting illegal funds and of giving bribes. One reason illegal practices continued was that most lower house politicians were in dire need of money: constituents visiting Tokyo had to be entertained, dinners and parties had to be arranged in the constituency, and gifts had to be given at proper times. Especially during election time, gift giving was very expensive.[22] These heavy expenses were met by political donations, by money from a political superior, and by commissions. Writing about this situation in the mid-1970s, Iga and Auerbach state, "When a Diet member gets a government subcontract or work from a large company for a constituent, the beneficiary is expected to pay at least 10% of the total price of his contract, and sometimes as much as 20%."[23] This statement could be applied aptly to the situation in the mid-1920s as well. As was noted in earlier chapters, a politician, a bureaucrat, or a businessman was occasionally indicted for bribery; some were even convicted; but the majority were not imprisoned and appeared to suffer no serious political ill effects. There were exceptions, of course, of which Ogawa Heikichi is the outstanding pre-1945 example. Ogawa had the misfortune of being exposed during a period when Tokyo procurators were aggressive. The postwar pattern with Tanaka Kakuei, the first former prime minister convicted of taking a bribe, was similar. Tanaka's legal problems arose from two factors: a semiopen shameless milking of the economy for political funds and a procuracy pressured by revelations in the United States about Japanese bribery. Yet even in these cases, the penalty was softened: Ogawa was reelected to office while on trial and pardoned by Prime Minister Konoe after leaving prison; Tanaka, who died before the Supreme Court pronounced a final verdict, was not only reelected but increased his political power.

Among national bureaucrats, procurators were the least tolerant of political bribery. Deals between those offering and those taking bribes, by their very nature secret, remained unknown unless someone exposed them. As was noted in earlier chapters, political opponents, journalists, and others sometimes pierced this veil of secrecy and exposed illegal acts. Procurators, however, had the right to prosecute or not prosecute bribery cases. This fact gave them political power, which they began to display from early in the twentieth century. It would be incorrect, however, to regard all the cases covered in this book as politically motivated. As one former procurator put it, "The general public had been very much concerned with the corruption of the political parties since the middle of the Taisho era. It was quite natural that the procurators inclined to correct the abuses from the standpoint of the maintenance of social justice, this being one of the purposes of the procuracy."[24] Nevertheless, restraints from within the Justice Ministry and pressure from the external political world did sometimes limit procurators' freedom of action.

Unfortunately for the procuratorial corps, the deep stain caused by the Teijin trial remains. This long, dramatic trial, in which all bribery defendants were acquitted, is lodged in public memory as an example of procurators violating suspects' procedural rights and is cited as an example of "fascism by the procuracy." The political critic Yayama Tarō, for example, began an article on the Recruit scandal with "The Lesson of the Teijin Affair." "The Teijin Affair is seen," he wrote,

> as a perfect example of procuratorial fascism, a case cooked up by right-wingers and reformist bureaucrats who were dissatisfied with party politics. . . . I am not suggesting that the Recruit scandal has been trumped up by the procurator's office, but I do think I can see many features in its handling of the affair that parallel the Teijin case. . . . In the Teijin Affair, the procurator's office leaked bits and pieces of what is called "confessions" until it had turned public opinion solidly against its opponents in the political, financial, and bureaucratic worlds. Much of what the procurator's office is doing now smacks of such practices.[25]

Suspects in recent political bribery cases have not hesitated to capitalize upon this image of Teijin case procurators who violated human rights by forcing confessions. Most of the accused in the Lockheed case, for instance, confessed to procurators and then repudiated the confessions at the trial. The charge of procuratorial fascism surfaced during the Tokyo Sagawa Express Company scandal as well.[26]

In recent years, a popular term used to explain the numerous official corruption scandals has been "structural corruption" *(kōzō oshoku)*. This term means "corruption that is inherent in the political and economic fabric of the nation, which is seen as being characteristically Japanese."[27] Murobushi Tetsurō, a sociologist of criminality who coined "structural corruption" in 1968, applied this label to corruption cases because in a typical case high-level government and financial-world figures were involved.[28] Other social critics follow Murobushi's lead but see structural corruption originating in the unusual economic and political conditions during the wartime and postwar eras. For example, one author writes,

> The immediate post-war years were very chaotic and the shortages of daily necessities and materials for industrial production together with a weakened governmental authority encouraged not only the disregard of legal restrictions but also of moral duties. During the war the munitions industry had resorted to bribing the all-powerful military bureaucracy in order to stay afloat while after the war businessmen were anxious to improve their chances by bribing Japanese officials. . . . Civil servants were all the more susceptible to this kind of persuasion because inflation pushed prices up relentlessly while salaries failed to keep pace with the erosion of purchasing power.[29]

Two questions need to be asked: is structural corruption unique to Japan and is it a strictly wartime and postwar phenomenon? As for the first point, the phenomenon called "structural corruption" is similar to political corruption found throughout the world at various stages of national development.[30] One Japanese journalist, "commenting on growing public awareness of this ubiquitousness in the wake of Tanaka's [Kakuei] arrest, noted that it had become clear that 'even the very corruption of political and business circles, which had long been considered to be particular to Japan, has deep connections with similar phenomena internationally.' "[31] As for the second point, readers need only reflect upon the fact that the Teijin incident involved two cabinet officers, a vice-minister in the Finance Ministry, important financiers in Baron Gō's club, and other business figures. Thus, corrupt practices, like political bribery, were deeply woven into the political fabric of the modern state.

The widespread use of political bribery during the pre-1945 era was a consequence, in part, of the institutional structure created in 1890 by the new government's architects. Itō Hirobumi and his helpers aimed to create a strong executive (i.e., cabinet), but the Meiji Constitution produced the reverse: a hybrid type of government in which the "executive could be made and unmade by all institutions that possessed a veto over its policy."[32] During the early years of the parliamentary era, the weak and unstable nature of cabinets was concealed by the prestige and power of Itō, Yamagata Aritomo, and the other elder statesmen who controlled cabinets and dominated the government. As other power centers arose and the elder statesmen's grip on government loosened, however, political conflict and deadlock increased. Expedients to solve these conflicts and to break deadlock between cabinets and the lower house included bribery and superior mediators like Hara Kei. During the so-called era of party government (1918–1932), cabinets, as before, were forced to compromise with other parts of the institutional structure or risk deadlock, which would result in a cabinet's fall.[33] "By the 1930s the leaders of Japanese governmental institutions had come to recognize that the 'normal course of constitutional government' made it futile to strive for anything more than sovereignty in the exercise of those functions they regarded as peculiarly their own. It was also futile to strive for control of the entire Cabinet. Having learned to live with the hybrid constitution, they jealously guarded their own functions and their share of Cabinet seats." Thus, the national unity cabinets of the 1930s "resulted not merely from constitutional forces that had been working themselves out since 1890. Only cabinets that represented each of the veto-possessing institutions could hope to retain a measure of their support, and the coalition cabinet became the logical way to make 'hybrid' constitutional government work." Furthermore, despite the accepted view that the army gained control of cabinets, in fact the situation in the 1930s remained about the same. "Neither the Army nor the House tolerated for long a prime minister who represented the other and the only 'successful' governments in the 1930s were led by more neutral men from the Navy, the Civil Service, the Upper House, and the Privy Council.... The power to raise a cabinet was therefore as far from the control of any one institution as ever, although cabinet-breaking power was less widely divided, since major influences from two institutions usually sufficed to force a cabinet out."[34]

One consequence of the parliamentary system outlined above was political corruption: "the flow of money from one institution to another or from electoral candidates to voters. In the absence of institutional incentives for harmony between the executive and legislature, the flow of money from one to the other became a *deus ex machina* to resolve deadlock."[35]

After the war, American reformers, who were aware of the Meiji system's serious flaws, tried to centralize the powers of the prime minister and to give the public the greatest possible voice in politics.

The early years under the new constitution witnessed considerable political party fluidity, but once the "1955 system" was locked in place, a single party dominated politics for nearly four decades. Given the nature of the constitution and the dominance of the Liberal Democratic Party, the prime minister and his party should have dominated the state. In fact, as Ozawa Ichirō points out, the prime minister exerted little power. Indeed, in some respects the power relationships in the postwar institutional structure are remarkably similar to those in the pre-1945 state. One long-time observer of Japan puts it this way: "There is, to be sure, a hierarchy or, rather, a complex of overlapping hierarchies. But it has no peak; it is a truncated pyramid. There is no supreme institution with ultimate policy-making jurisdiction."[36] He continues, "The bureaucrats tinker with the economy.... The politicians and almost everyone else keep out of their way. Parliamentary representatives ... attend mainly to the business of getting re-elected.... The industrialists continue to expand their foreign market shares.... They are kept in line by their peers; and they pay the politicians. Nobody is boss, but everybody, in some way or other, has leverage over somebody else, which helps ensure an orderly state of affairs."[37] Political bribery flourishes in this institutional structure where power is so diffuse, just as it did during the pre-1945 era.

Because cultural norms shape political behavior, reflections on "structural corruption" must not neglect traditional social practices. Two items are significant: the leader-follower or patron-client relationships and the deeply ingrained custom of gift giving.

Leader-follower relationships, which produce factions, are inherent in nearly all Japanese social organizations. Although contemporary political factions are not merely carbon copies of traditional patron-client formations, they are similar, and their existence is based on politicians' need to maintain close interpersonal relationships. Besides satisfying politicians' psychological needs, membership in a faction provides material benefits. For example, the faction leader acts as a sponsor and financial supporter of a member up for election and often provides a regular allowance to supplement a Dietman's salary. Membership in a faction is maintained through the exchange of favors and gifts.[38] Factionalism means that

> personal loyalties predominate over institutional loyalties.... In short, the leader-follower faction has transformed national politics into an exclusive, personalistic power game among elites which further inhibits popular participation in politics.... [Furthermore,] [t]he most damaging impact of personalistic norms ... is

found in their association with disquieting practices of political corruption. The cultural norms of reciprocity, exchange of favors, and gift-giving seem to legitimate influence peddling and bribery in the minds of many Japanese. Although the media have often highly publicized various corruption scandals, public officials have generally not been repudiated by the public for their malfeasance in office.[39]

Gift giving among the political elite has deep cultural roots. As was illustrated in chapter 1, the presentation of gifts of a prescribed nature was well formalized by the late Tokugawa, and the hairline boundary between etiquette and bribery was unclear. Gift giving was long prevalent among common people as well. One modern student of reciprocity writes,

> The full-page ads of midyear gift . . . sales by major department stores, the rows of gift shops in any resort town, the displays of gift-wrapped presents in stores at railroad stations, these are among the innumerable indications of the extent to which Japanese are involved in gift exchange. . . . Indeed, gift-giving is a minor institution . . . with complex rules defining who should give to whom, on what occasions he should give, what sort of gift is appropriate on any given occasion, and how the gift should be presented. . . . The moral obligation to give, to receive, and to return gifts is as much a part of traditional Japan as it is of the archaic societies with which Marcel Mauss concerned himself in his famous essay on the gift.[40]

Gift-giving customs in the general society influenced politicians throughout the modern era; indeed, because gift giving acts as a glue that bonds society, reciprocity was demanded of politicians. What the gift-giving custom meant for one typical lower house member in 1976 is illustrated by the ninety-three gifts he passed out in one month. These were gifts to groups for drinking and eating expenses; donations to formal organizations; wreaths sent for weddings, funerals, and other occasions; monetary gifts celebrating some occasion or expressing sympathy to a family; and so on. Besides these gifts, this politician gave gifts to superiors at least twice per year and, especially in an election year, gave gifts to local bosses.[41] Although voters and candidates everywhere have a relationship based on the principle of reciprocity, "Japanese voters' demands are more oriented to personal relationship and/or immediate profit than are American voters'."[42] Obviously, successful politicians must find ways, both legal and illegal, to provide enough income to meet expenditures. One method used to raise funds, which is well documented in this book, is to sell access based on personal connections to buyers who want something from the government. These transactions, if discovered and prosecuted, are categorized as bribes, but politicians like to call them "commissions" or an "introduction" fee.

As was noted in earlier chapters, traditional gift-giving customs influenced procurators and judges involved in political bribery cases. Ikeda Hayato, for example, escaped indictment because procurators accepted the claim that the money was a going-away gift before a trip to the United States (Shipbuilding scandal). Procurators agreed with Ōno Banboku that the money received was merely a friendship gift (Showa Electric Company scandal). These examples illustrate the difficulty procurators and judges have had in distinguishing between legal and illegal acts among government officials. Harumi Befu, who did field research on gift giving from the late 1960s, writes,

> In fact the more I learned about bribery, the less I could distinguish it from mundane and daily gift-giving. . . . It is interesting that in court hearings of bribery cases, the prosecutor asks in detail the manner in which bribes were given. Each little detail such as the use of wrinkled money, absence of gift-money envelope, etc., is additional evidence in support of the prosecutor's claim that money offered was a bribe. The assumption is that although acceptance of any gift by a public official for the execution of this [sic] public duty is bribery, in fact a court would not consider "customary" gift giving as constituting bribery. The court realizes that strict interpretation of the law is simply unwieldy and unmanageable because it is so contrary to the cultural norms regarding gift-giving. . . .
>
> [Crucial in separating gifts from bribes, writes Befu,] is the past relationship between the giver and the receiver. If they have long been friends or associates and have been in a gift-giving relationship and the gift involved in a bribery case was not too out of ordinary in comparison with the past gifts they have exchanged, then the prosecutor would have a hard time convincing the judge that the gift constitutes a bribe.[43]

Obviously, distinguishing between bribes and gifts has always been difficult (e.g., recall the low conviction rate in the major cases discussed in this book), but one rule of thumb used by procurators in spotting a potential bribery case is the "out of ordinary" cited by Befu. Justine Williams, a SCAP official who watched the Showa Electric Company scandal unfold, asked several knowledgeable Japanese about the amounts of money spread around by the company. They replied that the company paid excessive amounts for favors received. "As every Japanese knew, an obligation was to be met with the mathematical equivalent of the favor extended. But Showa Denko had repaid everyday favors with unheard of commissions. The gratuities were far out of proportion to the favors rendered. Lacking sophistication, the Showa Denko people were less concerned with meeting their obligations than with paying bribes for loans obtained."[44]

A proper analysis of political bribery in Japan demands comparison with other national experiences. Such a comparison is difficult given different social and political atmospheres, but it must be done to clarify what is typical and what atypical in the Japanese experience. China and Korea are obvious choices for a beginning.

Although the date of the earliest Chinese anti–political bribery regulation is unknown, it is known that penal law codes were in use as early as the sixth century B.C. and that by the time of the Ch'in dynasty (221–206 B.C.) officials were ordered not to accept bribes.[45] The T'ang dynasty (618–907) produced a comprehensive T'ang Penal Code: Articles 135 to 139 spelled out punishments for persons who offered bribes and officials who took them. Punishment depended upon personal status, value of the bribe, and whether the official subverted the law.[46]

Few books on traditional China neglect to mention official corruption. Indeed, the distinguished sinologist Etienne Balazs labeled bribery as one of the "congenital sores of officialdom."[47] According to Balazs, the source of the problem was not hard to find: officials spent many years preparing for the civil service examinations, and to gain official appointment they cultivated protectors and incurred debts. The degree of rapacity was dictated by the amount of debt incurred, the number of close kin, and the precariousness of the official's position.[48] During reform eras, reformers sought to solve this problem by urging an increase in official salaries. They also identified a major source of corruption: the runners, clerks, and servants gathered at each government office.[49] Corruption was stimulated during the Ming dynasty (1368–1643) by an inflation of paper currency; this inflation decreased the purchasing power of local officials, who were left without the means to finance their affairs unless they extorted more from the people.[50] Ch'ing dynasty (1644–1911) conditions were no better and perhaps worse by the nineteenth century. One outspoken district magistrate (the lowest-ranking official appointed by the central government) pointed out that corruption was a result of inadequate financial support:

> With the rise in the cost of living and the increasing importance of reliable secretarial services, the salaries of private secretaries alone could use up the district official's entire supplementary salary. . . . [Moreover,] the official also had to take care of his father and mother, his wife and children, the wages of his personal servants, the expenses of traveling on official business, the entertainment of superiors, presents for friends and fellow officials, and fees to superior offices for auditing district records and processing documents and registers. All these cost several times the amount of the supplementary salaries. . . . [Furthermore,] local officials continued to have to offer many customary contributions to superior officials. . . . [Therefore,] if given time they took from the people. If pressed they raided the treasury. Given the risks of the latter, the former was an obvious and irresistible alternative.[51]

A modern scholar, writing about roughly the same era, states, "The practice of paying inadequate salaries to government officials and permitting them to shift for themselves virtually forced them into graft and corruption."[52]

Like earlier dynasties, the Ch'ing outlined penalties for giving or receiving a bribe in a detailed penal code. Disciplinary regulations for officials also included punishments for using positions for private ends. Among the offenses listed was the one of giving a bribe or a gift to another official.[53] The giving of gifts to a superior, however, was such an ingrained habit that the government was powerless to stop it. Therefore, in mid-Ch'ing the regulations were somewhat softened to permit the innocent exchange of presents between officials who were friends or close relatives or who were born in the same place. It remained illegal to use occasions of gift exchange to ask for personal favors.[54]

The collapse of the last traditional dynasty ushered in a terrible period of disorder and expanded political corruption.[55] Indeed, a great attraction of the Chinese Communist Party was its attack upon political corruption. "The surprising achievement of the Communists was to be able to induce among their party members, who were after all thoroughly Chinese, a militant and puritanical hatred of the old system. . . . The Communist Party set out to hunt the corrupt; it disciplined its own members savagely if it caught them; it developed a steady pressure against corruption in all the administration—incidentally attaching charges of corruption to all of whom it disapproved upon other grounds."[56] Over the decades, however, the puritanical anticorruption zeal of Mao Tse-tung's revolution faltered. An American scholar who spent a year in China in the late 1980s notes that stories about political corruption among the elite leaders circulated and that they were believed by the common people and intellectuals. Older Chinese who recalled the 1940s claimed that the situation was worse than during the end of the Kuomintang era.[57] In January 1989 a senior Chinese scholar told the American, "I think they [the top leaders] want the best for China, just as I do. But many of the people right below them are out-and-out scoundrels, and the whole system is rotten to the core. It is beyond reform."[58] Another senior scholar said, "In China, politics is at the bottom of everything, including corruption. Every leader is jockeying to strengthen his own position. Just look how they feed dirt on one another's factions to the Hong Kong magazines."[59] After hearing these and similar comments from others, the American wrote, "The widespread perception that the top leadership was corrupt made it seem not only natural but almost justifiable that lower levels be corrupt as well."[60]

A report issued by the Chinese Academy of Social Science in mid-1993 confirms the above accounts. According to the report, the proportion of Communist Party members involved in bribery and embezzlement cases was increasing every year.[61] In August 1993, the Chinese Communist Party, seeing corruption as a threat to party control, launched the biggest anticorruption drive since 1949.[62] Over the next two years the campaign expanded, exposing high-level corruption among party officials.[63]

What conclusions may be drawn from comparing China with Japan? First, in traditional societies bribery, though illegal, was widespread. Second, the old custom of gift giving made it difficult for authorities to distinguish between legal gifts and illegal bribes. Third, the old regimes sometimes punished officials harshly with either exile or execution.[64] After the fall of the old regime in China, bribery and other forms of political corruption remained a social norm until the communist victory. Japan, during roughly the same years, experienced a number of sensational bribery cases, but China maintained a reputation as a more corrupt political environment. The death of Mao and the opening up of the Chinese economy resuscitated a traditional vice: political bribery. In Japan, despite a very different form of government, major corruption scandals pop up one after another.

It was pointed out earlier in this chapter that gift-giving customs are intimately connected with political bribery, to the point that Japanese justice authorities have a difficult time locating the thin margin between one and the other. The situation in China is similar. An important feature of Chinese social behavior is the stress on intimate personal relations. "Social and moral norms . . . are designed to maintain and enforce the particularistic-oriented Confucian values such as filial piety, affection, generosity, reciprocity, and fidelity. Particularism, therefore, plays an important role in daily interpersonal relationships. . . . As a result, the constant exchange of gifts and favors are [sic] considered not only desirable but also necessary, because these are concrete ways to express, and at the same time reinforce, the particularistic orientations."[65] Even though the deeply rooted gift-giving custom in both societies affects the political process, a word of caution is in order. The cultural norms of reciprocity in Japan do not necessarily stem from Confucianism: Japan was subjected to Buddhist and Shinto influences as well. John Hall writes, "Despite the victory of Neo-Confucianism in the realm of social and political ideas, the Buddhist establishment retained a good deal of its religious influences and some of its economic support." Shinto acted "as an institutional vehicle for the expression of deeply felt attitudes toward the homeland and the traditional social and political relationships."[66] Furthermore, Hall notes, "What is most impressive about the basic political institutions of the Tokugawa regime is that they owe little or nothing to Chinese models. The origins of Tokugawa political forms are clearly visible in the practices of the autonomous feudal houses which became the daimyo establishments of Tokugawa times."[67]

The pattern of political bribery in traditional Korea mirrors that of China. The government of the Yi dynasty (1392–1910) was copied from the Chinese administrative model; so was the legal code, which was copied from the Ming. As in China, local areas were governed by centrally appointed magistrates who were rotated frequently. To govern effectively the magistrate was forced to rely upon the permanent local officials and clerks. These administrators, however, received no regular salary; thus they were forced to live off bribery, extortion, and fees. They were in fact part of a nationwide system of institutionalized corruption.[68] Korean magistrates, like those in China, also found central government funds inadequate. They had to recover the purchase price of their office, acquire money to purchase a better position, and save money for retirement.[69] So pervasive was political corruption, at least during certain periods, that many folk tales and vernacular literature featured corrupt magistrates and rapacious underlings.[70]

We can suspect that during the Japanese occupation of Korea, from 1910 until 1945, the two currents of political corruption blended into one. At any rate, after 1945 the political-economic development of Korea followed a pattern similar to that of modern Japan. Out of the colonial era emerged Korean entrepreneurs who had learned, much as had the political merchants of Meiji Japan, to collaborate with political authority. Rhee Syngman, the first president of South Korea, built a powerful political machine by permitting foreign financing and bank credit for business leaders in return for political contributions and kickbacks. The overthrow of Rhee and his replacement by a militiary junta resulted in an anticorruption campaign. Soon, however, the generals swung the other way, striking a deal with the businessmen: all was forgiven if they established new companies in which the government held shares.[71] Given the legacy of the Japanese occupation and Japan's economic success, it is not surprising that the neighbor to the east was picked for the economic model.

In recent years, corruption scandals have appeard regularly. For example, one journal chronicled the following stories for the month of June 1993. Bribery charges were filed against Park Tae-joon, a former high official of the Pohang Steel and Iron Company. Kim Chong-in, a former economic adviser to former president Roh Tae-woo and a member of the ruling Democratic Liberal Party, was arrested for bribery. Prosecution officials planned to question former defense minister Lee Jong-koo and others about bribery in connection with the purchase of arms, Finally, the Board of Audits and Inspections was investigating General Dynamics for possible illegal payments in connection with the purchase of fighter planes.[72] In the face of these scandals, Kim Young-san, who in 1993 became the first civilian president in thirty-two years, launched a reform program to eliminate political corruption. Among other reforms, this program called for a declaration of assets by public officials and the use of real names in all financial transactions.[73] Thus political corruption in Korea, at least superficially, appears remarkably similar to corruption in Japan.

Another worthy choice for our comparison is England, where the first central government statute that defined corrupt electoral practices was issued in 1696. Members of Parliament lost their seats if they or persons acting for them gave or promised to give money or other rewards to any voter. The 1729 Bribery Act aimed at stopping corruption among electors. It appears that these laws were ignored.[74] Following the election of 1734, one observer wrote, "Notwithstanding the severe Act passed in the year 1729 to prevent bribery and corruptions in elections, yet money, though it had been formerly more openly given, was never more plentifully given than in these."[75] Because the law was ignored with impunity by electors and candidates, "the eighteenth-century politician came to believe that there was no effective way to end it [i.e., electoral corruption] and sighed with Sir William Yonge, 'The evil I am afraid is inevitable.' "[76]

By the eighteenth century, seats in Parliament were very expensive. Some wealthy members financed their own election campaigns; others accepted government support with the understanding that they would support government bills. Payments to the government's friends were made out of the king's secret service fund. Political parties as well established central election funds; candidates could also raise money by a subscription promoted by supporters. In spite of these various sources of funds, the increasing cost of elections sometimes made it difficult to find candidates. This rapid escalation in election expenses resulted from

> the corruptibility of the electorate and the willingness of candidates to take advantage of it. The opprobrium rained down upon the heads of the British electorate by politicians smarting under the cost of bribing and treating them is well known. . . . We should not, however, be too harsh in passing judgement upon the . . . voters of the pre-Reform era. . . . For centuries a limited electorate, a considerable part of which was composed of the poorer element of the population, accustomed to preying on the wealthy whenever possible, had been content for a consideration to allow the moneyed and landed upper classes to govern Britain.[77]

Although electoral corruption during the nineteenth century was attacked in newspapers and journals, it was accepted and even encouraged by most of society. Many voters continued to view elections as a time to make money and receive gifts. In some areas, voters had no desire to know about party platforms but were content to vote for the political party that would pay the most. It appears that corrupt electors saw nothing morally wrong with soliciting and accepting bribes. As for candidates, the century's permissive attitude toward electoral abuses produced members of Parliament who worried little about bribing their way into the House of Commons.[78] The *Westminister Review* (1862) summed up the situation: "It is a painful truth that a wealthy man, known to have bribed, nay actually convicted of bribery, is not the whit less respected by the majority of the House."[79]

Nevertheless, there was a growing consciousness during the nineteenth century that flagrant electoral corruption was not only illegal but immoral. This set of mind resulted in statutes in 1854 and 1868 that carefully defined electoral crimes such as bribery. According to the latter statute, anyone found guilty of bribery was prohibited from holding public office for seven years.[80]

The Reform Act of 1867 more than doubled the electorate. Although not yet universal male suffrage, it did give the vote to male household owners, household occupiers who paid rent, and lodgers. There was a residence qualification of one year. Adding a million working-class voters concerned some conservatives who worried about bribery and other forms of electoral corruption. One response was the Ballot Act of 1872, which introduced the secret ballot; it was hoped that the new system would decrease intimidation and corruption. Secret voting, however, did not reduce charges of corruption or reduce the cost of election, which continued to rise rapidly.[81]

A report by a royal commission investigating corrupt practices during the 1880 election led to the passage of the Corrupt and Illegal Practices Act of 1883. This act incorporated selected parts of all earlier legislation on this subject. Bribery and other illegal practices were punishable by severe fines and limits were placed on election expenses. Candidates were held liable not only for their own actions, but also for actions taken by their agents.[82] About ten years after the passage of this reform legislation, one observer noted that bribery and other illegal acts had in most areas ceased to exist and in others greatly diminished. Another source notes that during an investigation at the turn of the century no extensive electoral corruption was uncovered.[83] Although the 1883 act improved the method for detecting bribery and more harshly punished those apprehended, there was another reason for the decrease in this sort of crime: "[N]one of the statutes would have been effective had there not also occurred a revolution in the outlook of the mass of the people—admittedly very much influenced and enouraged by legislative reform—which gradually transformed their role in the government of the nation from a relatively passive to a relatively active one. In this mental transformation . . . lay a powerful force for bringing electoral corruption, and the huge expense it occasioned, to an end."[84]

In light of the English experience with electoral corruption, the attitudes of Japanese candidates and voters appear to follow a normal pattern of development. That electors expected and insisted upon bribery, and that candidates were happy to comply, during the early decades after the first election in 1890 is unremarkable. Moreover, over the decades the Japanese state passed antibribery regulations and ran clean election campaigns, following the English example (indeed, the first election law drew upon the 1883 English act for inspiration). In England, however, the last case of extensive electoral bribery occurred in 1906 in an area with a long tradition of corruption, where five hundred voters were found to have taken small bribes.[85] Thus, in just over twenty years after passage of the

1883 act, electoral bribery ceased to be important. That is not what happened in Japan. Some think that the large number of violations over many decades reflects overrestrictive regulations or overzealous enforcement by authorities. Others reply that the long-term continuation of corrupt practices is a reflection of a society in which electoral corruption is more tolerated than it is in some other countries.

The United States is our final example for comparison. Bribery and treason are the two crimes mentioned by name in the United States Constitution. Article 2, Section 4 reads, "The President, Vice-President and all civil officers of the United States shall be removed from office on impeachment for and conviction of treason, bribery, or other high crimes and misdemeanors."[86] This clause, however, did not cover members of Congress and probably was not intended to apply to judges. One scholar notes that this barrier to political bribery was modest. "A dichotomy was accepted. The chief magistrate could be removed for bribing Congress or anyone else. The Congress was subject to no sanction if it was bribed."[87] In 1789, the first federal antibribery law was enacted to punish customs inspectors and others involved in falsifying records; punishment was a monetary fine. The next year a law made it a crime to bribe federal judges and for judges to accept bribes: punishment was disqualification from federal office. Finally, in February 1853 a criminal statute was enacted to punish the bribing of a member of Congress. The scope of this law was expanded in 1862: punishment was a fine and two years in prison. Both the 1853 and 1862 laws were broad enough to cover any sort of bribe offered to legislators.[88]

The willingness of Congress to enforce the new antibribery law soon was tested. Newspaper reports in the autumn of 1872 charged that prominent congressmen took bribes, in the form of stock, in return for promises not to investigate Crédit Mobilier, a corporation created to construct the Union Pacific Railroad. One purpose of this corporation, said the newspapers, was to drain profits from building contracts into the pockets of the railroad promoters. Congressman Oakes Ames, who played a leading role in handing out stocks to buy colleagues' support to protect Crédit Mobilier, was the only House member censured.[89]

During the late nineteenth and early twentieth centuries, political corruption thoroughly permeated all levels of government; this phenomenon was tied to the growth of political parties, which needed money for expansion. "Massive contractor kickbacks for public works and payments to avoid the growing licensing and regulatory apparatus . . . were increasingly important sources of funds. And by the turn of the century large-scale corporate contributions had become a major source of money for state and national elections."[90] Although Lincoln Steffens and other muckrakers focused public attention on political corruption at all levels of government, and although some who gave and some who received bribes at local and state levels were convicted of wrongdoing, the federal government displayed little interest in the problem of political bribery. Even in the cases of a few judges impeached by the House of Representatives and convicted by the Senate, no criminal prosecution followed.[91]

In 1929 the traditional pattern of no criminal sanctions for high-ranking bureaucrats was broken, at least temporarily, by the conviction of former secretary of the interior Albert B. Fall. Fall's criminal act involved leasing naval oil reserves to oil companies owned by Edward L. Doheny and Harry F. Sinclair. A Senate investigation disclosed that Doheny loaned Fall $100,000 and that Sinclair gave him $85,000 in cash, $223,000 in bonds, and a herd of cattle. Although Doheny and Sinclair were acquitted of planning to defraud the government, Fall was convicted of bribery; he was sentenced to a year in prison and fined $100,000. His appeal was denied and he entered prison in July 1931. This scandal, which goes by the name of Teapot Dome, put a cabinet-level official in prison for the first time.[92] Fall's unprecedented conviction was the result of several factors: carelessness in displaying his new wealth; lies to the Senate committee; political vulnerability; a trial and appeal during the stock market collapse; and the Depression.[93]

The first federal judge convicted of bribery was Martin T. Manton, who was the ranking justice on the federal appeals court in New York City. Between 1932 and 1938, Manton received hundreds of thousands of dollars in payments from litigants. Given a two-year sentence, Manton entered prison in March 1940.[94]

The convictions of Fall and Manton were exceptions rather than the rule. Although politicians and judges sometimes resigned from office in the face of bribery charges, they did not face prison terms. "State enforcement of state criminal law against bribery," writes one scholar, "was not substantially different from the federal practice."[95]

Although no members of Congress were convicted of bribery before the twentieth century, ten had been convicted by 1970. The sentences in these cases were not severe: the main sanction was political oblivion. Although federal prosecutors became more active in indicting members of Congress after 1970, sentences remained mild. In 1978 the federal government launched the so-called Abscam operation. During this "sting," bribes of up to a hundred thousand dollars were paid by two imaginary wealthy Arabs to members of Congress who were to guide them around legal pitfalls as they invested in the United States. Caught by hidden cameras, all those targeted were convicted of criminal actions, six of them for bribery. Michael Myers, who refused to resign, became the first lower house member expelled for bribery. Senator Harrison A. Williams, Jr., also touched by this sting, resigned from the Senate.[96]

Efforts to purify corrupt federal election practices resulted in the Tillman Act of 1907: corporations were forbidden to provide money for candidates for federal offices. In 1910 Congress passed a Federal Corrupt Practices Act, which required reporting contributions given in national elections. Over the years other laws were added to close loopholes in the original statutes. Corporations, however, found numerous ways to bypass these laws, and in the main, enforcement of the laws was lax and penalties were light. In 1946 the Government Regulation of Lobbying Act was passed. Corporations subverted numerous loopholes in this law as well. Massive evasion of laws to control election crimes and illegal lobbying were mostly ignored until after the Watergate burglary in 1972. Because the special prosecutors for this affair had jurisdiction to investigate campaign finances, attention focused on the enforcement of the Tillman Act. By the conclusion of this investigation, many major corporations pleaded guilty to making illegal campaign contributions. As part of a settlement with the government, Gulf Oil Corporation agreed to an investigation of its political contributions. The committee charged with this task produced a detailed account of political payments among which were bribes paid overseas. Congress responded in 1977 by enacting the Foreign Corrupt Practices Act, which condemned efforts to influence an official act by giving any gifts, offers, or payments to any foreign official or to any person who might transmit such.[97]

Throughout American history the moral dimension of bribery was influenced by Christian religious teaching. "The imitation of God lies at the root of the bribery prohibition. . . . The God of Israel judges impartially. No human gift can blind God's eye or bind His judgement. . . . Fixed in the biblical basis of Western culture is the model of the Ruler-Judge who is above all attempts to bribe Him. We are to be like Him. . . . Generous gift and base bribe are demarcated forever by religious example and instruction."[98] The effect of the antibribery ideal on the Founding Fathers is demonstrated in the inclusion of "bribery" in the United States' basic legal document. Bribery was further criminalized in federal laws over the following years. Despite laxness in the enforcement of these laws until well into the twentieth century, the antibribery ethic remained strong among the general public. Commenting on the effort to root out bribery in Congress in the 1970s in the Abscam affair, one scholar notes, "It could not have taken place except in a society drenched in the antibribery ethic. No comparable antibribery effort had ever been mounted by any nation against criminal bribe takers among its own lawmakers."[99]

A comparison of political bribery in the United States and Japan results in the following conclusions. The history of political bribery in the United States is as old as the Republic, and examples of political corruption at both the national and local levels can match any examples produced by Japan. One difference, however, is worth noting: throughout American history, even in times of low enforcement of bribery laws, the idea that bribery was morally wrong remained widespread and deep rooted. The strong antibribery ethic provided a kind of punishment in lieu of criminal sanctions: public humiliation faced those who offered or took bribes. In the Japanese case, in contrast, the cultural context in which political bribery takes place results in a different outcome: a politician caught taking a bribe may feel shame at public exposure but may not feel a sense of moral guilt. Moreover, political careers flourish despite convictions for bribery.

Both nations have comprehensive penal codes and election regulations in which antibribery provisions are well established. Enforcement, too, follows a similar pattern, with more prosecution activity in some periods than in others; politics affects the process in both countries. Prosecution in Japan, however, is more difficult, because in the United States payment to an official is considered bribery: the prosecutor need not prove that the one offering the bribe received a favor from the official accepting it. This is not the case in Japan, where the procurator must prove that the official received the money, did a favor in return, and understood that the money was meant as a bribe. In both Japan and the United States, at least until the postwar era, the higher the status of the person being bribed, the less likely the person was to be prosecuted. Exceptions include Minister Ogawa and Secretary Fall, who were indicted in the same year (1929) and who both served short prison sentences. Unlike the United States, which imprisoned Judge Manton in 1940, Japan has no record of a bribed federal-level judge. There is, however, one dramatic difference between the nations: the series of postwar political bribery scandals in Japan, involving hundreds of politicians, bureaucrats, and businessmen. At the heart of these scandals is the pressing need of politicians for large sums of money for election campaigning and for maintaining political factions. Also central to each of these scandals is the different Japanese view of what constitutes political bribery.

There is widespread agreement that the Japanese political system needs reforming. Most reformers agree that something must be done to curb "money politics" (i.e., the dependence upon big business for funds), to rid parties of excessive factionalism, and to better integrate the general public into the political process. Of these three areas targeted by reformers, the most difficult to alter is factionalism, and because factions thrive on large sums of money, the link between big business and factions will be difficult to sever. One authority on factions *(habatsu)* notes,

> Given that the Japanese culture emphasizes personal ties more than institutionalized relations, the authority to which one is obedient and loyal would be embodied in a person rather than an institution. The party authority is a well-institutionalized, rather impersonal one. On the other hand, the authority of "oyabun" is based on traditional "giri-ninjō" relations. Thus, it is understandable that the conservative Japanese, who conform to traditional values and seek some sort of group authority to depend upon, will turn to the "habatsu," or more specifically to the boss of "habatsu," rather than to the party.[100]

Reformers behind the program of Prime Minister Miki (January 1977) reasoned that factions would decline if the party promoted a mass membership qualified to vote for the party president. Even though the mass membership was achieved, the factions continued to play a traditional role because the party members identified with their local Dietman, not with the party, and he in turn identified with his faction leader (see chapter 6). Given the nature of Japanese politics and the society of which it is a part, it is a serious error to underrate the lasting power of factions. Some social scientists, however, persist in the view that "modernization" will somehow remove factions from the political scene. Others, with a deeper understanding of Japan, think that factions, which serve a pragmatic purpose, will adjust to reformers' plans and survive.[101] All this brings us back to the key question of money, which factions must have. Obviously, faction leaders will try to maintain traditional links with big-business money sources. One scholar, writing about the electoral reform in January 1994, concluded, "Though a coalescence into two major political parties is quite possible, it is equally possible that it won't happen. Similarly, claims about the demise of money politics, factional politics, and personal support networks are questionable."[102]

Gunnar Myrdal, in a classic study about economic development (or lack of it) in South Asia, writes about the problem of corruption. Political corruption, he points out, is much on the mind of articulate people. Legislative assemblies and newspapers devote much time and space to this subject, and conversation between friends often turns to this subject. Occasionally, committees are established to study the problem and laws are passed to end it. Despite these measures and despite public concern about corruption, most people appear to believe that it is increasing, he notes, especially among highly placed officials.[103] "The ostentatious efforts to prevent corruption and the assertions that the corrupt are being dealt with as they deserve only seem to spread cynicism, especially as to how far all this touches the 'higher-ups.' "[104] Myrdal terms one thing he sees at work here the " 'folklore of corruption,' i.e., people's beliefs about corruption and the emotions attached to those beliefs, as disclosed in the public debate and in gossip."[105] This "folklore" influences the way people live their private lives and colors their very sense of loyalty to society. Thus, the "folklore of corruption" in a given society, even if that society is only moderately infected by the virus of bribery, can cause a widespread feeling that corruption is rampant, and this in turn can produce more individual corruption.[106] If Myrdal is correct, then the march of one after another scandal across Japan's political stage plus the numerous loudly announced plans to reform the political system must have shaken the faith of people in the integrity of public officials.

Political bribery will continue to flourish in Japan because electing new political leaders and enacting election reform laws will not alter the basic political culture. Successive reforms will, no doubt, make a dent in deeply rooted illegal practices, but meaningful reform must be directed at changing cultural values. Therefore, reform will be a long and painful process.

Appendix

YEN-DOLLAR EXCHANGE RATE

	¥	$
1900	2	1
1930	2.2	1
1946	50	1
1947	360	1
1970	360	1
1975	297	1
1980	227	1
1985	238	1
1990	145	1
1995	100	1

Notes

Introduction

1. *New York Times,* March 29, 1994, A4.
2. Ibid., May 17, 1995, A3.
3. Quoted in ibid.
4. Ibid., April 18, 1994, A3.
5. Kōdansha, *Japan: An Illustrated Encyclopedia,* 1:1211.
6. Edwin O. Reischauer, "The Lessons of the Lockheed Scandal," 20–21.
7. Jerome A. Cohen, "Japan's Watergate: Made in U.S.A.," 107.
8. *New York Times,* December 17, 1993, A17.
9. Bradley M. Richardson and Scott C. Flanagan, *Politics in Japan,* 190.
10. William Chapman, *Inventing Japan: The Making of a Postwar Civilization,* 155.
11. Edwin O. Reischauer, *The Japanese Today: Change and Continuity,* 283, 285.
12. Gerald L. Curtis, "Big Business and Political Influence," 51.
13. John W. Dower, *Origins of the Modern Japanese State: Selected Writings of E. H. Norman,* 365.
14. John T. Noonan, Jr., *Bribes: The Intellectual History of a Moral Idea,* xii.
15. Ibid., xiii–xiv.
16. Ibid., xi.
17. Gabriel Ben-Dor, "Corruption, Institutionalization, and Political Development: The Revisionist Theses Revisited," 63–64.
18. Michael Elliot, "Corruption," 40.
19. Yayama Tarō, "The Recruit Scandal: Learning from the Causes of Corruption," 93.
20. Itō Takashi, *Showa shi o saguru,* 1:143.

Chapter 1: Legacies

1. Inoue Mitsusada, "The Century of Reform," 1:163–164, 175–181; Tetsuo Najita, *Japan,* 13.

2. Inoue, 179–180.

3. Ienaga Saburō and Tsukishima Hiroshi, "Kenpō Jūnanajō," 15. A full translation of the injunctions appears in Ryūsaku Tsunoda et al., *Sources of Japanese Tradition*, 1:47–51. Article Five, however, is improperly translated.

4. Ishimoda Shō, *Nihon kodai kokka ron: Kanryōsei to hō no mondai*, 1:181.

5. George B. Sansom, *Japan: A Short Cultural History*, 165; Jeffrey P. Mass, "The Missing Minamoto in the Twelfth-Century Kanto," 123; Elizabeth Sato, "Ōyama Estate and *Insei* Land Policies," 89–96.

6. Kozo Yamamura, "The Decline of the Ritsuryō System: Hypotheses on Economic and Institutional Change," 19.

7. Nakase Katsutarō, *Tokugawa jidai no wairo shi kanken*, 1.

8. Quoted in Carl Steenstrup, "The Gokurakuji Letter: Hōjō Shigetoki's Compendium of Political and Religious Ideas of Thirteenth-Century Japan," 29.

9. Carl Steenstrup, "*Sata Mirensho*: A Fourteenth-Century Law Primer," 435.

10. Jeffrey P. Mass, *The Development of Kamakura Rule, 1180–1250: A History with Documents*, 131.

11. Steenstrup, "Gokurakuji Letter," 34 n. 87; George B. Sansom, *A History of Japan to 1334*, 460–461.

12. Quoted in Kenneth A. Grossberg, ed., *The Laws of the Muromachi Bakufu: Kemmu Shikimoku (1336) and Muromachi Bakufu Tsuikahō*, 20.

13. Kenneth A. Grossberg, *Japan's Renaissance: The Politics of the Muromachi Bakufu*, 6.

14. Paul Varley, *The Ōnin War: History of Its Origins and Background with a Selective Translation of the Chronicle of Ōnin*, 139.

15. Quoted in John S. Brownlee, "The Jeweled Comb-Box: Motoori Norinaga's *Tamakushige*," 54.

16. Quoted in Imatani Akira with Kozo Yamamura, "Not for Lack of Will or Wile: Yoshimitsu's Failure to Supplant the Imperial Lineage," 46 n. 3.

17. Kate Wildman Nakai, *Shogunal Politics: Arai Hakuseki and the Premises of Tokugawa Rule*, 202–205; J. C. Hall, "The Tokugawa Legislation, I," 303.

18. Nakai, *Shogunal Politics*, ix–x, 205.

19. Quoted in ibid., 207.

20. J. R. McEwan, *The Political Writings of Ogyū Sorai*, 38.

21. Quoted in Shigeru Matsumoto, *Motoori Norinaga, 1730–1801*, 146.

22. J. C. Hall, "The Tokugawa Legislation, IV," 712–713.

23. E. S. Crawcour, "Kawamura Zuiken, A Seventeenth-Century Entrepreneur, " 33; E. Herbert Norman, "Andō Shōeki and the Anatomy of Japanese Feudalism," 70; John McMaster, "The Japanese Gold Rush of 1859," 279; Arai Hakuseki, *Told Round a Brushwood Fire: The Autobiography of Arai Hakuseki*, 5; Dower, *Origins of the Modern Japanese State*, 365.

24. Arai, *Brushwood Fire*, 171, 266.

25. Quoted in ibid., 266.

26. Kōdansha, *Illustrated Encyclopedia*, 1:404; Shioya Sakae, *Chūshingura: An Exposition*, 9–11.

27. Ibid., 10.

28. Ibid., 11.

29. Kōdansha, *Illustrated Encyclopedia,* 1:404–405; Nakase, 20–21.

30. Kate Nakai, "Yanagisawa Yoshiyasu (1658–1714)," 8:314.

31. Beatrice Bodart-Bailey, "Councillor Defended: *Matsukage Nikki* and Yanagisawa Yoshiyasu," 467–468.

32. Nakai, "Yanagisawa Yoshiyasu," 314.

33. Bodart-Bailey, "Councillor Defended," 476–478.

34. Ibid., 468; Nakai, "Yanagisawa Yoshiyasu," 314.

35. Conrad D. Totman, *Early Modern Japan,* 341.

36. Dower, *Origins,* 365.

37. Quoted in ibid.

38. Conrad D. Totman, *Politics in the Tokugawa Bakufu, 1600–1843,* 222; idem, *Early Modern Japan,* 342.

39. John W. Hall, *Tanuma Okitsugu, 1719–1788: Forerunner of Modern Japan,* 142.

40. Anne Walthall, *Social Protest and Popular Culture in Eighteenth-Century Japan,* 11.

41. Herman Ooms, *Charismatic Bureaucrat: A Political Biography of Matsudaira Sadanobu, 1758–1829,* 78; Totman, *Early Modern Japan,* 346; Robert L. Backus, "Matsudaira Sadanobu as a Moralist and Litterateur," 33.

42. Hall, *Tanuma Okitsugu,* 141.

43. Isao Soranaka, "The Kansei Reforms—Success or Failure?" 154. Shogunal officials, who were used to bribes, reacted in panic, and Sadanobu was forced to relax the reform. For example, although they were not to take money they could accept goods. Nakase, *Tokugawa jidai,* 48–49.

44. Hiramatsu Yoshirō, "Summary of Tokugawa Criminal Justice," 107–108.

45. Ooms, *Charismatic Bureaucrat,* 106–119, 151.

46. Dower, *Origins,* 366. It is ironic that Sadanobu got promotions by giving "gifts" to Tanuma. Nakase, *Tokugawa jidai,* 49.

47. John W. Hall, *Government and Local Power in Japan, 500–1700: A Study Based on Bizen Province,* 364.

48. Hall, *Tanuma Okitsugu,* 156.

49. Ibid., 54–55.

50. Nakase, *Tokugawa jidai,* 52–53.

51. Hall, *Tanuma Okitsugu,* 56; Bodart-Bailey, "Councillor Defended," 476–477.

52. Quoted in Steenstrup, "*Sata Mirensho,*" 435.

53. Arai, *Brushwood Fire,* 5, 50, 164.

54. Charles D. Sheldon, *The Rise of the Merchant Class in Tokugawa Japan, 1600–1868,* 50.

55. Hall, *Tanuma Okitsugu,* 118.

56. Ooms, *Charismatic Bureaucrat,* 78.

57. Hall, *Tanuma Okitsugu,* 119.

58. Sansom, *Cultural History,* 164. Also see Yamamura, "Decline of the Ritsuryō System," 14, 17, 19.

59. Quoted in Hall, *Tanuma Okitsugu,* 117–118.

60. Noonan, *Bribes,* 697.

Chapter 2: The New State

1. Paul Heng-chao Ch'en, *The Formation of the Early Meiji Legal Order: The Japanese Code of 1871 and Its Chinese Foundation*, 11–16, 95, 159–164.

2. Wagatsuma Sakae, ed., *Kyū hōrei shū*, 431, 439–440.

3. Sterling Tatsuji Takeuchi, "The Japanese Civil Service," 515, 517–518.

4. Ibid., 549.

5. Ibid., 549, 551.

6. Thomas R. H. Havens, *Nishi Amane and Modern Japanese Thought*, 160.

7. William R. Braisted, trans., *Meiroku Zasshi: Journal of the Japanese Enlightenment*, 198.

8. Quoted in ibid.

9. Carol Gluck, *Japan's Modern Myths: Ideology in the Late Meiji Period*, 49–60; Ryūsaku Tsunoda et al., *Sources of Japanese Tradition*, 2:202.

10. Quoted in ibid., 206.

11. Arthur E. Tiedemann, "Big Business and Politics in Prewar Japan," 268.

12. Morikawa Hidemasa, *Zaibatsu: The Rise and Fall of Family Enterprise Groups in Japan*, 20.

13. Ibid., 5, 20; Robert A. Scalapino, *Democracy and the Party Movement in Prewar Japan: The Failure of the First Attempt*, 200 n. 29.

14. Byron K. Marshall, *Capitalism and Nationalism in Prewar Japan: The Ideology of the Business Elite, 1868–1941*, 29.

15. Andrew Fraser, "The Expulsion of Okuma from the Government in 1881," 227.

16. William D. Wray, *Mitsubishi and the N.Y.K., 1870–1914: Business Strategy in the Japanese Shipping Industry*, 197, 473–474.

17. Quoted in Walter W. McLaren, ed., "Government Documents, First Half of the Meiji Era," 185–186.

18. Wagatsuma, *Kyū hōrei shū*, 438.

19. R. H. P. Mason, *Japan's First General Election: 1890*, 219.

20. Gluck, *Modern Myths*, 66.

21. Mason, *General Election*, 167–169.

22. Ibid., 169.

23. Ibid., 170–173.

24. Banno Junji, *The Establishment of the Japanese Constitutional System*, 20–21.

25. Scalapino, *Democracy*, 154–155; Banno, *Constitutional System*, xii–xiii, 200–201; George Akita, *Foundations of Constitutional Government in Modern Japan, 1868–1900*, 76–77.

26. George Akita, "The Meiji Constitution in Practice: The First Diet," 31.

27. Ibid., 32, 36–37, 45–46.

28. R. H. P. Mason, "Changing Diet Attitudes to the Peace Preservation Ordinance, 1890–2," 113.

29. Banno, *Constitutional System*, xii.

30. Tsunoda, *Japanese Tradition*, 2:195.

31. Scalapino, *Democracy*, 157 n. 23.

32. Akita, "Meiji Constitution in Practice," 36.

33. Ibid., 36 n. 26.

34. Daniel B. Ramsdell, *The Japanese Diet: Stability and Change in the Japanese House of Representatives, 1890–1990.* For the bribery incident, see Hayashida Kametarō, *Nihon seitō shi* 1:311–312.

35. Akita, *Foundations*, 98, 104–105; Scalapino, *Democracy*, 160; Richard H. Mitchell, *Censorship in Imperial Japan*, 114–118; Andrew Fraser, "The House of Peers (1890–1905): Structure, Groups, and Role," 23–24.

36. Scalapino, *Democracy*, 176–177, 177 n. 80.

37. Oka Yoshitake, *Yamagata Aritomo*, 75–77; Nezu Masashi, *Nihon gendai shi* 1:40; David A. Titus, *Palace and Politics in Prewar Japan*, 128.

38. Quoted in Scalapino, *Democracy*, 178.

39. Oka Yoshitake, *Yamagata Aritomo*, 77–78.

40. Hayashida Kametarō, *Nihon seitō shi* 2:2–3; Scalapino, *Democracy*, 178; Akita, *Foundations*, 147.

41. Scalapino, *Democracy*, 179.

42. Hayashida, *Nihon seitō shi*, 2:3.

43. Ibid., 3–4.

44. Akita, *Foundations*, 158.

45. Scalapino, *Democracy*, 181; Fraser, "House of Peers," 29.

46. George Akita, "The Other Ito: A Political Failure," 353, 355; Tiedemann, "Big Business," 274–275.

47. Scalapino, *Democracy*, 167, 264; Wray, 595 n. 6.

48. Scalapino, *Democracy*, 264–265; Morikawa Tetsurō, *Nihon gigoku shi*, 113.

49. Yamamoto Taketoshi, *Shinbun kisha no tanjō: Nihon no medeia o tsukutta hitobito*, 254.

50. Mikiso Hane, *Modern Japan: A Historical Survey*, 169; Akita, *Foundations*, 257.

51. Morikawa Tetsurō, *Nihon gigoku shi*, 128–129, 135; Miyachi Tadashi, "Kyōkasho gigoku jiken: Kyōkasho kokutei e no katei to shite," 351, 357–358, 362; Chitoshi Yanaga, *Japan since Perry*, 272.

52. Herbert Passin, *Society and Education in Japan*, 233–236; Miyachi Tadashi, "Kyōkasho gigoku jiken," 372.

53. Robert M. Spaulding, Jr., *Imperial Japan's Higher Civil Service Examinations*, 86, 294–296.

54. Richard Yasko, "Hiranuma Kiichirō and Conservative Politics in Prewar Japan," 34.

55. Scalapino, *Democracy*, 258–260; Morikawa, *Zaibatsu*, 21, 36; Yokoyama Taiji, *Gendai no oshoku*, 58–60.

56. Scalapino, *Democracy*, 265.

57. Walter W. McLaren, *A Political History of Japan during the Meiji Era, 1867–1912*, 367. For early Meiji political corruption scandals touching Yamagata, Inoue Kaoru, and other important political leaders, see Donald Calman, *The Nature and Origins of Japanese Imperialism*, 256–267.

58. Oka Yoshitake, *Five Political Leaders of Modern Japan*, 69–70.

59. Nezu Masashi, *Nihon gendai shi*, 37–38; Murobushi Tetsurō, *Jitsuroku Nihon oshoku shi*, 32.

60. Nezu Masashi, *Nihon gendai shi,* 41.

61. Akita, "The Other Ito," 351–352.

62. Oka, *Five Political Leaders,* 33, 35.

63. Amemiya Shōichi, "Nittō jiken: Oshoku jiken to kensatsuken no kakudai," 486–487, 494, 502.

64. Ibid., 489–490.

65. Ibid., 490–492.

66. Ibid., 496; Nomura Masao, ed., *Hōsō fūunroku: Anohito konohito hōmonki* 1:69; Richard Yasko, "Bribery Cases and the Rise of the Justice Ministry in Late *Meiji–*Early *Taisho* Japan," 62–63.

67. Hiranuma Kiichirō kaikoroku hensan iinkai, *Hiranuma Kiichirō kaikoroku,* 54.

68. Amemiya Shōichi, "Nittō jiken," 486, 497, 499–500, 502, 505, 512.

69. Hiranuma, *Hiranuma Kiichirō kaikoroku,* 55.

70. Nomura *Hōsō fūunroku,* , 68–69.

71. Yasko, "Bribery Cases," 64.

72. Hiranuma, *Hiranuma Kiichirō kaikoroku,* 26, 30, 34, 39–40; Yasko, "Hiranuma Kiichirō," 29–32, 35–36.

73. Mc Laren, *Political History,* 369.

74. William J. Sebald, trans., *The Criminal Code of Japan,* 142–148.

75. Richardson and Flanagan, *Politics in Japan,* 22–23.

76. Mason, *First General Election,* 30–31; Tetsuo Najita, *Hara Kei in the Politics of Compromise, 1905–1915,* 59; Edward G. Griffin, "The Universal Suffrage Issue in Japanese Politics, 1918–1925," 275.

77. Peter Duus, *Party Rivalry and Political Change in Taishō Japan,* 19–20.

78. Hirata Naratarō, *Senkyo hanzai no kenkyū: Toku ni baishū hanzai ni tsuite,* 352.

79. Duus, *Party Rivalry,* 21.

80. R. L. Sims, *A Political History of Modern Japan, 1868–1952,* 97–98; Oka, *Five Political Leaders of Modern Japan,* 91; Janet E. Hunter, comp., *Concise Dictionary of Modern Japanese History,* 55.

81. Najita, *Hara Kei,* 15, 61, 77–78.

82. Akita, "The Other Ito," 354.

83. Ibid., 353–354; Najita, *Hara Kei,* 21; Oka, *Five Political Leaders,* 106–108.

84. Scalapino, *Democracy,* 204; Najita, *Hara Kei,* 188–189; Ōshima Tarō, "Shīmensu-Bikkāsu jiken: Tokaku gen'in to natta gunkaku ni yoru kaigun gigoku," 56–57; Kōdansha, *Illustrated Encyclopedia,* 1:1428.

85. Ōshima Tarō, "Shīmensu-Bikkāsu jiken," 56, 59–63; Ohara Naoshi kaikoroku hensankai, *Ohara Naoshi kaikoroku,* 49; Norman S. Hastings, "The Seiyūkai and Party Government in Japan, 1924–1932," 76 n. 53; Aritake Shūji, *Showa no saishō,* 147.

86. Ohara, *Ohara Naoshi kaikoroku,* 52, 60–61; Hiranuma, *Hiranuma Kiichirō kaikoroku,* 82–84.

87. Hastings, "Party Government," 47.

88. Ohara, *Ohara Naoshi kaikoroku,* 52, 60–61; Hiranuma, *Hiranuma Kiichirō kaikoroku,* 82–84; Ōshima Tarō, "Shīmensu-Bikkāsu jiken," 58, 65.

89. Ohara, *Ohara Naoshi kaikoroku*, 69.

90. Hiranuma, *Hiranuma Kiichirō kaikoroku*, 82.

91. Quoted in Eleanor M. Hadley, *Antitrust in Japan*, 42.

92. Ōshima Tarō, "Shīmensu-Bikkāsu jiken," 58.

93. Quoted in Andrew Gordon, *Labor and Imperial Democracy in Prewar Japan*, 40.

94. Quoted in ibid., 56.

95. A. Morgan Young, *Japan in Recent Times, 1912–1926*, 48.

96. Michael Lewis, *Rioters and Citizens: Mass Protest in Imperial Japan*, 5.

97. Najita, *Hara Kei*, 189–190.

98. Joyce C. Lebra, *Ōkuma Shigenobu: Statesman of Meiji Japan*, 116.

99. Najita, *Hara Kei*, 191–194.

100. Scalapino, *Democracy*, 205.

101. Tamiya Hiroshi, "Ōura jiken: Seifu no kōkan to kiso yūyo," 107–109.

102. J. Lebra, *Ōkuma Shigenobu*, 118, 124; Scalapino, *Democracy*, 206–207. On January 23, Ōura ordered Home Ministry personnel to carry out the election in a proper manner based on the law. Taikakai, ed., *Naimushō shi* 4: 382.

103. Tamiya, "Ōura jiken," 109.

104. Duus, *Party Rivalry*, 90; Najita, *Hara Kei*, 200.

105. Hirata, *Senkyo hanzai no kenkyū*, 351.

106. Tamiya, "Ōura jiken," 110; J. Lebra, *Ōkuma Shigenobu*, 124–125.

107. Tamiya, "Ōura jiken," 110, 114, 126, 133.

108. Ibid., 111; Suzuki Kisaburō sensei denki hensankai, *Suzuki Kisaburō*, 77–78.

109. Ibid., 77, 79; Tamiya, "Ōura jiken," 110–112.

110. Quoted in *Suzuki Kisaburō*, 79.

111. Tamiya, "Ōura jiken," 112.

112. J. Lebra, *Ōkuma Shigenobu*, 124, 128; Scalapino, *Democracy*, 207.

113. J. Lebra, *Ōkuma Shigenobu*, 125.

114. Najita, *Hara Kei*, 200.

115. J. Lebra, *Ōkuma Shigenobu*, 124.

116. Imai Seiichi, *Nihon no rekishi*, 23, 75.

117. *Suzuki Kisaburō*, 77.

118. Quoted in Imai Seiichi, *Nihon no rekishi*, 76.

119. Nezu, *Nihon gendai shi*, 209.

120. Murano Ren'ichi and Irokawa Daikichi, *Murano Tsuneemon den: Seiyūkai jidai* 2:83–86.

121. Ozaki Yukio, *Gakudō jiden*, 306–308.

122. Hiranuma, *Hiranuma Kiichirō kaikoroku*, 230–231.

123. Nomura, *Hōsō fūunroku*, 112–113.

124. Izawa Takio denki hensan iinkai, *Izawa Takio*, 115–117.

125. Hayashida, *Nihon seitō shi*, 2: 237.

126. *Suzuki Kisaburō*, 79; Isa Hideo, *Ozaki Yukio*, 198.

127. Aritake Shūji, *Showa no saishō*, 147.

128. Yasko, "Bribery Cases," 67 no. 37.

129. *Suzuki Kisaburō*, 79.

130. Kinbara Samon, *Taishoki no seitō to kokumin*, 75–77.

131. Tamiya, "Ōura jiken," 125.

132. Yasko, "Bribery Cases," 61–62.

133. Hiranuma, *Hiranuma Kiichirō kaikoroku*, 231.

134. See Tsunoda, *Japanese Tradition* 2:217–218.

135. Ibid., 232, 235.

136. John D. Vandenbrink, "State and Industrial Society in Modern Japan: The Liberal Critique, 1916–1926," 81–82.

137. George E. Uyehara, *The Political Development of Japan, 1867–1909*, 273.

138. Quoted in ibid., 258.

Chapter 3: The Era of Party Government

1. Norman S. Hastings, "The Seiyūkai and Party Government in Japan, 1924–1932," 129–130.

2. Quoted in Rikitaro Fujisawa, *The Recent Aims and Political Development of Japan*, 121.

3. Duus, *Party Rivalry*, 107; Sims, *Political History*, 153–154.

4. Tetsuo Najita, *Hara Kei*, 221; Duus, *Party Rivalry*, 136.

5. Quoted in Oka, *Five Political Leaders*, 119.

6. Scalapino, *Democracy*, 278–279.

7. Oka, *Five Political Leaders*, 119.

8. Quoted in ibid.

9. Quoted in ibid., 120.

10. Young, *Japan in Recent Times*, 240–243.

11. Kyoto daigaku bungakubu kokushi kenkyū shitsu, ed., *Nihon kindai shi jiten*, 573.

12. Ibid., 390; Scalapino, *Democracy*, 279.

13. Young, *Japan in Recent Times*, 240–244; Oka, *Five Political Leaders*, 120; Sanseidō henshūjo, ed., *Konsaisu jinmei jiten*, 445–446; Kyoto daigaku, *Nihon kindai shi jiten*, 14.

14. Young, *Japan in Recent Times*, 243.

15. Quoted in Scalapino, *Democracy*, 280.

16. Sharon Minichiello, *Retreat from Reform: Patterns of Political Behavior in Interwar Japan*, 64.

17. Scalapino, *Democracy*, 280.

18. Peter Duus, "Nagai Ryūtarō: The Tactical Dilemmas of Reform," *Personality in Japanese History*, 413.

19. Minichiello, *Retreat from Reform*, 134–135 n. 18.

20. Sims, *Political History*, 143; Hunter, *Modern Japanese History*, 248.

21. Oka, *Five Political Leaders*, 121–122; Sims, *Political History*, 154.

22. Duus, *Party Rivalry*, 199, 202–203; Sims, *Political History*, 159.

23. Mitani Taichirō, "The Establishment of Party Cabinets, 1898–1932," 71; for a complete text of the law, see Fujiike Kinroku, ed., *A Guide to the Imperial Japanese Diet*, 55–86; for Hara Kei's views on changes in 1919, see Mitani, "Party Cabinets," 85.

24. Hayashida Kazuhiro, "Development of Election Law in Japan," 38–39;

Harold S. Quigley, *Japanese Government and Politics: An Introductory Study,* 401–402; Hirata, *Senkyo hanzai no kenkyū,* 13, 17, 20; for the text of the 1925 law, see Quigley, *Japanese Government and Politics,* 401–402.

25. Uchida Mitsuru, "Changing Aspects of Spectatorial Democracy in Japan," 3.

26. Quigley, *Japanese Government and Politics,* 262.

27. Ibid., 257, 262–264.

28. Duus, *Party Rivalry,* 129–130.

29. Quoted in ibid., 130.

30. Tsurumi Yūsuke, "Universal Suffrage Seen as the Antidote to Big Money Elections (1924)," 61, 63.

31. Hastings, "Party Government," 44, 48.

32. Ibid., 78; also see Quigley, *Japanese Government and Politics,* 268–269.

33. Hastings, "Party Government," 48.

34. Ōshima Tarō, "Kunshō—tetsudō gigoku jiken: Seitō seiji ni okeru oshoku no rotei," 312; William F. Morton, *Tanaka Giichi and Japan's China Policy,* 45, 235 n. 36; Scalapino, *Democracy,* 286.

35. Koizumi Terusaburō, *Sanjūkyūken no shinsō: Hiroku Taisho Showa jidai shi,* 156.

36. Ōshima Mitsuko, "Matsushima Yūkaku iten jiken: Riken o meguru seitō no fuhai jiken," 100.

37. Ibid., 106.

38. Richard H. Mitchell, *Janus-Faced Justice: Political Criminals in Imperial Japan,* 44–45; Duus, *Party Rivalry,* 227–228.

39. Ōshima Mitsuko, "Matsushima Yūkaku," 97–98.

40. Ibid., 98–100; Sanseidō, *Konsaisu jinmei jiten,* 1007–1008.

41. Ōshima Mitsuko, "Matsushima Yūkaku," 100, 106, 108; Aritake Shūji, *Showa no saishō,* 44.

42. Kawasaki Takukichi Denki Hensankai, *Kawasaki Takukichi,* 330–332.

43. Ibid., 336–337.

44. Ōshima Mitsuko, "Matsushima Yūkaku," 105–106, 109, 111–112.

45. Hosono Nagamori, *Shisō akka no moto,* 321–322.

46. Shiono Suehiko kaikoroku kankōkai, *Shiono Suehiko kaikoroku,* 246–249, 439. Itō Takashi, *Showa shoki seijishi kenkyū,* 366–367.

47. Richard H. Mitchell, *Thought Control in Prewar Japan,* 82–86, 125.

48. Leonard A. Humphreys, *The Way of the Heavenly Sword: The Japanese Army in the 1920s,* 63, 198–199 n. 69.

49. Ōshima Tarō, "Kunshō," 312–313.

50. Shiono, *Shiono Suehiko kaikoroku,* 259–260.

51. Ibid., 260.

52. Ōshima Tarō, "Kunshō," 316.

53. Ibid., 317–318.

54. *Japan Weekly Chronicle,* July 18, 1935, 81.

55. Ibid.

56. Ogawa Heikichi bunsho kenkyūkai hen, *Ogawa Heikichi kankei bunsho* 1:91.

57. Quoted in ibid., 316.

58. Ibid.

59. Ōshima Tarō, "Kunshō," 320; Sanseidō, *Konsaisu jinmei jiten,* 248.

60. Ibid., 305–311, 313, 316; Shiono, *Shiono Suehiko kaikoroku,* 256, 259.

61. Kyoto daigaku, *Nihon kindai shi jiten,* 45; Sanseidō, *Konsaisu jinmei jiten,* 464.

62. Shiono, *Shiono Suehiko kaikoroku,* 261; Kyoto daigaku, *Nihon kindai shi jiten,* 45.

63. Matsuzaka Hiromasa den kankōkai, *Matsuzaka Hiromasa den,* 48.

64. Ōshima Tarō, "Kunshō," 311.

65. Hosono, *Shisō akka no moto,* 316.

66. Ibid.

67. Ibid., 316–317.

68. Quoted in ibid., 321.

69. Ibid., 322.

70. Shiono, *Shiono Suehiko kaikoroku,* 248–249.

71. Itō Takashi, *Showa shoki seijishi kenkyū,* 373–374.

72. Scalapino, *Democracy,* 288; Sims, *Political History,* 175; Quigley, *Japanese Government and Politics,* 418; Gordon M. Berger, *Parties Out of Power in Japan, 1931–1941,* 33.

73. Sims, *Political History,* 175.

74. Scalapino, *Democracy,* 237 n. 87; Hastings, "Party Government," 107.

75. Hirata, *Senkyo hanzai no kenkyū,* 21.

76. M. D. Kennedy, *The Changing Fabric of Japan,* 169.

77. Quoted in Tiedemann, "Business and Politics," 284.

78. Quoted in ibid., 285 n. 26.

79. Ibid.

80. Sims, *Political History,* 189.

81. Ibid., 178; Scalapino, *Democracy,* 289; Hunter, *Modern Japanese History,* 54, 281; William M. Fletcher III, *The Search for a New Order: Intellectuals and Fascism in Prewar Japan,* 41; idem, *The Japanese Business Community and National Trade Policy, 1920–1942,* 69–71.

82. Tiedemann, *Business and Politics,* 289, 292.

83. Sims, *Political History,* 187; Hane, *Modern Japan,* 252.

84. Quoted in *Japan Weekly Chronicle,* July 6, 1933, 22.

85. Hastings, "Party Government," 93–94, 96, 101–102, 285; Oka, *Five Political Leaders,* 170; Sims, *Political History,* 185–186; Hirata, *Senkyo hanzai no kenkyū,* 681.

86. David A. Sneider, "Action and Oratory: The Trials of the May 15th Incident of 1932," 6, 9, 34.

87. Hirata, *Senkyo hanzai no kenkyū,* 81; Rōyama Masamichi, *Nihon seiji dōkō ron,* 395.

88. Hastings, "Party Government," 44; also see Sheldon Garon, *The State and Labor in Modern Japan,* 148.

89. Hirata, *Senkyo hanzai no kenkyū,* 682.

90. Ibid., 493, 542, 682, 686–687.

91. Ibid., 79, 682.

92. Ibid., 78.

93. Tetsuo Najita, "Some Reflections on Idealism in the Political Thought of Yoshino Sakuzō," 56, 58–59.

94. Ibid., 56–57.

95. Quoted in Harada Kumao, *Fragile Victory: Prince Saionji and the 1930 London Treaty Issue from the Memoirs of Baron Harada Kumao*, 277.

96. Hastings, "Party Government," 79 n. 83; Sanseidō, *Konsaisu jinmei jiten*, 248.

97. Ibid., 464.

98. Ishida Takeshi, "Urbanization and Its Impact on Japanese Politics—A Case Study of a Late and Rapidly Developed Country," 5.

99. Itō Takashi, *Showa shoki seijishi kenkyū*, 353–356, 358–359. Although most books cite 1924 as the establishment date for the Kokuhonsha, Itō Takashi sees it as part of several earlier groups. At any rate, the first issue of *Kokuhon* was published on January 1, 1921. Ibid., 355.

100. Ibid., 361–363, 366–367.

101. Itō Takashi, "Conflicts and Coalitions in Japan, 1930: Political Groups [and] the London Naval Disarmament Conference," 165–166, 168–170, 172–173.

102. Christopher W. A. Szpilman, "The Politics of Cultural Conservatism: The National Foundation Society in the Struggle against Foreign Ideas in Prewar Japan, 1918–1936," 118, 118 n. 4, 122, 124, 126.

103. Quoted in ibid., 130–131.

104. Ibid., 135.

Chapter 4: Purifying Politics

1. Robert M. Spaulding, Jr., "The Bureaucracy as a Political Force, 1920–1945," 61–63; Berger, *Parties Out of Power*, 72.

2. Hirata, *Senkyo hanzai no kenkyū*, 23–24.

3. Hayashida, "Election Law," 7, 39; Gerald L. Curtis, *Election Campaigning Japanese Style*, 213–214; Charles B. Fahs, *Government in Japan: Recent Trends in Its Scope and Operation*, 74.

4. Ibid.

5. Susan B. Weiner, "Bureaucracy and Politics in the 1930s: The Career of Gotō Fumio," 135–137.

6. *Japan Weekly Chronicle*, August 22, 1935, 243; Obinata Sumio, *Tennōsei keisatsu to minshū*, 231.

7. Quoted in Weiner, "Bureaucracy and Politics," 138.

8. Ibid., 146–147.

9. *Japan Weekly Chronicle*, December 26, 1935, 806.

10. Ibid.

11. Quoted in Fletcher, *Search for a New Order*, 99.

12. Ibid., 80, 98.

13. Berger, *Parties Out of Power*, 73.

14. Weiner, "Bureaucracy and Politics," 148.

15. *Japan Weekly Chronicle*, May 14, 1936, 600.

16. Hirata, *Senkyo hanzai no kenkyū*, 79, 492, 682.

17. *Japan Weekly Chronicle*, May 13, 1937, 583.

18. Ibid.

19. Ibid.

20. Berger, *Parties Out of Power,* 74.

21. R. L. Sims, "National Elections and Electioneering in Akita Ken, 1930–1942," 99, 104, 274 n. 30.

22. Itō Takashi, *Showa shi o saguru,* 1:148.

23. *Japan Weekly Chronicle,* August 15, 1935, 211.

24. Ibid., March 26, 1936, 382.

25. Ibid., February 25, 1937, 237; Kazaba Gunzō, head of the Police Bureau, was grilled in the lower house about torture and other violations of human rights during and after the 1936 general election. Obinata, *Tennōsei keisatsu,* 232.

26. *Japan Weekly Chronicle,* May 13, 1937, 583.

27. Kawakami Kan, *Iwayuru jinken jūrin mondai ni tsuite,* 71–82.

28. *Japan Weekly Chronicle,* February 25, 1937, 237.

29. Mitchell, *Janus-Faced Justice,* 136.

30. Richard Storry, *The Double Patriots: A Study of Japanese Nationalism,* 54.

31. Quoted in Hane, *Modern Japan,* 248.

32. Storry, *Double Patriots,* 185–188; Ben-Ami Shillony, *Revolt in Japan: The Young Officers and the February 26, 1936, Incident,* 172–173; Stephen S. Large, *Emperor Hirohito and Showa Japan: A Political Biography,* 68–70.

33. Shillony, *Revolt,* 83–85; Tiedemann, "Business and Politics," 291–292, 296 n. 44, 300 n. 54.

34. Quoted in Tiedemann, "Business and Politics," 296 n. 44.

35. Hastings, "Party Government," 59, 79 n. 59; Shillony, *Revolt,* 89–92.

36. Ōshima Tarō, "Teijin jiken: Shōkanshū o mamotta ishoku no han-ketsu," 60.

37. Tiedemann, "Business and Politics," 295; for information about the attack on Minobe, see Frank O. Miller, *Minobe Tatsukichi: Interpreter of Constitutionalism in Japan,* 196–253.

38. For details about the intimate relationship between the Bank of Taiwan and the Suzuki Trading Company, see Morikawa, *Zaibatsu,* 175–177; for information on the financial panic of 1927, the failure of the Bank of Taiwan, the collapse of the Wakatsuki cabinet, and relief measures by the Diet to resuscitate the Bank of Taiwan, see Chō Yukio, "Exposing the Incompetence of the Bourgeoisie: The Financial Panic of 1927," 497–499.

39. *Japan Weekly Chronicle,* August 12, 1937, 231; Shiono, *Shiono Suehiko kaikoroku,* 259; Ōshima, "Teijin jiken," 310, 316; Akita, "The Other Ito," 352–353.

40. *Japan Weekly Chronicle,* January 3, 1935, 14.

41. Ōshima, "Teijin jiken," 55–56.

42. Ibid., 56–57; *Japan Weekly Chronicle,* January 3, 1935, 15; December 23, 1937, 835; Showa Ōkurashō gaishi kankōkai, *Showa Ōkurashō gaishi,* 571 (cited hereafter as SOG).

43. SOG, 482, 486–488, 492; Kyoto daigaku, *Nihon kindai shi jiten,* 592. As

late as February 1933, a lower house representative was interpellating Justice Minister Koyama Matsukichi on the Meitō tax settlement. *Japan Weekly Chronicle,* February 9, 1933, 188.

44. SOG, 498–499.
45. A. Morgan Young, *Imperial Japan, 1926–1938,* 187.
46. SOG, 517.
47. *Japan Weekly Chronicle,* April 15, 1934, 445.
48. SOG, 517.
49. Ōshima, "Teijin jiken," 57–59; Kawai Yoshinari, *Teijin jiken Sanjūnen-me no shōgen,* 21–22; Vandenbrink, "State and Industrial Society," 147; Kōdansha, *Illustrated Encyclopedia,* 2:1025.
50. Chitoshi Yanaga, *Big Business in Japanese Politics,* 57; *Japan Weekly Chronicle,* August 19, 1937, 270; Takenobu Y., ed., *The Japan Year Book, 1928,* appendix A, 17.
51. SOG, 523–524.
52. Ibid., 519, 521–522; Ōshima, "Teijin jiken," 58, Kawai, 51; Ōuchi Tsutomu, *Nihon no rekishi* 24, 374.
53. *Japan Weekly Chronicle,* January 3, 1935, 15; Ōshima, "Teijin jiken," 59.
54. SOG, 525.
55. Ibid., 573; Ōshima, "Teijin jiken," 59; *Japan Weekly Chronicle,* January 3, 1935, 15.
56. SOG, 526, 594–595.
57. Ibid., 535, 537; Ōshima, "Teijin jiken," 60.
58. Ibid., SOG, 531, 535, 537.
59. *Japan Weekly Chronicle,* December 6, 1934, 771; January 31, 1935, 125.
60. Ibid., January 10, 1935, 31.
61. Ibid., 126; Iwamura Michiyo den kankōkai, *Iwamura Michiyo den,* 88.
62. *Japan Weekly Chronicle,* February 7, 1935, 161.
63. Quoted in ibid.
64. Quoted in ibid., January 31, 1935, 134.
65. Ibid.
66. Ibid., 118.
67. SOG, 536–537, 563, 565, 567, 573, 575; Ōshima, "Teijin jiken," 67; Suzuki Yoshio denki kankōkai, *Suzuki Yoshio,* 101–102; *Japan Weekly Chronicle,* January 17, 1935, 76; June 27, 1935, 837.
68. Ōshima, "Teijin jiken," 52; SOG, 621.
69. *Japan Weekly Chronicle,* July 11, 1935, 48; August 15, 1935, 213.
70 *Suzuki Yoshio,* 406–407, 410, 412.
71. *Japan Weekly Chronicle,* August 15, 1935, 213; September 5, 1935, 310.
72. Ibid., September 12, 1935, 342; September 19, 1935, 374.
73. Quoted in ibid., February 25, 1937, 237.
74. Ibid.
75. Ibid., March 4, 1937, 251.
76. Ibid., May 27, 1937, 656.
77. Ibid., June 17, 1937, 750–751.

78. Ibid., 750.

79. Ibid.

80. Ibid., August 12, 1937, 231.

81. Ibid., August 19, 1937, 270.

82. Ibid., April 22, 1937, 494.

83. Quoted in SOG, 622.

84. Ibid.

85. Quoted in ibid., 621.

86. Matsuzaka, *Matsuzaka Hiromasa den*, 156–158.

87. Ohara, *Ohara Naoshi kaikoroku*, 256.

88. Quoted in ibid., 250.

89. SOG, 582.

90. Ohara, *Ohara Naoshi kaikoroku*, 257.

91. Shiono, *Shiono Suehiko kaikoroku*, 278–280.

92. Nomura, *Hōsō fūunroku*, 2:71.

93. Ibid., 291–293.

94. Morishita Sumio, "Imamura Rikisaburō," 135.

95. Imamura Rikisaburō, *Teijin jiken benron*, 9–10, 117–129, 132–133.

96. Kawai, *Teijin jiken*, 184, 186, 285.

97. Nonaka Moritaka, *Teijin o sabaku*, 11–12.

98. *Japan Weekly Chronicle*, December 23, 1937, 818.

99. Ibid., December 30, 1937, 873; February 3, 1938, 133.

100. Ibid., February 10, 1938, 170.

101. Ibid., February 3, 1938, 142.

102. Ibid., February 24, 1938, 238.

103. Ibid., January 19, 1939, 76.

104. Sanseidō, *Konsaisu jinmei jiten*, 801, 1073; *Japan Weekly Chronicle*, December 30, 1937, 873; Ohara, *Ohara Naoshi kaikoroku*, 474, 491; SOG, 584; Hunter, *Modern Japanese History*, 288, 299, 304; Iwamura, *Iwamura Michiyo den*, 563–569; Shiono, *Shiono Suehiko kaikoroku*, 902; Yanaga, *Big Business*, 56, 60, 93.

105. Ramsdell, *The Japanese Diet*, 47.

106. Murobushi Tetsurō, *Jitsuroku Nihon oshoku shi*, 244; *Japan Weekly Chronicle*, November 12, 1936, 637; March 2, 1939, 256.

107. Ibid.

108. Murobushi, *Jitsuroku Nihon*, 245; *Japan Weekly Chronicle*, August 3, 1939, 144.

109. Murobushi, *Jitsuroku Nihon*, 246–247.

110. Uchida Nobuya, *Fūsetsu gojūnen*, 235–236, 239, 246.

111. Edward J. Drea, "The Japanese General Election of 1942: A Study of Political Institutions in Wartime," 252–253.

112. Scalapino, *Democracy*, 388–389; Harold S. Quigley and John E. Turner, *The New Japan: Government and Politics*, 70–72; Hunter, 67.

113. Berger, *Parties out of Power*, 347.

114. Ibid., 348–349.

115. Drea, "General Election of 1942," 231, 238, 280, 282, 288, 296–298, 302–303, 305; Sims, "National Elections," 106; Ben–Ami Shillony, *Politics and Culture in Wartime Japan*, 23–25.

116. Japan, Prime Minister's Office, Statistics Bureau, ed., *Japan Statistical Yearbook, 1950*, 470.

117. Hadley, *Antitrust*, 42.

Chapter 5: Occupation Era

1. Gerald L. Curtis, *The Japanese Way of Politics*, 7.

2. Joseph A. Massey, "The Occupation of Japan and the Sheriff of Nottingham: The Legacy of Election Reform," 90; Curtis, *Election Campaigning*, 214; Kiyose Ichiro, "The New Election Law," 18, 21; Masumi Junnosuke, *Postwar Politics in Japan, 1945–1955*, 92–93; Hayashida, "Election Law," 40; Supreme Commander for the Allied Powers [hereafter SCAP], Government Section, *Political Reorientation of Japan, September 1945 to September 1948*, 2:832–833.

3. SCAP, *Political Reorientation*, 715.

4. Quoted in Masumi, *Postwar Politics*, 96–97.

5. Kenneth E. Colton, "Pre-war Political Influences in Post-war Conservative Parties," 948.

6. Ibid., 955–956.

7. Robert E. Ward, "Reflections on the Allied Occupation and Planned Political Change in Japan," 513; Curtis, *Japanese Way*, 10.

8. Hayashida, "Election Law," 8, 40; Curtis, *Election Campaigning*, 214.

9. Masumi, *Postwar Politics*, 138–140; T. A. Bisson, *Prospects for Democracy in Japan*, 57; Massey, "Occupation of Japan," 101.

10. SCAP, *The Japanese Elections, April 1947*, 99–100.

11. SCAP, *Political Reorientation*, 1:325, 336.

12. Russel Brines, *MacArthur's Japan*, 208.

13. Bradley Richardson, "Elections," 2:189.

14. Brines, *MacArthur's Japan*, 208.

15. Theodore Cohen, *Remaking Japan: The American Occupation as New Deal*, 338–339; William Costello, *Democracy vs. Feudalism in Post-war Japan*, 158; Bisson, *Prospects*, 113–114. For this report, see SCAP, *Political Reorientation*, 2:728–733.

16. SCAP, *Political Reorientation*, 308–311.

17. Quoted in ibid., 311.

18. T. Cohen, *Remaking Japan*, 343; SCAP, *Political Reorientation*, 1:312–313; Costello, *Democracy vs. Feudalism*, 171, 174; Masumi, *Postwar Politics*, 158.

19. T. Cohen, *Remaking Japan*, 315–316, 322.

20. Ibid., 324–325.

21. Itō Ushirō, "Yoyatō no gyakuten."

22. T. Cohen, *Remaking Japan*, 325.

23. Murobushi Tetsurō, *Sengo gigoku*, 87.

24. Ibid., 85–87.

25. Ibid., 90–91, 93–94, 100–101, 104.

26. Ibid., 99–100, 103.

27. Quoted in ibid., 103.

28. Ibid., 100–103.

29. SCAP, *Political Reorientation,* 1:352.

30. A few weeks after renouncing claim to divine status the emperor visited the Showa Electric Company factory in Kawasaki. This was the first of many trips designed to humanize the god-king. A picture of this visit is facing page 216 of Andrew Gordon, ed., *Postwar Japan as History.*

31. Masumi, *Postwar Politics,* 158–159.

32. Kōdansha, *Japan: An Illustrated Encyclopedia* 1:65.

33. Murobushi Tetsurō, *Sengo gigoku no kao,* 123, 126.

34. Nishio Suehiro, *Nishio Suehiro no seiji oboegaki,* 265.

35. Murobushi, *Sengo gigoku no kao,* 124–125.

36. Nishio, *Seiji oboegaki,* 266–267.

37. Quoted in ibid., 267.

38. Morikawa Tetsurō, *Nihon gigoku shi,* 229–230.

39. Masumi, *Postwar Politics,* 159; Aritake Shūji, *Seiji to kane to jiken to,* 263.

40. Quoted in Masumi, *Postwar Politics,* 137.

41. Ibid., 158.

42. Morikawa Tetsurō, *Nihon gigoku shi,* 230–234, 236–238.

43. Aritake, *Seiji,* 262–263, 267, 270; Harry E. Wildes, *Typhoon in Tokyo: The Occupation and Its Aftermath,* 127, 164; Justin Williams, Sr., *Japan's Political Revolution under MacArthur: A Participant's Account,* 251, Morikawa Tetsurō, *Nihon gigoku shi,* 236, 240; Kōdansha, *Illustrated Encyclopedia,* 1:1414.

44. Williams, *Political Revolution,* 251.

45. Nishio, *Seiji oboegaki,* 264.

46. Masumi, *Postwar Politics,* 159–160.

47. Nishio, *Seiji oboegaki,* 298, 302–304.

48. Ibid., 271–277. Although Hinohara told procurators that the million yen was a bribe, Fujii Takashi insisted it was a political contribution. Katō Hideo states that Hinohara lied. Katō Hideo, *Fūsetsu no hito Nishio Suehiro,* 103.

49. Quoted in Nishio, *Seiji oboegaki,* 265, 271.

50. Japanese Government, Attorney-General's Office, trans., *The Constitution of Japan and Criminal Laws,* 34.

51. Quoted in Tsuji Kan'ichi, *Seijika to iu mono,* 147.

52. Quoted in ibid.

53. Steven R. Reed, "The People Spoke: The Influence of Elections on Japanese Politics, 1949–1955," 319.

54. Sanseidō, *Konsaisu jinmei jiten,* 30, 415, 538, 842, 929; Hunter, *Modern Japanese History,* 310–317, 320; Theodore McNelly, *Contemporary Government of Japan,* 131; Edwin M. Reingold, *Chrysanthemums and Thorns: The Untold Story of Modern Japan,* 247; Morikawa Tetsurō, *Nihon gigoku shi,* 239.

55. SCAP, *Political Reorientation,* 2:1198–1206.

56. Hayashida, "Election Law," 24; Lawrence W. Beer, *Freedom of Expression in Japan: A Study in Comparative Law, Politics, and Society,* 372–374.

57. Curtis, *Election Campaigning,* 214.

58. Ikematsu Fumio, "Political Parties Today and Tomorrow," 390–391, 402.

59. Wildes, *Typhoon in Tokyo*, 127.

60. Herbert Passin, *The Legacy of the Occupation—Japan*, 27–28, 39.

Chapter 6: "New" Japan

1. Akira Kubota, "A Genuine Reform? The June–August 1993 Upheaval in Japanese Politics," 112.

2. Yanaga, *Big Business*, 83–85; 120–122; Masumi, *Postwar Politics*, 248–249, 276–277; Kōdansha, *Illustrated Encyclopedia* 1:888.

3. Morikawa Tetsurō, *Nihon gigoku shi*, 243–244.

4. Ibid., 244–245; Peter J. Herzog, *Japan's Pseudo-Democracy*, 153; Masumi, *Postwar Politics*, 298. Shipbuilding was a key industry targeted for government aid. Wartime losses left Japan with an acute shortage of merchant ships, which were needed to resume trade in the world economy. Tessa Morris-Suzuki, *The Technological Transformation of Japan: From the Seventeenth to the Twenty-first Century*, 187–188.

5. Herzog, *Pseudo-Democracy*, 298; Morikawa Tetsurō, *Nihon gigoku shi*, 246–247.

6. Morikawa Tetsurō, *Nihon gigoku shi*, 247; Kishimoto Yoshihiro tsuisōroku kankōkai, *Kishimoto Yoshihiro tsuisōroku*, 216. Murobushi, *Sengo gigoku*, 136.

7. Morikawa Tetsurō, *Nihon gigoku shi*, 251–252; Herzog, *Pseudo-Democracy*, 154.

8. Morikawa Tetsurō, *Nihon gigoku shi*, 252; Wildes, *Typhoon in Tokyo*, 141–142.

9. Morikawa Tetsurō, *Nihon gigoku shi*, 264; Aritake, *Seiji*, 289–290; Masumi, *Postwar Politics*, 298–299; Murobushi, *Sengo gigoku*, 166–167, 173.

10. Kishimoto, *Kishimoto Yoshihiro tsuisōroku*, 216; Morikawa Tetsurō, *Nihon gigoku shi*, 264; Murobushi, *Sengo gigoku*, 135–136, 170.

11. Yanaga, *Big Business*, 128–130; Lloyd A. Free, *The Dynamics of Influence in Today's Japan*, 1.

12. Allan B. Cole and Naomichi Nakanishi, eds., *Japanese Opinion Polls with Socio-Political Significance, 1947–1957* 1:164, 167.

13. Yanaga, *Big Business*, 129.

14. Free, *Dynamics of Influence*, 11.

15. Frank C. Langdon, "Part IV: Japan," 177–178.

16. Ibid., 178.

17. Chapman, *Inventing Japan*, 158.

18. Ibid.; Karel van Wolferen, *The Enigma of Japanese Power: People and Politics in a Stateless Nation*, 133.

19. Yoshida Shigeru, *The Yoshida Memoirs: The Story of Japan in Crisis*, 98–99.

20. B. J. George, Jr., "Discretionary Authority of Public Prosecutors in Japan," 61–62; Arthur T. von Mehren, "Commentary: Part II," 427–428.

21. Aritake, *Seiji*, 287–288.

22. Ushiomi Toshitaka, "The Prosecution at the Crossroads," 84–85.

23. Nomura, *Hōsō fūunroku,* 1:84.
24. Ibid., 2:223.
25. Ibid., 355, 369–370.
26. Masumi Junnosuke, "The 1955 System in Japan and Its Subsequent Development," 300.
27. Nobuo Tomita, Akira Nakamura, and Ronald J. Hrebenar, "The Liberal Democratic Party: The Ruling Party of Japan," 258–259.
28. Masumi, "The 1955 System in Japan," 292, 295.
29. Hans H. Baerwald, "Tento-Mura: At the Making of a Cabinet," 70–73; Herzog, *Pseudo-Democracy,* 158.
30. Marshall E. Dimock, *The Japanese Technocracy: Management and Government in Japan,* 85; Curtis, *Election Campaigning,* 28.
31. Haruhiro Fukui, "Postwar Politics, 1945–1973," 6:192, 195, 198, 210.
32. Masumi, "The 1995 System in Japan," 302–303.
33. Chalmers Johnson, "Tanaka Kakuei, Structural Corruption, and the Advent of Machine Politics in Japan," 11.
34. Michael K. Blaker, ed., *Japan at the Polls: The House of Councillors Election of 1974,* i.
35. Chapman, *Inventing Japan,* 159.
36. Herbert Passin, "The House of Councillors: Promise and Achievement," 34.
37. Ibid.; Blaker, *Japan at the Polls,* ii.
38. Johnson, "Machine Politics," 12; James L. Huffman, "The Idioms of Contemporary Japan XI," 509–511, 513; Takako Kishima, *Political Life in Japan: Democracy in a Reversible World,* 102, 104, 137.
39. Ronald J. Hrebenar, "The Money Base of Japanese Politics," 66–67; Johnson, "Machine Politics," 12; Huffman, "Idioms," 509–511.
40. Quoted in Hrebenar, "Money Base," 67.
41. Ibid.
42. Ibid., 68–69.
43. Kishimoto Kōichi, *Politics in Modern Japan: Development and Organization,* 137.
44. Curtis, *Japanese Way,* 164.
45. Ibid.
46. Ibid., 181. Kishimoto, *Politics in Modern Japan,* 137; Kōdansha, *Illustrated Encyclopedia,* 2:1212.
47. Taketsugu Tsurutani, "The LDP in Transition? Mass Membership Participation in Party Leadership Selection," 848.
48. Ibid.
49. Ibid., 851–852.
50. Ibid., 852–853.
51. Ibid., 856.
52. Herzog, *Pseudo-Democracy,* 161, 163–164; Johnson, "Machine Politics," 15.
53. David Boulton, *The Lockheed Papers,* 45, 241–250.
54. Herzog, *Pseudo-Democracy,* 163–167; Johnson, "Machine Politics," 15.
55. Herzog, *Pseudo-Democracy,* 168–170.

56. Johnson, "Machine Politics," 15.
57. Kōdansha, *Illustrated Encyclopedia*, 1:888; Johnson, "Machine Politics," 19.
58. Hrebenar, "Money Base," 64; Johnson, "Machine Politics," 16.
59. Hertzog, *Pseudo-Democracy*, 157.
60. Ibid., 175.
61. Ibid., 178; Yayama, "The Recruit Scandal," 101; William J. Holstein, *The Japanese Power Game: What It Means for America*, 110; Kōdansha, *Illustrated Encyclopedia*, 2:1248.
62. James W. White, "The Dynamics of Political Opposition," 446.
63. Herzog, *Pseudo-Democracy*, 186, 188.
64. Holstein, *Power Game*, 125; *Liberal Star*, June 15, 1989, 1, 3.
65. Quoted in *Liberal Star*, June 15, 1989, 1.
66. Holstein, *Power Game*, 125–127; Kubota, "Genuine Reform?" 96.
67. Holstein, *Power Game*, 131–132; Chalmers Johnson, "The People Who Invented the Mechanical Nightingale," 83.
68. Kenji Hayao, *The Japanese Prime Minister and Public Policy*, 93.
69. Scott C. Flanagan, "The Changing Japanese Voter and the 1989 and 1990 Elections," 445–446.
70. Quoted in *Liberal Star*, November 15, 1989, 2.
71. Ibid., March 15, 1990, 1.
72. Flanagan, "Changing Japanese Voter," 458–461.
73. Igarashi Akio, book review of *Jimintō: Chōki shihai no kōzō*, 21–23.
74. *Liberal Star*, February 15, 1991, 4; July 15, 1991, 2; August–September, 1991, 1; October 15, 1991, 2–3; November 15, 1991, 1; December 15, 1991, 3; April 15, 1992, 1; August–September, 1992, 1.
75. Herzog, *Pseudo-Democracy*, 189, 268; "Lurching toward Realignment," 6; Mizuguchi Hiroshi, "Political Reform: Much Ado about Nothing?" 253.
76. Quoted in *Liberal Star*, October 15, 1992, 2.
77. Ibid., November 15, 1992, 2.
78. Paul Blustein, "No Wonder U.S. Firms Couldn't Win: Rigged Contracts in Japan Shut Out Others," 19; Mizuguchi, "Political Reform," 253.
79. Kubota, "Genuine Reform?" 97.
80. "Lurching toward Realignment," 7; Kubota, 93.
81. Ibid., 93, 98.
82. *New York Times*, July 19, 1993, A1, A9.
83. Ibid., July 30, 1994, A1, A5.
84. *Japan Times*, January 30, 1994, 1, 3.
85. Paul Blustein, "In Japan, Will One Reform Beget Another? A Political Cleanup May Lead Economic Change," 16.
86. *Economist*, April 16, 1994, 16.
87. *Wall Street Journal*, January 31, 1994, A9.
88. Quoted in ibid.
89. *New York Times*, April 11, 1994, A3,; *Newsweek*, April 18, 1994, 31; Kubota, "Genuine Reform?" 123 n. 37.
90. *New York Times*, April 26, 1994, A1; *Newsweek*, July 4, 1994, 49.
91. *New York Times*, June 30, 1994, A1.

92. Ibid., A12.
93. *U.S. News and World Report,* July 11, 1994, 15.
94. *New York Times,* July 1, 1994, A3.
95. Chalmers Johnson, *Japan: Who Governs? The Rise of the Developmental State,* 219.
96. Robert C. Angel, "Implications of Japan's July 1993 General Election: 'The People Have Mumbled,' " unpublished paper, 5.
97. Ozawa, *Blueprint,* 23–24.
98. Ibid., 24–25.
99. Ibid., 29.
100. Ibid., 68–70.
101. Maruyama Masao, *Thought and Behaviour in Modern Japanese Politics,* 127.
102. Johnson, *Who Governs?* 231.
103. Yamaguchi Jirō, "The Book Forum of Political Reform," 4–5.
104. Quoted in Johnson, *Who Governs?* 226.
105. Ibid., 228.

Conclusion

1. Hiranuma, *Hiranuma Kiichirō kaikoroku,* 231.
2. Kōdansha, *Illustrated Encyclopedia,* 2:1368–1369; Yamamoto, *Shinbun kisha no tanjō,* 255.
3. Quoted in Tsunoda, *Japanese Tradition,* 2:140.
4. Japan, Ministry of Justice, Research and Training Institute, *Summary of the White Paper on Crime 1980,* 18. Judges are partial to suspended sentences in all criminal cases. See John O. Haley, *Authority without Power: Law and the Japanese Paradox,* 128–129.
5. Quoted in Najita, "Reflections on Idealism," 56.
6. Quoted in Haley, *Authority without Power,* 172–173.
7. Nathaniel B. Thayer, *How the Conservatives Rule Japan,* 26–27.
8. Quoted in ibid., 27.
9. Kubota, "Genuine Reform?" 109–110.
10. Richardson and Flanagan, *Politics in Japan,* 186.
11. Gary D. Allinson, "Politics in Contemporary Japan: Pluralist Scholarship in the Conservative Era—A Review Article," 331.
12. Chalmers Johnson, *MITI and the Japanese Miracle: The Growth of Industrial Policy, 1925–1975,* 39.
13. B. C. Koh, *Japan's Administrative Elite,* 229.
14. Ibid.
15. Ibid., 227–229.
16. Calman, *Japanese Imperialism,* 252–275.
17. Herzog, *Pseudo-Democracy,* 154–155.
18. Japan, *White Paper,* 18.
19. *New York Times,* February 17, 1994, A8.
20. Quoted in ibid.
21. Tamiya, "Ōura jiken," 112.
22. Mamoru Iga and Morton Auerbach, "Political Corruption and Social Structure in Japan," 558–560.

23. Ibid., 560.

24. Quoted in Hattori Takaaki, "The Legal Profession in Japan: Its Historical Development and Present State," 125 n. 50.

25. Yayama, "The Recruit Scandal," 93, 95–96.

26. Herzog, *Pseudo-Democracy*, 164, 269.

27. Karl Dixon, "Japan's Lockheed Scandal: 'Structural Corruption,' " 340.

28. Murobushi, *Jitsuroku Nihon*, 302, 309.

29. Herzog, *Pseudo-Democracy*, 152. The entry under "political corruption" in Kōdansha's *Illustrated Encyclopedia*, 2:1211, focuses exclusively on postwar corruption.

30. Ben-Dor, "Corruption, Institutionalization, and Political Development," 63–82; Arnold J. Heidenheimer, ed., *Political Corruption: Readings in Comparative Analysis*.

31. Quoted in Dixon, "Lockheed Scandal," 359–360.

32. R. P. G. Steven, "Hybrid Constitutionalism in Prewar Japan," 100.

33. Ibid., 114–115, 117, 119.

34. Ibid., 123–124.

35. Ibid., 132.

36. van Wolferen, *Enigma*, 5.

37. Ibid., 41.

38. Richardson and Flanagan, *Politics in Japan*, 100–105, 182.

39. Ibid., 182.

40. Harumi Befu, "Gift-Giving in a Modernizing Japan," 445, 450; also see Takie S. Lebra, *Japanese Patterns of Behavior*, 96–101.

41. Iga and Auerbach, "Political Corruption," 559–560.

42. Ibid., 563.

43. Harumi Befu, "From 'Bribery in Japan: When Law Tangles with Culture,' " 87, 92.

44. Williams, *Political Revolution*, 252.

45. Mayfair Mei-hui Yang, *Gifts, Favors, and Banquets: The Art of Social Relationships in China*, 217; N.H.K., *The First Emperor*, December 1994. This TV program was about the discovery of more than nineteen hundred bamboo strips in the grave of a Ch'in dynasty official. On these strips are orders from both the emperor and local government heads. Thus, for the first time, there are details about the Ch'in legal code and orders to officials.

46. Wallace Johnson, trans., *The T'ang Code*, vol. 1: *General Principles*, 23, 27, 127, 133–135, 206, 238, 278.

47. Etienne Balazs, *Chinese Civilization and Bureaucracy: Variations on a Theme*, ed. Arthur F. Wright, 12.

48. Ibid., 10.

49. Ibid., 223, 282; James T. C. Liu, *Reform in Sung China: Wang An-shih (1021–1086) and His New Policies*, 60, 80–85.

50. John R. Watt, *The District Magistrate in Late Imperial China*, 129–131.

51. Ibid., 209.

52. Kung-ch'uan Hsiao, *Rural China: Imperial Control in the Nineteenth Century*, 257.

53. Watt, *District Magistrate*, 171; Thomas A. Metzger, *The Internal Organi-*

zation of Ch'ing Bureaucracy: Legal, Normative, and Communication Aspects, 323 n. 82; George T. Staunton, trans., *Ta Tsing Leu Lee . . . Penal Code of China,* 379–382, 384–385.

54. Metzger, *Ch'ing Bureaucracy,* 323 n. 82.

55. O. Edmund Clubb, *Twentieth-Century China,* 75–77, 274; Gunnar Myrdal, *Asian Drama: An Inquiry into the Poverty of Nations* 2:938 n. 1.

56. Ibid.

57. Perry Link, *Evening Chats in Beijing: Probing China's Predicament,* 53, 55.

58. Quoted in ibid., 58.

59. Quoted in ibid.

60. Ibid.

61. Lena H. Sun, "High Anxiety: China Is Stressed by the Challenge of Change," 17.

62. Lena H. Sun, "Seeds of Revolt Sprouting among China's Peasants," 18.

63. *New York Times,* March 29, 1995, A1; July 15, 1995, A6.

64. For China, see Ichisada Miyazaki, *China's Examination Hell: The Civil Service Examinations of Imperial China,* 62–63, 120–121; Ping-ti Ho, *The Ladder of Success in Imperial China: Aspects of Social Mobility, 1368–1911,* 191–192; Mary C. Wright, *The Last Stand of Chinese Conservatisim: The T'ung-Chih Restoration, 1862–1874,* 81, 89–90.

65. Rance P. L. Lee, "The Folklore of Corruption in Hong Kong," 358.

66. John W. Hall, "The Confucian Teacher in Tokugawa Japan," 287, 290.

67. Ibid., 292.

68. James B. Palais, *Politics and Policy in Traditional Korea,* 12–13; Bong-Duck Chun et al., *Traditional Korean Legal Attitudes,* 25.

69. Pyong-choon Hahm, *The Korean Political Tradition and Law: Essays in Korean Law and Legal History,* 66–67.

70. Laurel Kendall, "Death and Taxes: A Korean Approach to Hell," 8.

71. Jung-en Woo, *Race to the Swift: State and Finance in Korean Industrialization,* 9, 81, 83–84.

72. *Korea Focus on Current Topics* 1:126–127, 129.

73. Ibid., 2:107.

74. William B. Gwyn, *Democracy and the Cost of Politics in Britain,* 12.

75. Quoted in ibid.

76. Quoted in ibid., 13.

77. Ibid., 19.

78. Ibid., 68–69, 72.

79. Quoted in ibid., 72.

80. Ibid., 85; R. K. Webb, *Modern England: From the Eighteenth Century to the Present,* 395.

81. Webb, *Modern England,* 326–327, 394–396.

82. Ibid. 396; Gwyn, *Democracy,* 89–91.

83. Gwyn, *Democracy,* 90.

84. Ibid., 92.

85. Ibid., 90 n. 1.

86. Edward S. Corwin, *The Constitution and What It Means Today,* 68.

87. Noonan, *Bribes,* 433.

88. Ibid., 434, 451, 453–455.

89. John M. Blum et al., *The National Experience: A History of the United States to 1877,* pt. 1, 405.

90. Morton Keller, "Corruption in America: Continuity and Change," 12.

91. John M. Blum et al., *The National Experience: A History of the United States since 1865,* pt. 2, 414; John A. Garraty, *A Short History of the American Nation,* 390; Noonan, *Bribes,* 526–534, 564.

92. Blum, *National Experience,* pt. 2, 627–628; Noonan, *Bribes,* 566.

93. Noonan, *Bribes,* 566–567.

94. Ibid., 568–569.

95. Ibid., 575.

96. Ibid., 601–619.

97. Ibid., 625–637, 677–678.

98. Ibid., 705.

99. Ibid., 604.

100. Kyoji Wakata, "Japanese Diet Members: Social Background, General Values, and Role Perception," 210.

101. J. A. A. Stockwin, "Factionalism in Japanese Political Parties," 165.

102. Raymond V. Christensen, "Electoral Reform in Japan: How It Was Enacted and Changes It May Bring," 605.

103. Myrdal, *Asian Drama,* 2:940.

104. Ibid.

105. Ibid.

106. Ibid., 941.

Bibliography

Akita, George. *Foundations of Constitutional Government in Modern Japan, 1868–1900.* Cambridge, Mass.: Harvard University Press, 1967.

———. "The Meiji Constitution in Practice: The First Diet." *Journal of Asian Studies* 22 (November 1962): 31–46.

———. "The Other Ito: A Political Failure." In *Personality in Japanese History,* ed. Albert M. Craig and Donald H. Shively. Berkeley: University of California Press, 1970.

Allinson, Gary D. "Politics in Contemporary Japan: Pluralist Scholarship in the Conservative Era—A Review Article." *Journal of Japanese Studies* 48 (May 1989): 324–332.

Amemiya Shōichi. "Nittō jiken: Oshoku jiken to kensatsuken no kakudai" (Nittō incident: Corruption incident and the expansion of procuratorial power). In *Nihon seiji saiban shiroku, Meijikō* (A history of political trials in Japan, latter Meiji), ed. Wagatsuma Sakae. Tokyo: Daiichi hōki shuppan kabushikikaisha, 1969.

Arai, Hakuseki. *Told Round a Brushwood Fire: The Autobiography of Arai Hakuseki.* Trans. Joyce Ackroyd. Princeton, N.J.: Princeton University Press, 1979.

Aritake Shūji. *Seiji to kane to jiken to* (Politics, money, incidents . . .). Tokyo: Keizai ōraisha, 1970.

———. *Showa no saishō* (Showa prime ministers). Tokyo: Asahi shinbunsha, 1967.

Backus, Robert L. "Matsudaira Sadanobu as a Moralist and Litterateur." Ph.D. dissertation, University of California, 1963.

Baerwald, Hans H. *Japan's Parliament: An Introduction.* London: Cambridge University Press, 1974.

———. "Tento-Mura: At the Making of a Cabinet." In *Cases in Comparative Politics: Asia,* ed. Lucian W. Pye. Boston, Mass.: Little, Brown, 1970.

Balazs, Etienne. *Chinese Civilization and Bureaucracy: Variations on a Theme.* Trans. H. M. Wright. New Haven, Conn.: Yale University Press, 1964.

Banno, Junji. *The Establishment of the Japanese Constitutional System.* Trans. J. A. A. Stockwin. London: Routledge, 1992.

Beer, Lawrence W. *Freedom of Expression in Japan: A Study in Comparative Law, Politics, and Society.* Tokyo: Kōdansha International, 1984.

Befu, Harumi. "From 'Bribery in Japan: When Law Tangles with Culture.' " In *The Self and the System: A View from the East,* ed. Elinor Lenz and Rita Riley. Los Angeles, Calif.: U.C.L.A. Extension, 1975.

————. "Gift-Giving in a Modernizing Japan." *Monumenta Nipponica* 23 (Winter 1968): 445–456.

Ben-Dor, Gabriel. "Corruption, Institutionalization, and Political Development: The Revisionist Theses Revisited." *Comparative Political Studies* 7 (April 1974): 63–83.

Berger, Gordon N. *Parties Out of Power in Japan, 1931–1941.* Princeton, N.J.: Princeton University Press, 1977.

Bisson, T. A. *Prospects for Democracy in Japan.* New York: Macmillan, 1949.

Blakemore, Thomas L., trans. *The Criminal Code of Japan (1947).* Tokyo: Nippon Hyoronsha, 1950.

Blaker, Michael K., ed. *Japan at the Polls: The House of Councillors Election of 1974.* Washington, D.C.: American Enterprise Institute for Public Policy Research, 1976.

Blum, John M., et al., eds. *The National Experience: A History of the United States to 1877.* Pt. 1. Orlando, Fl.: Harcourt Brace Jovanovich, 1985.

————. *The National Experience: A History of the United States since 1865.* Pt. 2. Orlando, Fl.: Harcourt Brace Jovanovich, 1985.

Blustein, Paul. "In Japan, Will One Reform Beget Another? A Political Cleanup May Lead Economic Change." *Washington Post National Weekly Edition,* February 7–13, 1994, 16.

————. "No Wonder U.S. Firms Couldn't Win: Rigged Contracts in Japan Shut Out Others." *Washington Post National Weekly Edition,* May 17–32, 1993, 19–22.

Bodart-Bailey, Beatrice. "Councillor Defended: *Matsukage Nikki* and Yanagisawa Yoshiyasu." *Monumenta Nipponica* 34 (Winter 1979): 467–478.

Boulton, David. *The Lockheed Papers.* London: Jonathan Cape, 1978.

Braisted, William R. trans. *Meiroku Zasshi: Journal of the Japanese Enlightenment.* University of Tokyo Press, 1976.

Brines, Russel. *MacArthur's Japan.* Philadelphia, Pa.: J. B. Lippincott, 1948.

Brownlee, John S. "The Jeweled Comb-Box: Motoori Norinaga's *Tamakushige.*" *Monumenta Nipponica* 43 (Spring 1988): 35–61.

Calman, Donald. *The Nature and Origins of Japanese Imperialism: A Reinterpretation of the Great Crisis of 1873.* London: Routledge, 1992.

Chapman, William. *Inventing Japan: The Making of a Postwar Civilization.* New York: Prentice-Hall, 1991.

Ch'en, Paul Heng-chao. *The Formation of the Early Meiji Legal Order: The Japanese Code of 1871 and Its Chinese Foundation.* Oxford: Oxford University Press, 1981.

Chō, Yukio. "Exposing the Incompetence of the Bourgeoisie: The Financial Panic of 1927." *Japan Interpreter* 8 (Winter 1974): 492–501.

Christensen, Raymond V. "Electoral Reform in Japan: How It Was Enacted and Changes It May Bring." *Asian Survey* 34 (July 1994): 589–605.

Chun, Bong-Duck, et al. *Traditional Korean Legal Attitudes.* Berkeley: Institute of East Asian Studies, University of California, 1980.

Clubb, O. Edmund. *Twentieth-Century China.* New York: Columbia University Press, 1964.

Cohen, Jerome A. "Japan's Watergate: Made in U.S.A." *New York Times Magazine,* November 21, 1976, 37, 104–119.

Cohen, Theodore. *Remaking Japan: The American Occupation as New Deal.* Ed. Herbert Passin. New York: Free Press, 1987.

Cole, Alan B., and Naomichi Nakanishi, eds. *Japanese Opinion Polls with Socio-Political Significance, 1947–1957.* Vol. 1. Boston: Tufts University Press, 1962.

Colton, Kenneth E. "Pre-war Political Influences in Post-war Conservative Parties." *American Political Science Review* 42 (October 1948): 940–957.

Corwin, Edward S. *The Constitution and What It Means Today.* Princeton, N.J.: Princeton University Press, 1930.

Costello, William. *Democracy vs. Feudalism: In Post-war Japan.* Tokyo: Itagaki Shoten, 1948.

Crawcour, E. S. "Kawamura Zuiken, A Seventeenth-Century Entrepreneur." *Transactions of the Asiatic Society of Japan,* 3d ser., 9 (1966): 28–50.

Curtis, Gerald L. "Big Business and Political Influence." In *Modern Japanese Organization and Decision-Making,* ed. Ezra F. Vogel. Berkeley: University of California Press, 1975.

———. *Election Campaigning Japanese Style.* New York: Columbia University Press, 1971.

———. *The Japanese Way of Politics.* New York: Columbia University Press, 1988.

Dimock, Marshall E. *The Japanese Technocracy: Management and Government in Japan.* New York: Walker/Weather Hill, 1968.

Dixon, Karl. "Japan's Lockheed Scandal: 'Structural Corruption.' " *Pacific Community* 8 (1977): 340–362.

Dower, John W. *Origins of the Modern Japanese State: Selected Writings of E. H. Norman.* New York: Pantheon, 1975.

Drea, Edward J. "The Japanese General Election of 1942: A Study of Political Institutions in Wartime." Ph.D. dissertation, University of Kansas, 1978.

Duus, Peter. "Nagai Ryūtarō: The Tactical Dilemmas of Reform." In *Personality in Japanese History,* eds. Albert M. Craig and Donald H. Shively. Berkeley: University of California Press, 1970.

———. *Party Rivalry and Political Change in Taishō Japan.* Cambridge, Mass.: Harvard University Press, 1968.

Economist. 1994.

Elliot, Michael. "Corruption." *Newsweek,* November 14, 1994.

Fahs, Charles B. *Government in Japan: Recent Trends in Its Scope and Operation.* New York: Institute of Pacific Relations, 1940.

Flanagan, Scott C. "The Changing Japanese Voter and the 1989 and 1990 Elections." In *The Japanese Voter,* ed. Scott C. Flanagan et al. New Haven, Conn.: Yale University Press, 1991.

Fletcher, William M., III. *The Japanese Business Community and National Trade Policy, 1920–1942.* Chapel Hill: University of North Carolina Press, 1989.

————. *The Search for a New Order: Intellectuals and Fascism in Prewar Japan.* Chapel Hill: University of North Carolina Press, 1982.

Fraser, Andrew. "The Expulsion of Okuma from the Government in 1881." *Journal of Asian Studies* 26 (February 1967): 213–236.

————. "The House of Peers (1890–1905): Structure, Groups and Role." In *Japan's Early Parliaments, 1890–1905: Structure, Issues and Trends,* ed. Andrew Frazer et al. London: Routledge, 1995.

Free, Lloyd A. *The Dynamics of Influence in Today's Japan.* Princeton, N.J.(?): Research Council, 1954.

Fujiike, Kinroku, ed. *A Guide to the Imperial Japanese Diet.* Tokyo: Fujiike Kinroku, 1905.

Fujisawa, Rikitaro. *The Recent Aims and Political Development of Japan.* New Haven, Conn.: Yale University Press, 1923.

Fukui, Haruhiro. "Postwar Politics, 1945–1973." In *The Cambridge History of Japan.* Vol. 6: *The Twentieth Century,* ed. Peter Duus. New York: Cambridge University Press, 1988.

Garon, Sheldon. *The State and Labor in Modern Japan.* Berkeley: University of California Press, 1987.

Garraty, John A. *A Short History of the American Nation.* New York: Harper and Row, 1985.

George, Jr., B. J. "Discretionary Authority of Public Prosecutors in Japan." *Law in Japan: An Annual* 17 (1984): 42–72.

Gluck, Carol. *Japan's Modern Myths: Ideology in the Late Meiji Period.* Princeton, N.J.: Princeton University Press, 1985.

Gordon, Andrew. *Labor and Imperial Democracy in Prewar Japan.* Berkeley: University of California Press, 1991.

————, ed. *Postwar Japan as History.* Berkeley: University of California Press, 1993.

Griffin, Edward G. "The Universal Suffrage Issue in Japanese Politics, 1918–1925." *Journal of Asian Studies* 31 (February 1972): 275–290.

Grossberg, Kenneth A. *Japan's Renaissance: The Politics of the Muromachi Bakufu.* Cambridge, Mass.: Harvard University Press, 1981.

Grossberg, Kenneth A., ed. *The Laws of the Muromachi Bakufu: Kemmu Shikimoku (1336) and Muromachi Bakufu Tsuikahō.* Tokyo: Sophia University Press, 1981.

Gwyn, William B. *Democracy and the Cost of Politics in Britain.* London: University of London, 1962.

Hackett, Roger. *Yamagata Aritomo in the Rise of Modern Japan, 1838–1922.* Cambridge, Mass.: Harvard University Press, 1971.

Hadley, Eleanor. *Antitrust in Japan.* Princeton, N.J.: Princeton University Press, 1970.

Hahm, Pyong-choon. *The Korean Political Tradition and Law: Essays in Korean Law and Legal History.* Seoul: Hollym, 1971.

Haley, John O. *Authority without Power: Law and the Japanese Paradox.* Oxford: Oxford University Press, 1991.

Hall, J. C. "The Tokugawa Legislation, I." *Transactions of the Asiatic Society of Japan* 38 (1911): 269–331.

———. "The Tokugawa Legislation, IV." *Transactions of the Asiatic Society of Japan* 41 (1913): 683–804 plus unnumbered pages.

Hall, John W. "The Confucian Teacher in Tokugawa Japan." In *Confucianism in Action*, eds. David S. Nivison and Arthur F. Wright. Stanford, Calif.: Stanford University Press, 1959.

———. *Government and Local Power in Japan, 500–1700: A Study Based on Bizen Province*. Princeton, N.J.: Princeton University Press, 1966.

———. *Tanuma Okitsugu, 1719–1788: Forerunner of Modern Japan*. Cambridge, Mass.: Harvard University Press, 1955.

Hane, Mikiso. *Modern Japan: A Historical Survey*. Boulder, Colo.: Westview, 1992.

Harada, Kumao. *Fragile Victory: Prince Saionji and the 1930 London Naval Treaty Issue from the Memoirs of Baron Harada Kumao*. Trans. Thomas F. Mayer-Oakes. Detroit, Mich.: Wayne State University Press, 1968.

Hastings, Norman S. "The Seiyūkai and Party Government in Japan, 1924–1932." Ph.D. dissertation, University of Kansas, 1977.

Hattori, Takaaki. "The Legal Profession in Japan: Its Historical Development and Present State." In *Law in Japan: The Legal Order in a Changing Society*, ed. Arthur von Mehren. Cambridge, Mass.: Harvard University Press, 1963.

Havens, Thomas R. H. *Nishi Amane and Modern Japanese Thought*. Princeton, N.J.: Princeton University Press, 1970.

Hayao, Kenji. *The Japanese Prime Minister and Public Policy*. Pittsburgh, Pa.: University of Pittsburgh Press, 1993.

Hayashida Kametarō. *Nihon seitō shi* (A history of Japanese political parties). Vol. 2. Tokyo: Dai Nihon yūbenkai kōdansha, 1927.

Hayashida, Kazuhiro. "Development of Election Law in Japan." *Hōsei-Kenkyū: Journal of Law and Politics* 34 (July 1967): 1–53.

Heidenheimer, Arnold J., ed. *Political Corruption: Readings in Comparative Analysis*. New York: Holt, Rinehart and Winston, 1970.

Herzog, Peter J. *Japan's Pseudo-Democracy*. New York: New York University Press, 1993.

Hiramatsu, Yoshirō. "Summary of Tokugawa Criminal Justice." Trans. Daniel H. Foote. *Law in Japan: An Annual* 22 (1989): 105–128.

Hiranuma Kiichirō kaikoroku hensan iinkai. *Hiranuma Kiichirō kaikoroku* (The memoirs of Hiranuma Kiichirō). Tokyo: Gakuyō shobō, 1955.

Hirata Naratarō. *Senkyo hanzai no kenkyū: Toku ni baishū hanzai ni tsuite* (A study on election crimes: Especially the crime of bribery). In *Shihō kenkyū* (Justice research) 19 (March 1935). Shihōshō chōsaka (Justice Ministry, research section).

Ho, Ping-ti. *The Ladder of Success in Imperial China: Aspects of Social Mobility, 1368–1911*. New York: Columbia University Press, 1962.

Holstein, William J. *The Japanese Power Game: What It Means for America*. New York: Charles Scribner's Sons, 1990.

Hosono Nagamori. *Shisō akka no moto* (The roots of becoming red). Tokyo: Ganshōdō, 1930.

Hrebenar, Ronald J. "The Money Base of Japanese Politics." In *The Japanese Party System*, ed. Ronald J. Hrebenar. Boulder, Colo.: Westview, 1992.

Hsiao, Kung-ch'uan. *Rural China: Imperial Control in the Nineteenth Century.* Seattle: University of Washington Press, 1960.

Huffman, James L. "The Idioms of Contemporary Japan XI." *Japan Interpreter: A Quarterly Journal of Social and Political Ideas* 9 (Spring 1975): 505–515.

Humphreys, Leonard A. *The Way of the Heavenly Sword: The Japanese Army in the 1920s.* Stanford, Calif.: Stanford University Press, 1995.

Hunter, Janet E., comp. *Concise Dictionary of Modern Japanese History.* Berkeley: University of California Press, 1984.

Ienaga Saburō and Tsukishima Hiroshi. "Kenpō Jūnanajō" (The seventeen-article constitution). In *Nihon shisō taikei: Shōtoku Taishi shū* (Systematization of Japanese thought: Shōtoku Taishi collection), comp. Ienaga Saburō, Fujieda Akira, Hayashima Kyōshō, and Tsukishima Hiroshi. Tokyo: Iwanami shoten, 1975.

Iga, Mamoru, and Morton Auerbach. "Political Corruption and Social Structure in Japan." *Asian Survey* 18 (June 1977): 556–564.

Igarashi, Akio. Book review of *Jimintō: Chōki shihai no kōzō. Japan Foundation Newsletter* 18 (January 1991): 21–23.

Ikematsu, Fumio. "Political Parties Today and Tomorrow." *Contemporary Japan* 21, nos. 7–9 (1952): 390–400.

Imai Seiichi. *Nihon no rekishi* (A history of Japan). Vol. 23. Tokyo: Chūō kōronsha, 1966.

Imamura Rikisaburō. *Teijin jiken benron* (Summation on the Teijin incident). Tokyo: Kanaishi Kazuo, 1938.

Imatani, Akira, with Kozo Yamamura. "Not for Lack of Will or Wile: Yoshimitsu's Failure to Supplant the Imperial Lineage." *Journal of Japanese Studies* 18 (Winter 1992): 45–78.

Inoue, Mitsusada. "The Century of Reform." In *The Cambridge History of Japan.* Vol. 1: *Ancient Japan,* ed. Delmer M. Brown. Cambridge: Cambridge University Press, 1993.

Isa Hideo. *Ozaki Yukio.* Tokyo: Yoshikawa kōbunkan, 1960.

Ishida, Takeshi. "Urbanization and Its Impact on Japanese Politics—A Case of a Late and Rapidly Developed Country." *Annals of the Institute of Social Science,* no. 8 (1967): 1–11.

Ishimoda Shō. *Nihon kodai kokka ron: Kanryōsei to hō no mondai* (Essay on the ancient Japanese state: The problem of the bureaucratic system and law). Vol. 1. Tokyo: Iwanami shoten, 1973.

Itō, Takashi. "Conflicts and Coalitions in Japan, 1930: Political Groups [and] the London Naval Disarmament Conference." In *The Study of Coalition Behavior: Theoretical Perspectives and Cases from Four Continents,* ed. Sven Groennings et al. New York: Holt, Rinehart and Winston, 1970.

———. *Showa shi o saguru* (Searching for the history of Showa). Vol. 1. Tokyo: Mitsumura tosho shuppan kabushikikaisha, 1984.

———. *Showa shoki seijishi kenkyū* (Research in the political history of early Showa). Tokyo: Tokyo daigaku shuppankai, 1969.

Itō Ushirō. "Yoyatō no gyakuten" (Reversal of the government and opposition parties). In *Mizutani Chōsaburō den* (Biography of Mizutani Chōsaburō), ed. Nagamatsu Eiichi. Tokyo: Minshu shakaitō honbu kyōsen-kyoku, 1963.

Iwamura Michiyo den kankōkai. *Iwamura Michiyo den* (Biography of Iwamura Michiyo). Tokyo: Iwamura Michiyo kankōkai, 1971.

Izawa Takio denki hensan iinkai. *Izawa Takio.* Tokyo: Haneda shoten, 1951.

Japan. Ministry of Justice. Research and Training Institute. *Summary of the White Paper on Crime 1980.* Tokyo: Ministry of Justice, 1980.

Japan. Prime Minister's Office. Statistics Bureau. *Japan Statistical Yearbook, 1950.* Tokyo: Nihon Statistical Association, 1951.

Japan Times, 1994.

Japan Weekly Chronicle, 1933–1939.

Japanese Government, Attorney-General's Office, trans. *The Constitution of Japan and Criminal Laws.* Tokyo: Japan Trade Guide Publishing, 1951.

Johnson, Chalmers. *Japan: Who Governs? The Rise of the Developmental State.* New York: W. W. Norton, 1995.

———. *MITI and the Japanese Miracle: The Growth of Industrial Policy, 1925–1975.* Stanford, Calif.: Stanford University Press, 1982.

———. "The People Who Invented the Mechanical Nightingale." In *Showa: The Japan of Hirohito,* ed. Carol Gluck and Stephen R. Graubard. New York: W. W. Norton, 1992.

———. "Tanaka Kakuei, Structural Corruption, and the Advent of Machine Politics in Japan." *Journal of Japanese Studies* 12 (Winter 1986): 1–28.

Johnson, Wallace, trans. *The T'ang Code.* Vol. 1: *General Principles.* Princeton, N.J.: Princeton University Press, 1979.

Katō Hideo. *Fūsetsu no hito Nishio Suehiro* (Nishio Suehiro: A man under severe distress). Tokyo: Nekko bunko taiyōsha, 1966.

Kawai Yoshinari. *Teijin jiken: Sanjūnen-me no shōgen* (Teijin incident: Testimony on the thirtieth anniversary). Tokyo: Kōdansha, 1970.

Kawakami Kan. *Iwayuru jinken jūrin mondai ni tsuite* (About the so-called infringement of human rights). In Shihōshō chōsaka (Justice Ministry, research section), *Shihō kenkyū (hōkokusho)* (Justice research, report). 24 (14) (February 1938).

Kawasaki Takukichi denki hensankai. *Kawasaki Takukichi.* Tokyo: Kawasaki Takukichi denki hensankai, 1961.

Keller, Morton. "Corruption in America: Continuity and Change." In *Before Watergate: Problems of Corruption in American Society,* ed. Abraham S. Eisenstadt et al. New York: Brooklyn College Press, 1978.

Kendall, Laurel. "Death and Taxes: A Korean Approach to Hell." *Transactions: Royal Asiatic Society, Korea Branch* 60 (1985): 1–13.

Kennedy, M. D. *The Changing Fabric of Japan.* London: Constable, 1930.

Kinbara Samon. *Taishoki no seitō to kokumin* (Political parties and the people during the Taisho era). Tokyo: Hanawa shobō, 1973.

Kishima, Takako. *Political Life in Japan: Democracy in a Reversible World.* Princeton, N.J.: Princeton University Press, 1991.

Kishimoto, Kōichi. *Politics in Modern Japan: Development and Organization.* Tokyo: Japan Echo, 1988.

Kishimoto Yoshihiro tuisōroku kankōkai. *Kishimoto Yoshihiro tsuisōroku* (Reminiscences about Kishimoto Yoshihiro). Tokyo: Kishimoto Yoshihiro tsui-sōroku kankōkai, 1971.

Kiyose, Ichiro. "The New Election Law." *Contemporary Japan* 15 (January–April 1946): 1–23.

Kōdansha, ed. *Japan: An Illustrated Encyclopedia.* 2 vols. Tokyo: Kōdansha, 1993.

Koh, B. C. *Japan's Administrative Elite.* Berkeley: University of California Press, 1989.

Koizumi Terusaburō. *Sanjūkyūken no shinsō: Hiroku Taisho Showa jidai shi* (True facts about thirty-nine cases: The secret record history of Taisho and Showa incidents). Tokyo: Yomiuri shinbunsha, 1970.

Korea Focus on Current Topics 1, no. 3 (1993); 2, no. 2 (1994).

Kubota, Akira. "A Genuine Reform? The June–August 1993 Upheaval in Japanese Politics." *Asian Thought and Society: An International Review* 18 (May–December 1993): 93–125.

Kyoto daigaku bungakubu kokushi kenkyū shitsu, ed. *Nihon kindai shi jiten* (A dictionary of modern Japanese history). Tokyo: Tōyō keizai shinpōsha, 1958.

Langdon, Frank C. "Part IV: Japan." In *Business Associations and the Financing of Political Parties: A Comparative Study of the Evolution of Practices in Germany, Norway, and Japan,* ed. Arnold J. Heindenheimer and Frank C. Langdon. The Hague: Martinus Nijhoff, 1968.

Large, Stephen S. *Emperor Hirohito and Showa Japan: A Political Biography.* London: Routledge, 1992.

Lebra, Joyce C. *Ōkuma Shigenobu: Statesman of Meiji Japan.* Canberra: Australian National University Press, 1973.

Lebra, Takie S. *Japanese Patterns of Behavior.* Honolulu: University of Hawai'i Press, 1976.

Lee, Rance P. L. "The Folklore of Corruption in Hong Kong." *Asian Survey* 21 (March 1981): 355–368.

Lewis, Michael. *Rioters and Citizens: Mass Protest in Imperial Japan.* Berkeley: University of California Press, 1990.

Liberal Star, 1989, 1991–1992.

Link, Perry. *Evening Chats in Beijing: Probing China's Predicament.* New York: W. W. Norton, 1992.

Liu, James T. C. *Reform in Sung China: Wang An-shih (1021–1086) and His New Policies.* Cambridge, Mass.: Harvard University Press, 1959.

"Lurching toward Realignment." *Japan Echo* 20 (Spring 1993): 6–7.

Marshall, Byron K. *Capitalism and Nationalism in Prewar Japan: The Ideology of the Business Elite, 1868–1941.* Stanford, Calif.: Stanford University Press, 1967.

Maruyama, Masao. *Thought and Behaviour in Modern Japanese Politics.* Ed. Ivan Morris. London: Oxford University Press, 1963.

Mason, R. H. P. "Changing Diet Attitudes to the Peace Preservation Ordinance, 1890–2." In *Japan's Early Parliaments, 1890–1905: Structure, Issues and Trends,* ed. Andrew Fraser et al. London: Routledge, 1995.

———. *Japan's First General Election, 1890.* Canberra: Australian National University, 1969.

Mass, Jeffrey P. *The Development of Kamakura Rule, 1180–1250: A History with Documents.* Stanford, Calif.: Stanford University Press, 1979.

——. "The Missing Minamoto in the Twelfth-Century Kanto." *Journal of Japanese Studies* 19 (Winter 1993): 121–145.

Massey, Joseph A. "The Occupation of Japan and the Sheriff of Nottingham: The Legacy of Election Reform." In *The Occupation of Japan: Impact of Legal Reform,* ed. L. H. Redford. Norfolk, Va.: The MacArthur Memorial, n.d.

Masumi, Junnosuke. "The 1955 System in Japan and Its Subsequent Development." *Asian Survey* 28 (March 1988): 286–306.

——. *Postwar Politics in Japan, 1945–1955.* Trans. Lonny E. Carlile. Berkeley: Institute of East Asian Studies, University of California, 1985.

Matsuzaka Hiromasa den kankōkai. *Matsuzaka Hiromasa den* (Biography of Matsuzaka Hiromasa). Osaka: Dai Nihon insatsu kabushikikaisha, 1969.

Matsumoto, Shigeru. *Motoori Norinaga, 1730–1801.* Cambridge, Mass.: Harvard University Press, 1970.

McEwan, J. R. *The Political Writings of Ogyū Sorai.* Cambridge: Cambridge University Press, 1962.

McLaren, Walter W. *A Political History of Japan during the Meiji Era, 1867–1912.* New York: Charles Scribner's Sons, 1916.

McLaren, Walter W., ed. "Government Documents, First Half of the Meiji Era." *Transactions of the Asiatic Society of Japan* 42, pt. 1 (1914): 185–186.

McMaster, John. "The Japanese Gold Rush of 1859." *Journal of Asian Studies* 19 (May 1960): 273–287.

McNelly, Theodore. *Contemporary Government of Japan.* Boston: Houghton Mifflin, 1963.

Metzger, Thomas A. *The Internal Organization of Ch'ing Bureaucracy: Legal, Normative, and Communication Aspects.* Cambridge, Mass.: Harvard University Press, 1973.

Miller, Frank O. *Minobe Tatsukichi: Interpreter of Constitutionalism in Japan.* Berkeley: University of California Press, 1965.

Minichiello, Sharon. *Retreat from Reform: Patterns of Political Behavior in Interwar Japan.* Honolulu: University of Hawai'i Press, 1984.

Mitani, Taichirō. "The Establishment of Party Cabinets, 1898–1932." In *The Cambridge History of Japan.* Vol. 6: *The Twentieth Century,* ed. Peter Duus. New York: Cambridge University Press, 1988.

Mitchell, Richard H. *Censorship in Imperial Japan.* Princeton, N.J.: Princeton University Press, 1983.

——. *Janus-Faced Justice: Political Criminals in Imperial Japan.* Honolulu: University of Hawai'i Press, 1992.

——. *Thought Control in Prewar Japan.* Ithaca, N.Y.: Cornell University Press, 1976.

Miyachi Tadashi. "Kyōkasho gigoku jiken: Kyōkasho kokutei e no katei to shite" (Textbook scandal incident: Toward the process of nationalizing textbooks). In *Nihon seiji saiban shiroku, Meijikō* (A history of political trials in Japan, latter Meiji), ed. Wagatsuma Sakae. Tokyo: Daiichi hōki shuppan kabushikikaisha, 1969.

Miyazaki, Ichisada. *China's Examination Hell: The Civil Service Examinations of Imperial China.* Trans. Conrad Schirokauer. New York: Weatherhill, 1976.

Mizuguchi, Hiroshi. "Political Reform: Much Ado about Nothing?" *Japan Quarterly* 40 (July–September 1993): 246–257.

Morikawa, Hidemasa. *Zaibatsu: The Rise and Fall of Family Enterprise Groups in Japan.* Tokyo: University of Tokyo Press, 1992.

Morikawa Tetsurō. *Nihon gigoku shi* (A history of Japanese scandals). Tokyo: Sanichi shobō, 1976.

Morishita Sumio. "Imamura Rikisaburō". In *Nihon no bengoshi* (Japanese lawyers), ed. Ushiomi Toshitaka. Tokyo: Nippon hyōronsha, 1972.

Morris-Suzuki, Tessa. *The Technological Transformation of Japan: From the Seventeenth to the Twenty-first Century.* Cambridge: Cambridge University Press, 1994.

Morton, William F. *Tanaka Giichi and Japan's China Policy.* New York: St. Martin's Press, 1980.

Murano Ren'ichi and Irokawa Daikichi. *Murano Tsuneemon den: Seiyūkai jidai* (Biography of Murano Tsuneemon: Seiyūkai era). Vol. 2. Tokyo: Murano Ren'ichi, 1971.

Murobushi Tetsurō. *Jitsuroku Nihon oshoku shi* (A history of Japanese corruption: An authentic account). Tokyo: Chikuma bunko, 1988.

———. *Sengo gigoku* (Postwar scandals). Tokyo: Ushio, 1968.

———. *Sengo gigoku no kao* (The postwar face of scandals). Tokyo: Asahi shinbun sha, 1967.

Myrdal, Gunnar. *Asian Drama: An Inquiry into the Poverty of Nations.* Vol. 2. New York: Twentieth-Century Fund, 1968.

N.H.K. *The First Emperor.* December 1994.

Najita, Tetsuo. *Hara Kei in the Politics of Compromise, 1905–1915.* Cambridge: Harvard University Press, 1967.

———. *Japan.* Englewood Cliffs, N.J.: Prentice-Hall, 1974.

———. "Some Reflections on Idealism in the Political Thought of Yoshino Sakuzō." In *Japan in Crisis: Essays on Taisho Democracy,* ed. Bernard S. Silbermann and H. D. Harootunian. Princeton, N.J.: Princeton University Press, 1974.

Nakai, Kate Wildman. *Shogunal Politics: Arai Hakuseki and the Premises of Tokugawa Rule.* Cambridge, Mass.: Harvard University Press, 1988.

———. "Yanagisawa Yoshiyasu (1658–1714)." In *Encyclopedia of Japan,* ed. Itasaka Gen, 8:314. Tokyo: Kōdansha, 1983.

Nakase Katsutarō. *Tokugawa jidai no wairo shi kanken* (My views of the history of bribery during the Tokugawa era). Tokyo: Keizaikurabu, 1935.

Newsweek, 1994.

New York Times, 1993–1995.

Nezu Masashi. *Nihon gendai shi* (Modern Japanese history). Vol. 1. Tokyo: Sanichi shobō, 1966.

Nishio Suehiro. *Nishio Suehiro no seiji oboegaki* (Political memoir of Nishio Suehiro). Tokyo: Mainichi shinbunsha, 1968.

Nomura Masao, ed. *Hōsō fūunroku: Anohito konohito hōmonki* (Record of affairs in judicial circles: Interviews of various people). Vols. 1 and 2. Tokyo: Asahi shinbunsha, 1966.

Nonaka Moritaka. *Teijin o sabaku* (Judgment on Teijin). Tokyo: Heibonsha, 1938.

Noonan, John T., Jr. *Bribes: The Intellectual History of a Moral Idea.* Berkeley: University of California Press, 1984.

Norman, E. Herbert. "Andō Shōeki and the Anatomy of Japanese Feudalism." *Transactions of the Asiatic Society of Japan,* 3d ser., 2 (December 1949): 1–340.

Obinata Sumio. *Tennōsei keisatsu to minshū* (Emperor system police and the people). Tokyo: Nippon hyōronsha, 1987.

Ogawa Heikichi bunsho kenkyūkai hen. *Ogawa Heikichi kankei bunsho* (The archives of Ogawa Heikichi). Vol. 1. Tokyo: Misuzu shobō, 1973.

Ohara Naoshi kaikoroku hensankai. *Ohara Naoshi kaikoroku* (The memoirs of Ohara Naoshi). Tokyo: Ohara Naoshi kaikoroku hensankai, 1966.

Oka, Yoshitake. *Five Political Leaders of Modern Japan.* Trans. Andrew Fraser and Patricia Murray. Tokyo: University of Tokyo Press, 1986.

———. *Yamagata Aritomo.* Tokyo: Iwanami shoten, 1958.

Ooms, Herman. *Charismatic Bureaucrat: A Political Biography of Matsudaira Sadanobu, 1758–1829.* Chicago: University of Chicago Press, 1975.

Ōshima Mitsuko. "Matsushima Yūkaku iten jiken: Riken o meguru seitō no fuhai jiken (Relocating the Matsushima Brothels incident: Political parties' corruption incident over vested interests). In *Nihon seiji saiban shiroku, Showazen* (A history of political trials, early Showa), ed. Wagatsuma Sakae. Tokyo: Daiichi hōki shuppan kabushikikaisha, 1970.

Ōshima Tarō. "Kunshō—tetsudō gigoku jiken: Seitō seiji ni okeru oshoku no rotei" (Decorations—railways scandals incidents: Exposing corruption in political party politics). In *Nihon seiji saiban shiroku, Showazen* (A history of political trials, early Showa), ed. Wagatsuma Sakae. Tokyo: Daiichi hōki shuppan kabushikikaisha, 1970.

———. "Shīmensu-Bikkāsu jiken: Tōkaku gen'in to natta gunkaku ni yoru kaigun gigoku" (Siemens-Vickers incident: Because of military expansion a navy scandal became a factor in the overthrow of the cabinet). In *Nihon seiji saiban shiroku, Taisho* (A history of political trials, Taisho), ed. Wagatsuma Sakae. Tokyo: Daiichi hōki shuppan kabushikikaisha, 1969.

———. "Teijin jiken: Shōkanshū o mamotta ishoku no hanketsu" (Teijin incident: A unique judgment protected commercial practices). In *Nihon seiji saiban shiroku, Showakō* (A history of political trials, latter Showa), ed. Wagatsuma Sakae. Tokyo: Daiichi hōki shuppan kabushikikaisha, 1970.

Ōuchi Tsutomu. *Nihon no rekishi* (A history of Japan). Vol. 24. Tokyo: Chūō kōronsha, 1967.

Ozaki Yukio. *Gakudō jiden* (Gakudō's autobiography). Tokyo: Gakudō jiden kankokai, 1937.

Ozawa, Ichirō. *Blueprint for a New Japan: The Rethinking of a Nation.* Tokyo: Kōdansha, 1994.

Palais, James B. *Politics and Policy in Traditional Korea.* Cambridge, Mass.: Harvard University Press, 1975.

Passin, Herbert. "The House of Councillors: Promise and Achievement." In *Japan at the Polls: The House of Councillors Election of 1974*, ed. Michael K. Blaker. Washington, D.C.: American Enterprise Institute for Public Policy Research, 1976.

————. *The Legacy of the Occupation—Japan*. New York: Columbia University Press, 1968.

————. *Society and Education in Japan*. New York: Columbia University Press, 1965.

Quigley, Harold S. *Japanese Government and Politics: An Introductory Study*. New York: Century, 1932.

Quigley, Harold S., and John E. Turner. *The New Japan: Government and Politics*. Minneapolis: University of Minnesota Press, 1956.

Ramsdell, Daniel B. *The Japanese Diet: Stability and Change in the Japanese House of Representatives, 1890–1990*. Lanham, Md.: University Press of America, 1992.

Reed, Steven R. "The People Spoke: The Influence of Elections on Japanese Politics, 1949–1955." *Journal of Japanese Studies* 14 (Summer 1988): 309–339.

Reingold, Edwin M. *Chrysanthemums and Thorns: The Untold Story of Modern Japan*. New York: St. Martin's Press, 1992.

Reischauer, Edwin O. *The Japanese Today: Change and Continuity*. Cambridge, Mass.: Belknap Press, 1988.

————. "The Lessons of the Lockheed Scandal." *Newsweek*, May 10, 1976, 20–21.

Richardson, Bradley. "Elections." In *Encyclopedia of Japan*, ed. Itasaka Gen, 2:188–190. Tokyo: Kōdansha, 1983.

Richardson, Bradley M., and Scott C. Flanagan. *Politics in Japan*. Boston: Little, Brown, 1984.

Rōyama Masamichi. *Nihon seiji dōkō ron* (Commentary on tendencies in Japanese politics). Tokyo: Kōyō shoin, 1936.

Sanseidō henshūjo, ed. *Konsaisu jinmei jiten* (A concise biographical dictionary). Tokyo: Sanseidō kabushikikaisha, 1976.

Sansom, George. *A History of Japan to 1334*. Stanford, Calif.: Stanford University Press, 1958.

————. *Japan: A Short Cultural History*. New York: Appleton-Century-Crofts, 1962.

Sato, Elizabeth. "Ōyama Estate and *Insei* Land Policies." *Monumenta Nipponica* 34 (Spring 1979): 73–99.

Scalapino, Robert A. *Democracy and the Party Movement in Prewar Japan: The Failure of the First Attempt*. Berkeley: University of California Press, 1975.

Sebald, William J., trans. *The Criminal Code of Japan*. Kobe: Japan Chronicle Press, 1936.

Sheldon, Charles D. *The Rise of the Merchant Class in Tokugawa Japan, 1600–1868*. Locust Valley, N.Y.: J. J. Augustin, 1958.

Shillony, Ben-Ami. *Politics and Culture in Wartime Japan*. Oxford: Clarendon Press, 1981.

————. *Revolt in Japan: The Young Officers and the February 26, 1936, Incident.* Princeton, N.J.: Princeton University Press, 1973.

Shiono Suehiko kaikoroku kankōkai. *Shiono Suehiko kaikoroku* (The memoirs of Shiono Suehiko). Tokyo: Shiono Suehiko kaikoroku kankōkai, 1958.

Shioya, Sakae. *Chūshingura: An Exposition.* Tokyo: Hokuseido Press, 1956.

Showa Ōkurashō gaishi kankōkai [SOG]. *Showa Ōkurashō gaishi* (An unofficial history of the Finance Ministry). Tokyo: Showa Ōkurashō gaishi kankōkai, 1967.

Sims, R. L. "National Elections and Electioneering in Akita Ken, 1930–1942." In *Modern Japan: Aspects of History, Literature and Society,* ed. W. G. Beasley. Berkeley: University of California Press, 1975.

————. *A Political History of Modern Japan, 1868–1952.* New Delhi: Vikas, 1991.

Sneider, David A. "Action and Oratory: The Trials of the May 15th Incident of 1932." *Law in Japan: An Annual* 23 (1990): 1–66.

Soranaka, Isao. "The Kansei Reforms—Success or Failure?" *Monumenta Nipponica* 33 (Summer 1978): 151–164.

Spaulding, Robert M., Jr. "The Bureaucracy as a Political Force, 1920–1945." In *Dilemmas of Growth in Prewar Japan,* ed. James W. Morley. Princeton, N.J.: Princeton University Press, 1971.

————. *Imperial Japan's Higher Civil Service Examinations.* Princeton, N.J.: Princeton University Press, 1967.

Staunton, George T., trans. *Ta Tsing Leu Lee . . . Penal Code of China.* Taipei: Ch'eng-wen, 1966.

Steenstrup, Carl. "The Gokurakuji Letter: Hōjō Shigetoki's Compendium of Political and Religious Ideas of Thirteenth-Century Japan." *Monumenta Nipponica* 32 (Spring 1977): 1–34.

————. "*Sata Mirensho:* A Fourteenth-Century Law Primer. *Monumenta Nipponica* 35 (Winter 1980): 405–435.

Steven, R. P. G. "Hybrid Constitutionalism in Prewar Japan." *Journal of Japanese Studies* 3 (Winter 1977): 99–133.

Stockwin, J. A. A. "Factionalism in Japanese Political Parties." *Japan Forum* 1 (October 1989): 161–171.

Storry, Richard. *The Double Patriots: A Study of Japanese Nationalism.* Westport, Conn.: Greenwood, 1973.

Sun, Lena H. "High Anxiety: China Is Stressed by the Challenge of Change." *Washington Post National Weekly Edition,* July 5–11, 1993, 17.

————. "Seeds of Revolt Sprouting among China's Peasants." *Washington Post National Weekly Edition,* May 9–15, 1994, 18.

Supreme Commander for the Allied Powers [SCAP]. Government Section. *The Japanese Elections, April 1947.* Tokyo: June 20, 1947.

————. *Political Reorientation of Japan, September 1945 to September 1948.* 2 vols. Washington, D.C.: U.S. Government Printing Office, 1949.

Suzuki Kisaburō sensei denki hensankai. *Suzuki Kisaburō.* Tokyo: Suzuki Kisaburō sensei denki hensankai, 1945.

Suzuki Yoshio denki kankōkai. *Suzuki Yoshio.* Tokyo: Suzuki Yoshio denki kankōkai, 1964.

Szpilman, Christopher W. A. "The Politics of Cultural Conservatism: The National Foundation Society in the Struggle against Foreign Ideas in Pre-war Japan, 1918–1936." Ph.D. dissertation, Yale University, 1993.

Taikakai, ed. *Naimushō shi* (A history of the Home Ministry). Vol. 4. Tokyo: Chihō zaimu kyōkai, 1971.

Takenobu, Y., ed. *The Japan Year Book, 1928*. Tokyo: Japan Year Book Office, 1928.

Takeuchi, Sterling Tatsuji. "The Japanese Civil Service." In *The Civil Service in the Modern State: A Collection of Documents*, ed. Leonard D. White. Chicago: University of Chicago Press, 1930.

Tamiya Hiroshi. "Ōura jiken: Seifu no kōkan to kiso yūyo" (Ōura incident: High government officials and a suspension of indictment). In *Nihon seiji saiban shiroku, Taisho* (A history of political trials in Japan, Taisho), ed. Wagatsuma Sakae. Tokyo: Daiichi hōki shuppan kabushikikaisha, 1969.

Thayer, Nathaniel E. *How the Conservatives Rule Japan*. Princeton, N.J.: Princeton University Press, 1969.

Tiedemann, Arthur E. "Big Business and Politics in Prewar Japan." In *Dilemmas of Growth in Prewar Japan*, ed. James W. Morley. Princeton, N.J.: Princeton University Press, 1971.

Titus, David A. *Palace and Politics in Prewar Japan*. New York: Columbia University Press, 1974.

Tomita, Nobuo; Akira Nakamura; and Ronald J. Hrebenar. "The Liberal Democratic Party: The Ruling Party of Japan." In *The Japanese Party System*, ed. Ronald J. Hrebenar. Boulder, Colo.: Westview, 1992.

Totman, Conrad D. *Early Modern Japan*. Berkeley: University of California Press, 1993.

———. *Politics in the Tokugawa Bakufu, 1600–1843*. Berkeley: University of California Press, 1967.

Tsuji Kan'ichi. *Seijika to iu mono* (To be called a politician). Tokyo: Gakufu shoin, 1955.

Tsunoda, Ryūsaku, et al., comps. *Sources of Japanese Tradition*. Vols. 1 and 2. New York: Columbia University Press, 1958.

Tsurumi, Yūsuke. "Universal Suffrage Seen as the Antidote to Big Money Elections (1924)." In *Democracy in Prewar Japan: Groundwork or Facade?*, ed. George C. Totten. Lexington, Mass.: D. C. Heath, 1965.

Tsurutani, Taketsugu. "The LDP in Transition? Mass Membership Participation in Party Leadership Selection." *Asian Survey* 20 (August 1980): 844–859.

Uchida, Mitsuru. "Changing Aspects of Spectatorial Democracy in Japan." *Waseda Political Studies*, March 1974, 1–14.

Uchida Nobuya. *Fūsetsu gojūnen* (Fifty years of wind and snow). Tokyo: Jitsugyō no Nihonsha, 1951.

U.S. News and World Report, 1994.

Ushiomi, Toshitaka. "The Prosecution at the Crossroads." *Annals of the Institute of Social Science*, no. 9 (1968): 84–85.

Uyehara, George. *The Political Development of Japan, 1867–1909*. New York: E. P. Dutton, 1910.

Vandenbrink, John D. "State and Industrial Society in Modern Japan: The Liberal Critique, 1916–1926." Ph.D. dissertation, University of Chicago, 1985.

van Wolferen, Karel. *The Enigma of Japanese Power: People and Politics in a Stateless Nation*. New York: Alfred A. Knopf, 1989.

Varley, Paul. *The Ōnin War: History of Its Origins and Background with a Selective Translation of the Chronicle of Ōnin*. New York: Columbia University Press, 1967.

von Mehren, Arthur T. "Commentary: Part II." In *Law in Japan: The Legal Order in a Changing Society*, ed. Arthur T. von Mehren. Cambridge, Mass.: Harvard University Press, 1963.

Wagatsuma Sakae, ed. *Kyū hōrei shū* (A collection of old laws and regulations). Tokyo: Yūhikaku, 1968.

Wakata, Kyoji. "Japanese Diet Members: Social Background, General Values, and Role Perception." Ph.D. dissertation, Rice University, 1977.

Wall Street Journal, 1994.

Walthall, Anne. *Social Protest and Popular Culture in Eighteenth-Century Japan*. Tucson: University of Arizona Press, 1986.

Ward, Robert E. "Reflections on the Allied Occupation and Planned Political Change in Japan." In *Political Development in Modern Japan*, ed. Robert E. Ward. Princeton, N.J.: Princeton University Press, 1968.

Watt, John R. *The District Magistrate in Late Imperial China*. New York: Columbia University Press, 1972.

Webb, R. K. *Modern England: From the Eighteenth Century to the Present*. New York: Dodd, Mead, 1973.

Weiner, Susan B. "Bureaucracy and Politics in the 1930s: The Career of Gotō Fumio." Ph.D. dissertation, Harvard University, 1984.

White, James W. "The Dynamics of Political Opposition." In *Postwar Japan as History*, ed. Andrew Gordon. Berkeley: University of California Press, 1993.

Wildes, Harry E. *Japan in Crisis*. New York: Macmillan, 1934.

———. *Typhoon in Tokyo: The Occupation and Its Aftermath*. New York: Macmillan, 1954.

Williams, Sr., Justin. *Japan's Political Revolution under MacArthur: A Participant's Account*. Athens: University of Georgia Press, 1979.

Woo, Jung-en. *Race to the Swift: State and Finance in Korean Industrialization*. New York: Columbia University Press, 1991.

Wray, William D. *Mitsubishi and the N.Y.K., 1870–1914: Business Strategy in the Japanese Shipping Industry*. Cambridge, Mass.: Harvard University Press, 1984.

Wright, Mary C. *The Last Stand of Chinese Conservatism: The T'ung-Chih Restoration, 1862–1874*. New York: Atheneum, 1969.

Yamaguchi, Jirō. "The Book Forum of Political Reform." *Japanese Book News*, no. 6 (Spring 1994), 4–5.

Yamamoto Taketoshi. *Shinbun kisha no tanjō: Nihon no medeia o tsukutta hitobito* (Birth of newspaper reporters: Creators of Japanese media). Tokyo: Shinyōsha, 1991.

Yamamura, Kozo. "The Decline of the Ritsuryō System: Hypotheses on Economic and Institutional Change." *Journal of Japanese Studies* 1 (Autumn 1974): 3–37.

Yanaga, Chitoshi. *Big Business in Japanese Politics*. New Haven, Conn.: Yale University Press, 1968.

———. *Japan since Perry*. Hamden, Conn.: Archon, 1966.

———. *Japanese People and Politics*. New York: John Wiley and Sons, 1956.

Yang, Mayfair Mei-hui. *Gifts, Favors, and Banquets: The Art of Social Relationships in China*. Ithaca, N.Y.: Cornell University Press, 1994.

Yasko, Richard. "Bribery Cases and the Rise of the Justice Ministry in Late *Meiji*–Early *Taisho* Japan." *Law in Japan: An Annual* 12 (1979): 57–68.

———. "Hiranuma Kiichirō and Conservative Politics in Pre-war Japan." Ph.D. dissertation, University of Chicago, 1973.

Yayama, Tarō. "The Recruit Scandal: Learning from the Causes of Corruption." *Journal of Japanese Studies* 16 (Winter 1990): 93–114.

Yokoyama Taiji. *Gendai no oshoku* (Corruption of modern times). Tokyo: Sanichi shobō, 1967.

Yoshida, Shigeru. *The Yoshida Memoirs: The Story of Japan in Crisis*. Trans. Yoshida Ken'ichi. Boston: Houghton Mifflin, 1962.

Yoshimura, Tadashi. "Conservative Parties during the First Ten Years of Postwar Japan." *Waseda Political Studies* 1 (1957): 1–25.

Young, A. Morgan. *Imperial Japan, 1926–1938*. New York: William Morrow, 1938.

———. *Japan in Recent Times, 1912–1926*. New York: W. Morrow, 1929.

Index